Haunted City

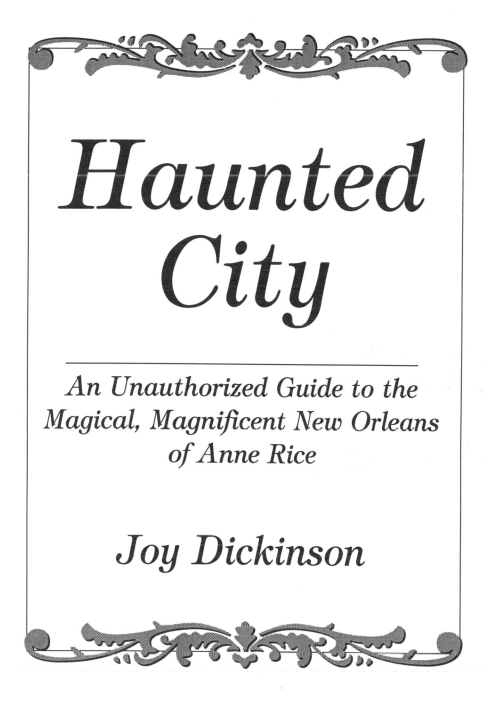

Haunted City

An Unauthorized Guide to the Magical, Magnificent New Orleans of Anne Rice

Joy Dickinson

A Citadel Press Book
Published by Carol Publishing Group

A Citadel Press Book

Published by Carol Publishing Group

Citadel Press is a registered trademark of Carol Communications, Inc.

Editorial Offices: 600 Madison Avenue, New York, N.Y. 10022
Sales and Distribution Offices: 120 Enterprise Avenue, Secaucus, NJ 07094
In Canada: Canadian Manda Group, One Atlantic Avenue, Suite 105, Toronto, Ontario M6K 3E7

Queries regarding rights and permissions should be addressed to Carol Publishing Group, 600 Madison Avenue, New York, N.Y. 10022

Carol Publishing Books are available at special discounts for bulk purchases, sales promotion, fundraising, or educational purposes. Special editions can be created to specifications. For details, contact: Special Sales Department, Carol Publishing Group, 120 Enterprise Avenue, Secaucus, NJ 07094.

Manufactured in the United States of America

10 9 8 7 6 5 4 3 2 1

Library of Congress Cataloging-in-Publication Data
Dickinson, Joy.
    Haunted city : an unauthorized guide to the magical, magnificient New Orleans of Anne Rice / Joy Dickinson.
       p.   cm.
    "A Citadel Press book."
    ISBN 0-8065-1696-8 (pbk.)
    1. Rice, Anne, 1941-   —Knowledge—Louisiana—New Orleans.
2. Literary landmarks—Louisiana—New Orleans—Guidebooks.
3. Horror tales. American—History and criticism.   4. New Orleans (La.)—In literature.   5. Rice, Anne, 1941-   —Settings.
6. Witchcraft in literature.   7. Vampires in literature.   I. Title.
PS3568.I265Z63   1995
813'.54—dc20   95-19914
                                                       CIP

For my mother,
Marjorie Dickinson Wilson,
who made sure I had the two essential elements
for a happy life—her unconditional love and
belief in me, and a public library card

Contents

Acknowledgments

Without the support and encouragement of those listed here, *Haunted City* forever would have remained an unrealized dream. But thanks to these family and dear friends, to whom I am abidingly and humbly grateful, my dream came true. I hope someday to return the favor.

Special thanks and admiration for the skills and patience of Dena Hill, whom I am blessed to call "best friend." Dena provided the book's delightful maps and also doled out endless supplies of reassurance and cheerleading ("You can do it, Joy. Remember, you're fast!"). Appreciation, too, to her husband, Michael Bennett, for putting up with Dena while she was putting up with me, and for his own words of encouragement (often helpfully translated into Latin. *Carpe diem*, Michael!).

In New Orleans, special thanks to Beverly Gianna at the New Orleans Convention and Tourism Bureau, Mike Carr at the New Orleans Film Commission, Claire and Jacques Creppel at The Columns Hotel, Carole Lubritz and Michael Dietrich at The Pontchartrain Hotel, Myrna Bergeron at Pitot House and Susan Levy of Friends of St. Alphonsus, all of whom contributed seemingly inexhaustible knowledge and inimitable Southern hospitality. My phenomenally patient friends Bert Pigg and Adriana Bate gave shelter and sympathetic ears, and Daisy the Cat provided much-needed on-site fur therapy.

At home, deep gratitude to my parents, Marjorie and Gene Wilson, who cheerfully endured my most annoying "writer moods"; fellow authors Victoria Chancellor Huffstutler and Amy Plummer for saying "Joy, that's a book!"; Kathy Hartley (my other "best friend"), Brenda Barrett, Julia and Joseph Battino (a.k.a. the Moomuls), Paula Johnson, Lori Racine, Melinda Rice, and Marilyn Stults; my writing mentors, Dr. Richard Wells (University of North Texas) and Jane Roberts Wood; the staff of the Craft of Writing Conference; and the *Richardson News* gang (especially Lois Brown and Sharon McCann).

Last, but most certainly not least, heartfelt thanks and recognition to my wise and spirited agent, Linda M. Kruger of The Fogelman Literary Agency; agency president Evan Fogelman; and my extraordinarily patient and enthusiastic editor, Kevin McDonough at Carol Publishing Group. And, of course, my gratitude and eternal respect to Anne Rice, whose magical literary portrayal of New Orleans inspired me in the first place.

February 1995
Richardson, Texas

Introduction

This was New Orleans, a magical and magnificent place to
live. In which a vampire, richly dressed and gracefully walking through the pools of light of one gas lamp after another
might attract no more notice in the evening than hundreds
of other exotic creatures. . . .

—Anne Rice, *Interview With the Vampire*, 1976

My initial impression of New Orleans was formed almost solely through
the works of Anne Rice. Sure, I'd heard about Louisiana's "Crescent
City," just a short flight from my North Texas hometown of Richardson, and it probably had occurred to me to visit someday, but it was
never a consuming passion. That is, until—at the impressionable, in-
curably romantic age of sixteen—I picked up a copy of *Interview With
the Vampire*. Intoxicated with author Anne Rice's vivid descriptions of
an almost foreign-sounding city, equal parts exotic and eerie, I became
completely obsessed with New Orleans. No other contemporary writer
comes close to Rice in capturing the sensual, ripe, decaying atmosphere
of America's most European city. Throughout my late teens and young
adulthood, I read, with equal ardor, each new Rice book as well as histories, fiction, and anything else I could find about New Orleans. Before I ever set eager feet on Louisiana soil, I knew New Orleans far better
than any part of Texas.

Coming from an Anne Rice–influenced perspective, I especially
relished what little I could glean about the actual locations Rice used
in her books. From book reviews, published and broadcast interviews
with Rice, and an occasional guidebook reference to a certain house,

church, or cemetery, I made mental notes of every "Rice connection" I could find to New Orleans's Old World–style architecture and culture.

Interview aroused my love for New Orleans and served eventually as the impetus for *Haunted City*. But my first encounter with Louis and Lestat, the aristocratic vampires of the book, was memorable for other reasons as well. During English class one day at Richardson High School, having already finished the assigned reading of *An American Tragedy*, I turned my rapt attention to *Interview*. Spying its Gothic, gold-and-red, anything-but-unassuming cover in my hands, my teacher pounced. "What," she demanded in whispered indignation, "are you doing reading that trashy horror in my class?"

Blood pressure rising, I explained that I had finished with Theodore Dreiser and moved on, thank you very much. Was there another assignment that she would prefer I read? No, but I was *not*, she declared, going to read *that*. The woman clearly had no taste or sense of adventure, which I suppose can be forgiven as the result of reading nothing but approved "literature," but never in my life had anyone told me I *couldn't* read something. The Richardson school district had never banned a book, and at home, reading was as much a part of each day as brushing my teeth. Forbidden books were something I had encountered only through the pages of *Fahrenheit 451*. When I politely (well, perhaps I did raise my voice above a whisper) explained this to the teacher, it earned me a hasty trip to the principal's office. He looked a little troubled and chuckled some at my audacity, but I didn't get in any trouble. And I went back to English class, *Interview* firmly in hand, and never heard another word about it.

Eighteen years later, it does my heart good to think of that teacher, cruising the aisles of her favorite bookstore, inundated by images of Anne Rice books. Pity the Anne Rice detractor in the mid-1990s—she's everywhere, and the 1994 release of the film version of *Interview* only fueled the frenzy. My ex-English-teacher's righteous indignation, if still active, has undoubtedly undergone a rather strenuous workout lately.

Sweet vindication, of a sort, came my way a lucky thirteen years after that English class. In 1990, while perusing the Sunday book section of *The Dallas Morning News*, I read that Anne Rice would be in town the following week signing copies of *The Witching Hour*. Alas, I couldn't go to the signing; it conflicted with "deadline day" in my job at the *Richardson News*. I was disappointed, but still elated by the throw-away phrase *The Morning News* had inserted to localize the story: "Anne Rice, who graduated from Richardson High School, will sign copies of her latest book. . . .'

My senses reeled. Could this possibly be true? My literary idol had graduated from *my* high school? The irony was delicious, especially recalling my traumatic *Interview* incident there. Hoisting my courage to full sail, I called Rice's publicist, explained that I was lifestyles editor for the *Richardson News* (and then explained that Richardson is a Dallas suburb), took a deep breath, and asked for an interview.

"Sure," came the unexpected reply, "but her schedule doesn't allow for in-person interviews. Would a phone call be acceptable?" I think I stammered something eloquent, along the lines of "Uh-huh," and before I quite had time to adjust to the idea, I was on the phone chatting with "Anne," as she firmly instructed me to call her. She seemed happy to talk with another Richardson High alumna, and was especially tickled to hear that she had motivated rebellion in a younger reader. She described the intense culture shock she had experienced upon moving from the quirky contradictions of New Orleans—sin, seduction, and open eroticism played out in America's only predominantly Catholic city—to the flat, excruciatingly neutral, and politically conservative plains of North Texas. "Richardson was like a whole new world for me," she said. "It was like stepping into a TV set—*Father Knows Best*, live. It was the American dream come true."

She also empathized with my own astonishment, coming from the opposite perspective, upon first visiting New Orleans. To a girl accustomed to scrubby trees and the occasional glorious sunset providing most of the color, New Orleans loomed like an almost painfully vivid hallucination, both visually and aurally noisy at a deafening level. Even for someone with a vigorous, if undeveloped, imagination, New Orleans took on a surreal quality. It was about as far from *Father Knows Best* as you could get and still be in the United States.

I'd had to wait a good while for a firsthand glimpse of my dream city. Eight long, longing years passed between my first reading of *Interview* and my first unforgettable trip, in December 1984, to Rice's "haunted city," as it is described by a character in *The Witching Hour.* My best friend, Dena Hill, took me there as a surprise gift for my twenty-fourth birthday. Until we were at the airport, I had no idea where we were going. Then Dena produced from her purse, with magician-worthy flourish, a copy of an historical romance novel we'd both guiltily enjoyed. It featured, along with the requisite heaving chests and burst bodices, a large section set in nineteenth-century New Orleans. Dena hadn't yet read Rice's books, much to my dismay, but she had caught, through some sort of psychic osmosis (and that romance novel, no doubt), my fascination for the city. When Dena told me we were going to New Orleans, I don't remember much other than her wild outbreak of giggles over the look on my face. I do recall an inability to breathe, followed by hopping up and down and much arm waving. I must have been quite a sight.

During the brief flight south and east, my thoughts whirled—I had to see the St. Louis No. 1 and Lafayette cemeteries, of course, and I racked my brain for the name of the historic house that had served as the model for Louis and Lestat's townhouse in *Interview*. I knew I'd read it somewhere. And, of course, I'd have to visit the outlying estates, like the indigo plantation where Louis lived. First thing when we landed, I'd have to find a bookstore and get a copy of *Interview*. Oh, my thoughts raced with "must dos," each inspired by Anne Rice and her irresistible vampires.

Dena thought I'd lost what was left of my mind—she was looking forward to a weekend of jazz, *beignets*, and riverboat cruises. And I wanted to spend all my time in the *cemeteries*, for heaven's sake? Being my best friend, however, she indulged me, and we compromised. I got a moonlight glance at some of New Orleans's "cities of the dead," and several "this might be it" glimpses of French Quarter townhouses, and Dena got her breakfasts at Café du Monde and evenings on Bourbon Street. We didn't sleep much. In New Orleans's overstimulating atmosphere, eating dinner at 2 A.M. suddenly seemed quite normal.

From the moment I stepped off the airport shuttle and onto Royal Street, New Orleans seemed my spiritual home. The city's moods and influences create a vivid undercurrent—every conversation, every gesture, every incident seems somehow more "on" in New Orleans, more brilliantly lucid. The city's blazing physical and emotional color can drain the uninitiated or unprepared; New Orleans does not long tolerate the timid or unadventurous. Its residents, however, bear none of the standoffish attitude toward nonnatives so common in other large cities. If you've got the spirit, they've got the welcome mat.

Over the course of several subsequent trips to New Orleans, my initial enthusiasm has not waned. My first, and most eagerly anticipated, "duty" of every trip is to ferret out and experience for myself the locales of the latest Rice works. Each new *Vampire* or *Witching* sequel provides intriguing new tidbits that simply beg to be investigated. Although Rice's other novels frequently use New Orleans as a setting, in the *Vampire* and *Mayfair Witches* series, the city literally *becomes* a character. The books are unimaginable without the city.

I'm far from alone in my fascination. Every time I've ventured to "stake out" the haunting grounds of Louis, Lestat, and the Mayfair Witches, I've been startled and charmed to find others doing the same thing. On a tour sponsored by the Voodoo Museum, a fellow fan who happened to be our guide was fiendishly thrilled to point out an unusual feature of the St. Louis No. 1 cemetery. "Ooh, an Anne Rice fan. Me too," he said, brimming with the sort of instant, confiding companionship one feels with other Americans when meeting them abroad. "Then you'll *definitely* want to see this," he continued excitedly. Somewhat nervously, we followed as he explored the deserted (as far as we could tell, anyway) burial ground for several minutes, until he finally found the tomb he'd been seeking.

Desecrated by weather, vandalism, and just plain neglect, some of New Orleans's once stately tombs, mostly built above-ground because of the city's high water table, have cracked open. The curious can get an unprecedented view of the, well, *interiors* of certain graves. "Look here at this one," our guide said, pointing gleefully. "There's nothing there—no bones or anything, just dust. And doesn't it kind of look like the top has been *slid* off, rather than just cracking open?" We knew what he meant: *just like a vampire's coffin.* Logically speaking, of course, it didn't hold up. We were there in bright daylight, when any self-respecting (and health-conscious) vampire would be slumbering away in his casket. If this were a vampire lair, the least we would have found, surely, would have been the smoldering remains of a sun-charred immortal. Besides, Rice's vampires prefer the comforts of indoor storage, with their coffins neatly secured in their French Quarter townhouse.

Still, it was a fascinatingly macabre encounter, and not all that unusual among the faithful Rice legions. Again and again—at the Gallier House (*that's* the name of Louis and Lestat's townhouse), on the St.

Charles streetcar, and at the corner of Chestnut and First in the Garden District, where Anne Rice lives and housed her Mayfair Witches—I have met, conversed and exchanged "clues" with, and been surprised and delighted by the spirited determination of, fellow Rice fans.

Logic reared its ugly head again a few years ago, when I asked a French Quarter tour leader whether any sort of organized guide existed for the "Anne Rice sights." The woman looked at me as though I might be a bit mad, certainly odd at the very least. She meandered away to ask a fellow guide, apparently got a negative response, and pointedly avoided me during the rest of the tour. We Rice fans shudder with pleasure at the eerie and unusual; it still comes as a shock to realize that some people merely shudder. Oh, well . . . So my friend and I set off, as I'd done dozens of times before, determined to find the latest Rice "sets" ourselves.

Haunted City grew out of those often frustrating, but always exhilarating quests for Rice locales. Her fans are legion—strolling through the Garden District, sipping coffee in Jackson Square, whirling through a Cajun-style dance at Tipitina's, you're as likely to overhear animated discussions of Lestat's motivations and Rowan Mayfair's latest whereabouts as the outcome of a Saints game or the city's all-too-familiar problem of violent crime. Striking up a conversation with a fellow Rice fan doesn't take much initiative; just mention the name Lestat and listen as the discussion comes alive with talk of the undead.

In addition to my early captivation with Rice's locations simply because they were in her books, I also found myself increasingly intrigued by the historical aspects of the sites. The Gallier House, for instance, was built in 1857 by the son of Irishman James Gallier Sr., who had been born James Gallagher and "French-ified" the name upon arrival in London (such was the status of the Irish at the time, and Gallier would find it wasn't much better in New Orleans). It seems a bit of fine irony that his house would be fictitiously immortalized by Anne O'Brien Rice, who grew up near the working-class Irish Channel, just blocks from the mansions of the Garden District. Just down the street from Gallier House in the French Quarter is the supposedly haunted house of a certain Madame Delphine LaLaurie, whose chained and starving slaves were discovered during a deadly fire. To this day, people insist they hear mournful shrieks coming from the house on stormy nights. Never dull, the French Quarter.

The churches and cemeteries of Rice's childhood and books also resonate with rich histories. In Lafayette Cemetery, just blocks from Rice's home and the burial site of her Mayfair Witches, one can still see the "yellow fever graves" of nineteenth-century epidemic victims. In St. Louis No. 1, the "oven" tombs along the walls were regularly "recycled" to accommodate more than one occupant. So intrinsic to Rice's works are the cemeteries, in fact, that in October (naturally) 1988, the City of New Orleans bequeathed her an honorary deed to a plot in St. Louis No. 1.

Haunted City also includes information on Rice's own coming-of-age—the schools, parks, and churches where she spent her childhood, many of which turn up, sometimes pseudonymously, in her books. St. Joseph's Academy in the French Quarter, for example, where Anne unhappily attended school for a time, became St. Rose de Lima's in *The Witching Hour.*

Haunted City is divided by geographical sectors for sightseeing and reading ease. A St. Charles Streetcar tour in chapter 3 gives a quick overview of many of the non–French Quarter sites. The French Quarter, to be fully appreciated, simply must be strolled. Also included are suggested tours of the swamps, bayous, and restored plantation homes surrounding New Orleans—if the indigo plantations like Louis's Pointe du Lac are long gone, one can at least envision where they might have been. Anne Rice fans, certainly, find imagination at least as potent as reality, and in cases where actual locations were simply the product of the author's fertile mind, *Haunted City* speculates on what might have been.

For those who'd like to further the fantasy of entering Rice's world, *Haunted City* also explores the hotels, bed-and-breakfasts, vintage clothing and jewelry stores, and antique outlets conducive to the feeling of stepping back in time. In chapter 7, you'll find lodgings, restaurants, shopping, and a few hints about the more practical, prudent aspects of New Orleans tourism.

Haunted City also ventures forward in time, to what may lurk for Rice fans in upcoming books and film adaptations of her works. The much-anticipated, controversial movie of *Interview*, starring Tom Cruise as Lestat and directed be Neil Jordan (who won fame with *The Crying Game*), hit theaters in the fall of 1994 to a remarkably glowing reception by Rice and her fans. Rice, who initially had vehemently (and publicly) protested the casting of Cruise as her vampire-hero, changed her tune dramatically after seeing the film, even taking out ads urging fans to see it. *Interview* producer David Geffen also owns the rights to *The Vampire Lestat* and *The Witching Hour*, and the success of *Interview* virtually guarantees more Rice-inspired cinema. The fifth *Vampire Chronicles* book, *Memnoch the Devil*, was released in July 1995.

My goal with *Haunted City* is to provide an atlas for the faithful, the curious wanderers like myself who want to go beyond simply reading Rice's books and into experiencing them. For those actually planning a trip to New Orleans, *Haunted City* serves as an easy-to-carry, illustrated guide, complemented with simple maps (designed to be used in conjunction with more detailed city maps, which are available free of charge at the Jackson Square tourist center). This is not meant to be a coffee table book; tuck it in your purse or pocket and take it along. After a few days in the New Orleans humidity, it'll probably start to have that crumpled, vaguely historic "pirate map" look. So much the better—a crumpled book is a happy book; that means it has been opened often.

For those whose current travels are via armchair only, *Interview* also gives an in-depth look into the history and anecdotes surrounding Rice's locales. Whether you're sitting on a plane headed for the Crescent City or cuddled on a Seattle couch savoring a rainy day at home, I hope *Haunted City* will bring you a bit closer to unveiling the mysteries of these cemeteries and churches, vampires and witches, Anne Rice and her city. Each chapter begins by discussing the sites most closely related to Rice's works, then moves to other locales of particular historical significance. In the interest of simplicity, the maps are restricted almost entirely to the "Rice sights." As with most guidebooks, you will notice some repetition from chapter to chapter—St. Louis No. 1, for instance, is mentioned in both the French Quarter chapter and the chapter on cemeteries. Addresses, tour information, and other "practical stuff" have been compiled in chapter 7.

In references to Rice's books, the titles are abbreviated as follows:

Interview With the Vampire—*Interview*

The Vampire Lestat—*Lestat*

Queen of the Damned—*Queen*

The Tale of the Body Thief—*Body Thief*

Map Legend

⬡ cemeteries

✝ churches

ᴟ other points of interest

The Witching Hour—Witching
Lasher and *Taltos* conveniently serve as their own abbreviations.

Admittedly, my view of New Orleans always has been and remains somewhat skewed. Fans of the modern aspects of the city—Saints football, the Aquarium of the Americas, the downtown revival, etc.—will think me hopelessly caught up in the past. They're probably right. My fundamental conception of New Orleans is as the setting for Anne Rice's books—a grand-scale theatrical production of sumptuous costumes, exquisite decor, and fascinating characters, just waiting for the next *Vampire* or *Witching* saga to throw on the stagelights of imagination. And in New Orleans, the curtain never descends.

I have heard other authors say that books take on their own personalities, despite the writer's valiant struggles to retain control, and *Haunted City* certainly was no exception to that rule: It steadfastly refused to be written by sunlight, firmly establishing a nocturnal affinity that threw my schedule into considerable chaos. I wrote it almost entirely after dark, and I would like to think Rice's night-loving characters—Lestat, Louis, and all of the Mayfairs—would enjoy reading it.

Ah, here comes the sunset, so let's begin our journey. Please keep your necks well-covered to protect them from the . . . elements.

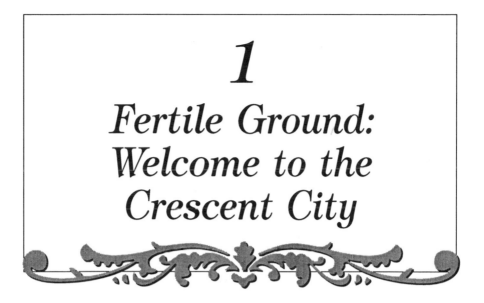

1
Fertile Ground: Welcome to the Crescent City

Night comes quickly in New Orleans. Crimson-and-gold-flecked sunsets flicker intensely, lingering long enough only to tease, then vanish as glistening blackness drops rapidly and remorselessly over the city. And that's when the true life of the Crescent City begins—like the shadow-dwelling protagonists of Anne Rice's books, New Orleanians convey a distinct preference for darkness over light.

This is fertile ground, both geographically and spiritually. Seeds planted here sprout with wild profusion, and the landscape remains lushly verdant at least nine months of the year—locals insist it's actually harder *not* to garden in New Orleans. Children, likewise, blossom into exotic creatures filled with curiosity and daring. It seems almost inevitable that Anne Rice, blessed with an imagination bathed in moonlight and growing up within shouting distance of Lafayette Cemetery, would take a dark, distinctly nontraditional direction in her writing.

A New Orleans native, Anne Rice was born Howard Allen Frances O'Brien at the old riverfront Mercy Hospital (since demolished) in the month of All Hallow's Eve—on October 4, 1941. In fact, Rice shares a birth date with one of her Mayfair heroines, the sad and doomed Deirdre, whose death at age forty-eight echoes Rice's mother's death at the same

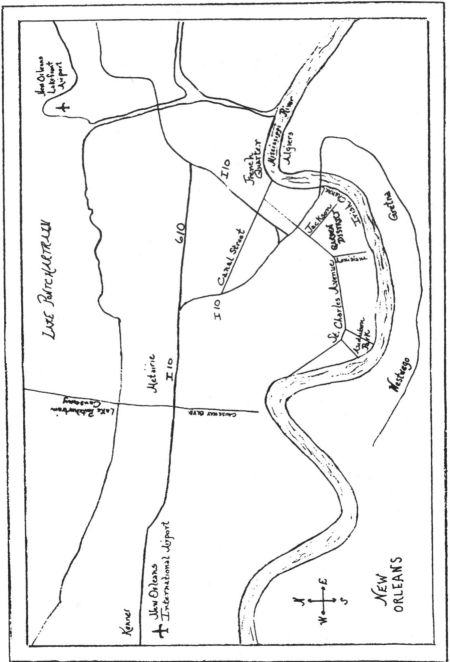

Overview

age. Anne's given name incorporates both her father's given name (Howard) and her mother's maiden name (Allen). Already headstrong and determined (desirable qualities for a future author), the little girl didn't like "Howard Allen," so she simply changed it, test-running several more feminine names before settling on "Anne" in first grade.

Rice is hardly the first great writer weaned on the muggy days and foggy nights of New Orleans, but many modern critics have dubbed her the best at capturing the city's uncanny combination of romance and menace, and of both physical and moral sophistication and decay. Other writers, both native and "foreign," who found inspiration here include John Kennedy O'Toole (whose *A Confederacy of Dunces* is considered must-reading for the true New Orleans fan), Frances Parkinson Keyes, Truman Capote, Lillian Hellman, Sherwood Anderson, George Washington Cable, and, of course, Tennessee Williams. Lafcadio Hearn and Lyle Saxon, like Rice, were especially renowned for their vivid written portraits of the city.

Onetime resident William Faulkner could have been describing the New Orleans of Louis and Lestat when he wrote of the city, "She lives in an atmosphere of a bygone and more gracious age. And those whom she receives are few in number, and they come to her through an eternal twilight." Faulkner, whose name now adorns the Pirates Alley house where he wrote his first novel, contributed the lively "New Orleans Sketches" column to the *Times-Picayune* in the 1920s.

Rice moved to Texas as a teenager, then lived in San Francisco for a quarter century, but she remained passionately bound in spirit to the city of her birth. *Interview With the Vampire* begins in San Francisco, but the action moves to New Orleans within the first ten pages. Although other locales are used, New Orleans and *Interview* seem fatally bonded; Rice fans can't envision it set anywhere else, and imagine the uproar if the makers of the film version had dared shoot elsewhere. They did, in fact, construct fake swamps and antebellum ballrooms at a British studio, but used enough "real" locations to satisfy the faithful. Production designer Dante Ferretti did such a skillful job, in fact, it's nearly impossible to distinguish the genuine Louisiana from the cinematic fabrication.

Rice herself has often discussed New Orleans's unique lure to those enchanted by the macabre. In a 1993 *Playboy* interview, she said, "I have met countless people in New Orleans who told me their personal experiences of seeing ghosts. I never met those people in California. . . . And since I've been here, people look me right in the eye and describe the ghost's clothes and what it did as it came up the stairs."

Early Inspiration

Although Rice did not actually grow up in the Irish Channel, the riverfront area near the Garden District on the "wrong side" of Magazine Street, her roots were firmly enmeshed within its immigrant Celtic traditions. Her parents, Katherine and Howard O'Brien, were married at St. Alphonsus Church, the spiritual heartbeat of the Irish Catholic community. As a child, Rice attended both St. Alphonsus and St. Mary's Assumption, the German Catholic church right across the street. Many of Rice's Mayfairs, including Deirdre and Rowan, were baptized in St. Alphonsus's gilt-covered Victorian baptismal font, which recently was restored.

Howard O'Brien grew up in a large Irish Channel family, one of nine children. Katherine Allen also came from a large family, but of its eight children, only Katherine, one sister, and one brother survived to maturity. After Katherine's father died of tuberculosis and alcoholism (at age forty-eight, something of an unlucky number in this family), Katherine's mother, Alice, did domestic work in the Garden District, where her granddaughter Anne would one day own an historic First Street townhouse.

Howard and Katherine married on Thanksgiving Day 1938. Their first house was at 2301 St. Charles, at the corner of Philip, now beautifully renovated. In the October 1994 Lifetime special *Anne Rice: Birth of the Vampire*, Rice took viewers on a nostalgic tour through her childhood home, which is within walking distance of her most famous residence, the brooding violet mansion at First and Chestnut immortalized in *The Witching Hour*. In *Prism of the Night*, Rice's biography by Katherine Ramsland, the author recounts a tale sure to delight fans: As a child, Anne and one of her sisters scandalized the neighborhood one sunny afternoon by romping naked in the backyard. Their mother, with typical aplomb, replied to the indignant neighbors, "That's why we have a fence! Just don't look out your window."

Anne's formal education began at Redemptorist School, referred to in *Prism* as "the poorest white school in the city." The building, which sits directly to the left of St. Alphonsus Church, has now been converted to public housing. From fourth through ninth grades, Anne attended the Holy Name of Jesus School, affiliated with Holy Name Church near Loyola and Tulane universities.

This put her in daily proximity to Audubon Park, where she took to wandering among the ancient moss-hung oaks, listening to the distinct Southern song of the cicadas. Nearer home, Anne frequented the public library at Lee Circle, since torn down (the K&B Building now stands on the site). There, *Prism* recounts, the little girl with the straight dark hair and huge brown eyes would "ask for books about big houses and creepy things."

A couple of blocks behind the O'Brien house was the Granada Theatre (also a victim of the wrecking ball), where little Anne bravely faced a rerelease of 1933's *The Mummy* from the front row, but eventually succumbed to terror, burst into tears, and fled. (More recently, much the same reaction was had by talk-show host Oprah Winfrey on seeing *Interview With the Vampire*.)

Soon after Anne entered her teens, the family moved a short distance uptown to 2524 St. Charles, which was owned by Catholic priests and had served variously as a school, convent, and rectory. It even included a room that had once been a private chapel. When Anne was in high school, Katherine died from complications of alcoholism. She is buried with her mother's family, the Connels, in St. Joseph Cemetery on Washington Avenue. Anne returned to Redemptorist School in 1956 for tenth grade. She helped raise money to build the Redemptorist gym, and was aghast to learn that although boys *and* girls had pitched in with the fund-raising, girls could use the gym only after the boys were finished with their activities.

To get to Redemptorist School from the O'Brien home on St. Charles, Anne regularly walked through the Garden District, one of America's most stunningly gorgeous residential areas, replete with block after block of Greek Revival, Italianate, and mixed-style antebellum homes. This was the area settled in the nineteenth century by the wealthy Americans who swarmed into the city after the Louisiana Purchase. It was their retort to the rich Creole mansions of Esplanade Avenue, on the downriver edge of the French Quarter.

Anne's strolls through the Garden District undoubtedly inspired the similar walks and yearning feelings of Michael Curry in *The Witching Hour*. Real-life Currys, incidentally, are one of Anne's ancestral families. Michael grows up on Annunciation Street, his love of architecture and design fueled by saunters through the Garden District, physically just across Magazine Street but economically and emotionally on the other side of the world. Michael eventually opens a restoration firm, Great Expectations (named for his favorite Dickens novel), in a Magazine Street storefront.

Anne's return to Redemptorist School was fairly short-lived. Soon after Katherine's death, Howard moved the family from St. Charles to an apartment on St. Mary Street, and Anne and her sisters went as boarders to St. Joseph's Academy in the French Quarter, on Ursulines near Esplanade. In *Prism*, Anne describes the school as "like something out of *Jane Eyre*, a dilapidated, awful, medieval type of place." The boarders slept on the top floor of the four-story brick building. In *The Witching Hour*, St. Joseph's is resurrected as St. Rose de Lima's, one of the many learning forums from which the unruly Deirdre Mayfair is expelled.

Culture Shock: From the Big Easy to Big D

The O'Briens, now including stepmom Dorothy Van Bever O'Brien (who bought Anne her first typewriter), moved to Richardson, Texas, in the summer of 1958. Howard's employer, the U.S. Post Office, had transferred him to the Dallas regional office, and Richardson was the closest suburb north of Dallas.

So at sixteen, Anne was transported from the lush, mist-caressed banks of the Mississippi to the flat, dry plains of North Texas. The physical differences between the two areas were striking, with New Orleans the clear winner in terms of charm if not climate. Humidity is a pervasive problem in both cities, but it is possible to have a dry moment or two in Dallas, whereas one never feels completely moisture-free in New Orleans (one former resident nailed it when she described it as "living in a terrarium"). The sun shines mercilessly on both locales, but Dallas can't compete with New Orleans's seductively balmy nights, which compensate for the blistering days, and its frequent Caribbean-style afternoon rain showers that bring brief, deceptive coolness.

Other disparities were even more startling. Richardson, once known as the "City of Churches," sits smack in the navel of the Bible Belt. It was (and still is) Baptist, Methodist, and Lutheran country, with few Catholics and still scarcer opportunity for Catholic education. So for the first time in her life, Anne O'Brien enrolled in a public, coeducational school, Richardson High School. It was there, in a journalism class, that she met her future husband, artist-poet Stan Rice, whose family hails from Dallas. The summer after Anne graduated (Stan, a year younger, graduated the following year), she, Stan, and another male friend went to New Orleans for a week. Stan and the friend stayed at 2301 St. Charles, Anne's old childhood home, which had been turned into a boardinghouse.

After graduation, Anne briefly attended Texas Woman's University, in Denton, about twenty-five miles north of Dallas via Interstate 35E. A secluded garden at the school plays an eerie role in *The Witching Hour*, as the site where Aaron Lightner has a frightening encounter with Deirdre Mayfair. Anne transferred to North Texas State University (now the University of North Texas), also in Denton, her sophomore year, and Stan also enrolled at NTSU.

But Anne had endured Texas long enough and yearned for adventure and travel. She and a school friend moved to San Francisco, alighting in the boisterous Haight district. A year later, Anne returned to Denton to marry Stan Rice in a civil ceremony at the home of one of Stan's English professors, and then the newlyweds headed back to the West Coast.

The Rices would stay in San Francisco for twenty-five years, with ups and downs to rival the fiercest roller coaster—Stan's success as a poet and professor; the joy of parenthood with Michele, born September 21, 1966; the devastation of her death from leukemia at age five;

Anne's burgeoning writing career; a second chance at parenthood with Christopher, born March 11, 1978. Michele Rice, although she died a child, is the spiritual mother to Anne's vampires, Louis, Lestat, and Claudia. *Interview* was written in a five-week flurry of grief following Michele's death, and features the five-year-old vampire Claudia (whose September 21 "birth date"—the day she's made a vampire—coincides with Michele's birthday.)

Home at Last: Return to New Orleans

The Rice clan returned to New Orleans in 1988. The old house at Philip and St. Charles was a depressing sight to Anne's eyes; it had fallen to near ruins due to the neglect of an absentee landlord. The Rices found a home on the other side of the Garden District, a 131-year-old pink house at 1020 Philip Street in the Irish Channel. It was near the residence of one of Anne's cousins, and from its windows, the steeples of St. Alphonsus and St. Mary's peeked through the trees.

The Rices maintained their house in San Francisco, but for all practical purposes had come home to the South. At this time, Anne was working on *The Witching Hour*, which featured an imaginary setting in a house a few blocks away on Philip Street. In October, New Orleans officially welcomed Anne back with a gift that might have struck "outsiders" as somewhat odd, but was in its way a perfect tribute: She was given an "honorary deed" to a plot in St. Louis Cemetery No. 1, as well as a small, discreet garlic wreath. Though surely well-meaning, somebody goofed with the garlic—Anne's vampires are immune to the repellent qualities of that herb.

Anne, Stan, and Christopher Rice returned to New Orleans permanently in 1989, more than thirty years after the O'Briens' exodus to Texas. Anne once more took to strolling around the Garden District, à la Michael Curry, and was particularly drawn to the historic Brevard-Clapp House at 1239 First Street on the Chestnut Street corner. An architectural concoction blending Greek Revival and Italianate styles, the house was built in 1857 by Charles Pride. Its intricate cast-iron fence,

Anne Rice's Garden District townhouse, the home of her fictional Mayfair Witches.

twined with roses, inspired the house's nickname, Rosegate. Anne said in interviews at the time that the house "called to her" to buy it. She answered its summons, and honored her new dwelling by reworking *Witching* to make the First Street house the residence of the Mayfairs. It may be "Rosegate" or "the Brevard-Clapp House" in many of the old guidebooks, but to Anne Rice fans, this corner will forever be known simply as "the Mayfair house."

The townhouse, which does indeed sport the "Egyptian keyhole" doorway so prominently mentioned in the Mayfair books, came complete with what some might consider an essential element for any Anne Rice home: its own reputed ghost. A woman named Pamela Starr, whose initials are carved into the ballroom mirrors, lived in the home from age seventeen to ninety-two. She died there in the 1930s. In addition to tales of Pamela, stories have circulated about a man who supposedly committed suicide by shooting himself on the staircase—the same twenty-seven-step flight on which Arthur Langtry sees Stuart Townsend's ghost in *Witching*.

Rice's elation at coming home is evident in *Witching*, the "city-bridging" book that she started in San Francisco and completed in New Orleans. An entire chapter of *Witching* concentrates on lovingly describing the Crescent City, especially the Garden District. "Was there anyplace in the world where the air was such a living presence, where the breeze kissed you and stroked you, where the sky was pulsing and alive?" Michael Curry muses as he wanders the streets, following his own arrival home after years in (no coincidence) San Francisco.

Through her evocative descriptions and an uncanny ability to re-create space and mood, Anne Rice has intellectually ferried millions of fans to the Crescent City. Some are content with armchair adventuring, believing that they can capture much of the city's ambiance via Rice's works, through a sort of literary transfusion. To some extent, they're absolutely correct: New Orleans is so well-described by Rice that on my first visit I saw almost exactly what I expected.

On the other hand, it was so much more. You can intellectually understand, and imagine, a moonlight saunter through the Garden District. But to actually experience it—to skitter with fear when a flutter of crisp, stray magnolia leaves mimic a stranger's footsteps behind you, to gasp aloud at your first sight of *that house*—is a wholly emotional endeavor. Like great bliss or sorrow, it simply cannot be adequately preimagined.

In a way, the city bears much in common with Rice's view of immortality. It's irresistibly seductive, blessed with a delicate, frequently astonishing beauty. Yet the price must be paid, and in New Orleans it has been extracted through an unending cycle of heat, humidity, decay, and disease. But once New Orleans has captured your heart, you'll never again be safe from her charms. The city is like a moody lover: You know the heat and humidity and insects and rich food are bad for you. But just when you're ready to bail out, it turns all sweetly caressing, murmuring in your ear with silky breezes and velvet strains of jazz, and you're lost again. Be prepared.

Hopefully, *Haunted City* will help evoke those feelings for those who, for whatever reason, cannot actually visit New Orleans. But I hope it also will urge those on the fence about traveling to hop an airplane, train, horse and buggy, or roller skates, to experience New Orleans's bittersweet brew with their own lips and noses and the very pores of their skin.

New Orleans 101

First, a quick explanation of New Orleanians' unique sense of direction. You may have puzzled over it when reading Rice's works. In *Witching*, for instance, she refers to the Mayfair house as being on the "riverside downtown corner" of First and Chestnut. Understandable reaction of those unfamiliar with the Crescent City: "Huh?"

That nifty compass watch won't help you navigate New Orleans. East, west, north, and south might be used to refer to points outside the city—"Oh, those folks back east don't understand about Southern tradition"—but that's not what you'll hear if you ask for directions. And it's utterly futile to try to thrust your directional biases on New Orleanians; they'll just laugh good-naturedly and try to enlighten you on the error of your ways.

The original colony's geographical position, perched on a carved-out arc of the Mississippi River, renders it a bit off-center in terms of traditional directional points. New Orleanians, typically, have simplified things for themselves without worrying too much about the reaction, or confusion, of outsiders. So here, everything is "uptown" or "downtown," "riverside" or "lakeside." The easiest way to deal with this directional schizophrenia is this: Upon arrival, locate your "home base" on a map that shows both the river and Lake Pontchartrain. Then scope out the French Quarter and the Garden District.

Now imagine you're on the streetcar heading from the French Quarter to the Garden District. You're going uptown, as well as up-river—St. Charles Avenue visually mimics the curves of the Mississippi. The lake would be to your right (the opposite side of St. Charles from the Garden District). The river lies beyond the Garden District and the Irish Channel to your left. You'll notice that Garden District homes usually have broad galleries on the river side (toward Magazine Street), to catch the refreshing breezes stirred by "Old Muddy."

Okay, so you're standing at First and Chestnut, still wondering which is the "riverside downtown corner." It's the corner toward the French Quarter (downtown) and toward Magazine Street (riverside). Totally confused yet? Don't worry. After a couple of days, it becomes almost natural to think of directions this way. But you might be in trouble when you return home, trying to readjust to navigation by compass points. Just think of it as directional jet lag.

New Orleanians also play fast and loose with traditional pronunciation, giving every street name its own distinctive spin. If you took a year or two of high school French, don't make the mistake of trying to impress anyone with your perfectly accented versions of Vieux Carré street names. Chartres, for example, here is pronounced plain old "Charters." For Burgundy, the accent is put on the *second* syllable—"Bur-*gun*-dee." *Lagniappe*, the local expression for "a little something extra"—that third *beignet* or chocolate mint after a meal—is pronounced "lan-yap." The all-time tongue scrambler to many nonresidents is Tchoupitoulas— "Chop-a-*tool*-us." Perhaps the best advice is just to pronounce everything exactly opposite of the way you think it should be.

For newcomers, the following orientation should help you maneuver the New Orleans streets, many of which follow the ancient curve of the Mississippi River. A sketch of the city's past will help you put the lives of Louis, Lestat, Claudia, and the Mayfairs into historical perspective. A word of warning, however: Discretion is recommended when publicly discussing, for instance, the potential impact of the Civil War on the Mayfairs, or whether Lestat and Louis made any attempt to learn English after the Louisiana Purchase. Make sure you're among fellow Rice fans (and they're everywhere, so that shouldn't be too difficult), or you risk some strange looks.

Ancient Origins

The swampy wilderness that would become New Orleans was bred some 25,000 years ago, after the Ice Age zapped drainage systems throughout the midwestern United States and rerouted drainage in the direction of the previously puny Mississippi River.

The Mississippi Delta's southern end was filled in by the resultant debris and silt, eventually wrestling Lake Pontchartrain from the arms of its mother, the Gulf of Mexico, a relatively recent 5,000 years ago. The soft, mosquito-infested swampland left between the lake and river became the unlikely site for New Orleans. In *Interview*, when Claudia and Louis dump Lestat's body in the swamps "just beyond the city's north gate," they are returning him to the city's geographic womb. In fact, Lestat's fate, if temporary, was not uncommon in early New Orleans. In a Catholic city, suicide was considered the most heinous violation of both church and municipal law. Those who dared take their own lives had their bodies dragged through the streets of the Vieux Carré, presumably to elicit postmortem humiliation and to serve as a deterrent to anyone else contemplating this mortal sin. Furthermore, suicide victims were denied burial in consecrated ground, and their bodies were tossed without final rites into the outlying swamps.

Louisiana was first scouted by Spanish explorers in the sixteenth century, but ultimately was claimed by a Frenchman, René-Robert Cavelier, sieur de la Salle. (Despite eventual Spanish reign over the territory, French influence over Louisiana and New Orleans never waned; the culturally stubborn French influenced their Spanish "rulers" far more than the other way around.) In 1682, La Salle led an expedition of fifty-six intrepid explorers down the Mississippi to its mouth, about ninety miles below present-day New Orleans. In early April of that year, La Salle plunged a cross into the mud at the river's mouth and declared the entire valley to be the property of the Sun King, Louis XIV of France. La Salle called the site "Louisiane," which, mingled with the Spanish "Luisiana," became today's "Louisiana."

La Salle was followed by French Canadian brothers Pierre le Moyne, sieur d'Iberville, and Jean Baptiste le Moyne, sieur de Bienville, who landed in what is now Mississippi. In 1699, they, too, sailed to the mouth of the Mississippi River, naming the point where they landed Pointe du Mardi Gras because that year, the Catholic holiday of "Fat Tuesday" fell the day after their landing. That fall, a pair of British ships appeared at the river's mouth, but the French brothers convinced them they were in the wrong spot. The point in the river where the dejected Brits reversed their course is still called English Turn.

Parlez-vous Français?

The first permanent French settlement in the boundaries of present-day Louisiana was founded in 1715 at Natchitoches. Three years later, in the spring of 1718, the Ville de la Nouvelle Orleans was founded by Jean-Baptiste le Moyne, sieur de Bienville, who named it for Phillipe II, duc d'Orleans, regent (and *de facto* ruler) of France during the minority of the child king Louis XV. Bienville's brother, Iberville, had died of yellow fever in 1706 in Cuba. New Orleans's locale, in a natural curve of the Mississippi River, quickly earned it the nickname "the Crescent City."

Meanwhile, control of the economically unsuccessful Louisiana colony had been transferred by France to the Company of the West (later known as the Company of the Indies), headed by Scottish financier John Law. The deal was simple: The company would have authority for twenty-five years, including a trade monopoly and appointment of the governor and the other leaders. Law, in return, agreed to send Louisiana 6,000 white colonists and 3,000 blacks during the first decade. That would require considerable effort on his part: A 1721 census revealed a distinctly skimpy population of free whites: 290 men, 140 women, and 96 children. Another 156 colonists were listed as indentured white servants, with 533 black and 50 Indian slaves.

Law mounted a marketing campaign that makes twentieth-century advertising tactics look saintly by comparison. His plan, later called "the Mississippi Bubble" for the way it eventually burst, promised those willing to invest in the New World fertile fields, gold mines, seas full of pearls, and a heavenly climate that virtually eradicated old age and disease. The best part was this: The "shareholders" themselves need only put up the money and send the requisite warm bodies to work; they need not necessarily venture into this uncivilized outpost themselves.

Hence many of New Orleans's first citizens were paupers, prostitutes, and jail or hospital inmates. Some came willingly, deeming even a savage wilderness more agreeable than the ghastly European prisons of the time. Those who declined were put in shackles and sent anyway. New laws were enacted in France to expedite Law's plans—one allowed that anyone out of work for four consecutive days could be shipped to Louisiana; another gave total freedom to any French jail inmate, provided he agree to marry a prostitute and move to Louisiana. The lack of women, something of a stumbling block to increasing population, also was alleviated by releasing dozens of "professional" girls from Parisian prisons and sending them into the eager arms, and huts, of New Orleans's lovelorn men.

Perhaps because they already were accustomed to less-than-ideal conditions, those first New Orleanians were remarkably resilient, blithely reconstructing from the ground up every time a hurricane, flood, or fire destroyed the city. The hurricane of 1721 conveniently wiped the slate clean for Adrien de Pauger's city plan (the old buildings most certainly would not have met with the royal engineer's orderly ideal). Pauger laid out a formal grid pattern, with four blocks above and below the central square, the Place d'Armes. During Spanish rule, the square was called Plaza de Armas, and in 1851 it was renamed for Andrew Jackson, hero of the Battle of New Orleans during the War of 1812.

With the eventual addition of extra blocks, the city extended from Iberville Street uptown to Esplanade Avenue downtown. The area between Iberville and Canal Street originally was not included in the town plan, and the "official" Vieux Carré (meaning "old square") still ends at Iberville. The town ran six streets deep, from the Rue de la Levee (later changed to Decatur) at riverside, to Rampart Street on the lakeside. The less-than-flawless environs were succinctly described by one eighteenth-century scribe: "Those living in the city dedicated to the Duke of Orleans feel as if they were living on an island in the middle of a mud puddle."

Most of the original Vieux Carré streets were approximately thirty-eight feet wide, resulting in the intimate scale still treasured by French Quarter walkers and cursed by those trying to drive (or, heaven forbid, park) within its narrow confines. Orleans Street, extending directly behind St. Louis Cathedral, was envisioned as the main thoroughfare and consequently is seven feet wider. Blocks were subdivided into twelve rectangular lots each, surrounded by deep drainage ditches.

The streets were named for their primary buildings, and for saints, French aristocracy, and royalty. Those running "vertically," when looking at a map, are (starting at the uptown edge of the Quarter) Iberville, Bienville, Conti, St. Louis, Toulouse, St. Peter, Orleans, St. Ann, du

Maine (now Dumaine), Clermont (St. Philip), Rue Arsenal (Ursulines), Hospital (Governor Nicholls), Barracks, and Esplanade. The "horizontal" streets, starting closest to the river, were Rue de la Levee (now Decatur), Condé (Chartres), Royal, Bourbon, Vendome (Dauphine), Bourgogne (Burgundy), and Rampart. Pauger's plan called for stockade fences and five forts surrounding the city, but fortification did not begin until 1760, when Quebec fell to the British (making other French colonies, no matter how distant, nervous). The battlements never were completed.

In 1727, the first Ursuline nuns arrived in New Orleans, attempting to impart some reverence and dignity, not to mention nursing and education, to the reckless inhabitants of the city. The sisters took care of orphans, set up a school and hospital, and gave shelter to the immigrant *filles à la cassette* ("casket girls"), the middle-class, well-bred French girls whose government-provided trousseaus gave them their nickname. The casket girls, arriving from 1728 to 1751, provided respectable marriage opportunities for the gentlemen of the colony. The Ursuline Convent, designed in 1745 and completed in 1752, is generally recognized as the oldest building in the Mississippi Valley.

In 1729, Indians raided Fort Rosalie at Natchez, killing some 200 men and taking more than 400 women, children, and slaves prisoners. The Indian attacks so close to New Orleans tested the nerves of the already tense citizenry, and in 1731, John Law's Company of the Indies gladly returned the unruly town to the hands of the French crown. Bienville was called out of retirement to serve as governor.

By then, however, Law's plan had gone to work, almost in spite of itself. Through stubborn persistence backed by not much else, Law's outlaw colonists had built a thriving city of some 7,000, with burgeoning businesses dealing in everything from lumber and bricks to sugar and rum.

Spanish Acquisition

In November 1762, King Louis XV ceded Louisiana to Spain in the secret (to all but the Spanish) Treaty of Fontainbleau. France neglected to inform its colonial subjects of this minor detail until April 1764, when Louis finally caught up on his correspondence and sent a letter to Jean-Jacques Blaise D'Abbadie, governor of Louisiana. New Orleanians finally heard about the deal in October 1764. Needless to say, they were not amused.

It was another eighteen months before a Spanish official set foot in Louisiana. Don Antonio de Ulloa, appointed governor by Carlos III of Spain, arrived in March 1766 with ninety infantrymen. He was met with unbridled hatred. Not only did New Orleanians dislike the idea of becoming Spanish, they found trade increasingly difficult since no one was clear whose laws, French or Spanish, were to be followed.

In 1768, some 600 New Orleanians (mostly Germans and Acadians, the French-speaking immigrants from Canada who became today's "Cajuns"), led by Nicolas Chauvin de Lafreniere, rebelled against the Spanish, forcing Ulloa to flee to Havana. Spain's King Carlos responded decisively, sending 2,600 troops to New Orleans, a contingent larger than the entire male population of the city. The leader of the mercenary unit, Don Alexander O'Reilly (an Irishman in Spanish service), earned the nickname Bloody O'Reilly by putting all the revolutionaries to death before firing squads. Although unsuccessful, this uprising was the first example of colonial rebellion in what would become the United States. (Rice may have had Lafreniere in mind in naming Louis's River Road neighbors, the Frenieres, in *Interview*.)

It was during the nearly forty years of Spanish rule that New Orleans was struck with two disastrous fires. For a city that has steadfastly retained its inherent Catholicism, New Orleans has had particularly bad luck on religious holidays. On Good Friday, March 21, 1788, more than four-fifths of the city was reduced to ashes in a raging blaze that began in the private chapel of Don Vincente Jose Nunez, the city's military treasurer. The flames, ignited by a falling altar candle, raged through the city like vengeful demons, burning 865 buildings (out of a total of some 1,100), including the parish church on the plaza. Many residents didn't know about the fire until it was upon them; the parish priests were reluctant to ring the church bells on a holy day. Ever resilient, burned-out New Orleanians pitched tents in the plaza and on the river levee and started to rebuild.

Rebuilding was advancing nicely when, just six years later, in 1794, on the Feast of the Immaculate Conception, another fire destroyed more than 200 buildings. This blaze was accidentally set by children playing in a hay store on Royal Street. City leaders finally recognized that they couldn't keep rebuilding the town every few years, and passed an ordinance mandating that all structures of more than one story must be brick.

Tile roofs became common, and two- and three-story houses of masonry and stucco replaced the simpler wooden Creole cottages. The most popular type of construction, *briquete-entre-poteaux* ("bricks-between-posts"), featured diagonal crossbeam braces made of cypress planks, with the inner space filled in with native brick. A still-visible example of this type of construction is Lafitte's Blacksmith Bar on Bourbon Street. The cypress beams and bricks can be seen on the side of the building, where patches of the stucco overcoat have been chipped away by time and vandals.

Although the Spanish were distinctly unsuccessful in influencing the French-drenched culture and language of New Orleans, they did bring their style of building, and the French Quarter as we see it today is, ironically, almost entirely Spanish architecture. The Spanish brought their penchant for ornate decoration—wrought iron began to spring up in the form of lanterns, arches, gates, latches, door handles, and keyholes. They also painted their stucco homes in pastel colors recalling the waters and sunsets of the Mediterranean—turquoise, apricot, buttercup, mint, sky blue, and petunia pink bloomed above the grimy streets.

Most nineteenth-century Creole homes were L-shaped, with the short side on the street, and the long side running along inner gardens, called courtyards by the French and patios by the Spanish. The word *courtyard* stems from the French *coeur* for "heart," since the private, enclosed areas served as the heart of the household. The word *Creole*, by the way, has been attributed to a variety of origins, including *crioulo*, meaning a slave of African descent born in the New World. In New Orleans, it came to mean a New Orleans–born person descended from one of the original French or Spanish colonists.

It was also during the Spanish period that "Bronze John," or yellow fever, made its most frequent and deadly visits to the city. A 1796 outbreak led to thirty-eight more epidemics throughout the nineteenth century (twenty-three between 1817 and 1860 alone) and into the twentieth, finally ending with the epidemic of 1905. Early colonists, having no idea that the often lethal disease was spread by the ubiquitous moisture-loving mosquitoes, were virtually helpless to stop it. The early 1850s were particularly lethal, with yellow fever outbreaks in four out of five years, and some 12,000 deaths in 1853 alone. One minister described, with appalling precision, the devastation: "A private hospital was found deserted; the physicians, nurses and attendants were all dead, or had run away. Not a living person was in it. The wards were filled with putrid bodies."

So the nineteenth century New Orleans inhabited by Rice's Louis, Lestat, and Claudia was far from idyllic, although as vampires they at least had immortality on their side. Their New Orleans was pestilence- and insect-ridden, un-air-conditioned, and rife with crime. Most streets remained unpaved, muddy ruts through the 1890s. Wide, deep gutters edging the streets were lined with stone and bridged by granite or wooden slabs to allow crossing. These little bridges were called *banquettes*, the word still used by New Orleanians to describe their sidewalks.

Invasion of the Americans

In 1803, New Orleanians experienced triple culture shock, going from bad to much worse, in their opinion. To hallelujahs all around, the city was transferred back to French rule under Napoleon Bonaparte. But the French flag had barely had time to flutter a couple of times in the Place d'Armes before New Orleans became the crown jewel in the best dollar-for-acre land deal of all time: the Louisiana Purchase. The transfer from France to the United States included more than 800,000 square miles, bought at less than five cents an acre. The New Orleans citizenry hadn't been happy about Spanish rule, but at least the Spaniards were European and Catholic. Now the French and Spanish were united in indignant fury that their city was going to be governed by *Americans*, and worse, *Protestants*. Residents reacted with nothing less than abject horror, and the Ursuline nuns were so traumatized that they temporarily retreated to Cuba. One extremely consequential fragment of the three-week (November 30–December 20, 1803) French resurgence still remains, however: The Napoleonic Code was established as the legal norm, in contrast to the British-inspired legal system throughout the rest of the country.

After the Louisiana Purchase, U.S. President Thomas Jefferson appointed twenty-eight-year-old William Charles Cole Claiborne as governor of the Territory of Orleans. The Marquis de Lafayette and James Monroe had both declined the "honor." Claiborne was a Protestant from Virginia who spoke not a single word of French, and although New Orleans's official language was now English, most of its inhabitants spoke only *Français*. Claiborne tried to diffuse tensions by retaining French mayor Etienne de Boré, who had been appointed by Napoleon, but a frustrated Boré resigned only six months later.

The term *dixie* came into usage following the Louisiana Purchase, when bilingual ten-dollar notes nicknamed dixies were printed in New Orleans. They read "10 dollars" on one side for the Americans, and "dix," French for "ten," on the other for the Creoles. The word *dixie*, originally used only in New Orleans, eventually came to be associated with the entire South, particularly during the Civil War (or "War Between the States," as it is still called by many stalwart Southerners. Some still bristle at anything less than "War of Northern Aggression.").

New Orleans boomed under U.S. rule, bolstered by the explosion of trade down the Mississippi River. By 1810, New Orleans was the largest city in the South and the fifth largest in the United States. In April 1812, Louisiana became the nation's eighteenth state, just in time to be official when, little more than a month later, America once more went to war with Great Britain. New Orleanians had avoided any participation in the Revolutionary War, distanced as they were by both geography and nationality. This time, however, they were Americans, and the conflict roared down the river to them. By early 1814, rumors were flying that the British were advancing toward New Orleans. By December, it was clear that an attack was imminent. Andrew Jackson, a forty-seven-year-old major general in the U.S. Army, was ill and recuperating at his Royal Street home in the French Quarter. From his sickbed, Jackson declared martial law and recruited assistance from anyone who could fire a gun, including the local Choctaw Indians and pirate Jean Lafitte and his crew.

General Jackson attacked the British, who were camped on the banks of the Mississippi, on December 23, 1814. The British got reinforcements and charged back against the Americans on New Year's Day, 1815. The final battle began January 8 at Chalmette Plantation, with the scroungy Jackson-led militia facing the highly organized British. Jackson's troops may have been ragtag, but they were better shots. When the final volleys had been fired, the British had lost 858 men and seen another 2,500 wounded. The Americans lost 15 and suffered another 40 injuries. Soon after the British sailed away in defeat, word reached New Orleans that the Treaty of Ghent, officially ending the War of 1812, had been signed on Christmas Eve, 1814, two weeks *prior* to the Battle of New Orleans.

During the early to mid 1800s, tension increased between the Catholic Creoles of the French Quarter and the Protestant Americans who were settling upriver in the Faubourg (suburb) St. Marie. In 1807, a strip of land between the two sectors was designated as "neutral ground"; we now know it as Canal Street. Today, all medians throughout New Orleans are still called neutral ground. Original plans for Canal Street called for it to connect to the Carondelet Canal (the Old Basin Canal), which ran to Bayou St. John and then Lake Pontchartrain, thus creating a complete river-to-lake water route. Fifty feet of Canal Street's 171-foot width was designated for the canal, which never materialized— a short-lived drainage ditch was as close as Canal Street ever came to its original intent. But because of that ambitious goal, New Orleans ended up with what is still the United States' widest thoroughfare.

The nearly half-century between the War of 1812 and the War Between the States—the prime years for Lestat, Louis, and Claudia's sixty-five-year experiment as a "family"—was arguably New Orleans's most successful era, a certifiable "Belle Epoque" with a growing economy, glittering society on both sides of the neutral ground, and an outburst of architectural activity. By the early 1830s, "King Cotton" was the main crop of Southern planters, with sugar a close second. The ongoing need for cheap labor on Louisiana plantations made New Orleans the biggest slave market in the South, with human cargo being bought and sold with abandon at the sweaty Camp Street auctions.

A crop of talented and energetic architects arrived in New Orleans in the early 1800s, including Henry Latrobe, followed by his famous father, Benjamin, and Irish-born James Gallier. Many of the city's most recognized and acclaimed buildings were constructed during this period, including the first St. Charles Hotel (which burned in 1851), Gallier Hall (originally the Americans' City Hall), and many of the still-standing buildings of the French Quarter. Major civic improvements took place during this period, including some street-lighting, although lighting one's own way by lantern was still common until the late 1830s.

Merchants, who once clustered exclusively on Royal and Chartres streets, moved uptown to Canal and Camp in the American sector. During the 1850s, Judah Touro (by all accounts the city's wealthiest man) donated $10,000 to beautify Canal Street, which was then briefly named Touro Avenue. Citizens, while no doubt grateful, persisted in calling it Canal, and it was officially changed back a few years later.

As population and prosperity grew, though, so did crime. The night-seeing vampires of Rice's books would have had no trouble gliding through the inky darkness that must have typified New Orleans nights of the early nineteenth century, but it was tougher going for the ordinary mortals of the city. Today, a nighttime stroll down Pirates Alley or Père Antoine Alley (the pedestrian streets along the sides of St. Louis Cathedral) still can bring a feeling of instant isolation and irrational terror. Don't wander alone after dark, however, or that feeling might not be so irrational—Père Antoine Alley, on the downriver side of the cathedral, has an especially unsavory reputation.

By 1840, New Orleans had a population of more than 102,000 and was the United States' fourth-largest city and second-busiest port. La Belle Epoque's bustling commerce and heady optimism would come to a stunning halt just twenty years later, however, when the Civil War forced Louisianians to ally with a South they'd never completely felt part of—much of New Orleans's agricultural and commercial success was due to ties with the North. Nevertheless, in January 1861, an Order of Secession was passed by a large majority, and Louisiana existed for nine days as an independent republic before joining the Confederacy in early February. Trade and commerce ground to a halt due to a federal blockade of the Mississippi, and two months later, Union captain David Glasgow Farragut and his fleet took possession of the Crescent City.

New Orleans remained occupied until deep into Reconstruction; it wouldn't rid itself of the last Union soldier until mid-1877. Much of the city's Reconstruction era was overseen by General Benjamin Butler, who arrived in May 1861 with 15,000 federal troops. Butler was probably the most hated man in Louisiana, and much of the rest of the South, during the nineteenth century. You won't see any buildings named after him or appreciative monuments in his honor in New Orleans. If Lestat had actually existed, New Orleanians probably would have gladly paid him to dispose of Butler.

The bleak years of Reconstruction—at one point Louisiana was bankrupt with a debt of $53 million—eventually gave way to renewed optimism and progress. By 1882, Canal Street was completely lit by electricity, and by 1887, most of the city was bathed in an electric glow. In 1892, the first electric streetcars began running, replacing the mule-drawn cars that had been used since the Civil War (the mules undoubtedly rejoiced).

The late 1890s also spawned one of the city's most notorious experiments—the thirty-eight-block area known as Storyville, where controlled (if not actually legalized) prostitution was allowed between 1897 and 1917. The ordinance creating the district was introduced by Alderman Sidney Story, who regretted his innovative thinking when the area became known, much to his embarrassment, as Storyville. All that remains today of the infamous red-light district is a small sign on Rampart Street pointing out the area, which was completely torn down and rebuilt with an equally notorious (for its crime rate) public-housing complex.

At the dawn of the twentieth century, New Orleans finally saw the end of the horrific yellow fever epidemics that had cursed nineteenth-century city dwellers. The death rate dropped dramatically—from 28 per 1,000 annually in the 1890s to 18 per 1,000 in the early 1920s, a rate comparable to the rest of the nation. The twenties and thirties brought a flurry of building activity in the American section, now called the Central Business District. Concerned citizens formed the Vieux Carré Commission to encourage revitalization of the city's most historically important sector, which had fallen into disrepair, disfavor, and near-slum conditions in some areas. The commission's efforts halted demolition of some buildings and helped restore others; today's French Quarter residents and visitors owe much of what they cherish to the commission's work.

Anne Rice's *Vampire Chronicles* and *Mayfair Witches* series focus more on the unique, ethereal atmosphere of the "City That Care Forgot" (as it was dubbed during World War I) than actual historic events. But Rice's deep knowledge of and respect for New Orleans's past is always evident, if skillfully subtle. Her vampires trod the muddy, mucky streets of the early-nineteenth-century Quarter; her witches on the more solid, if equally muggy, streets of the late 1800s and the modern era. Louis and Lestat traveled by horse and carriage; Julien Mayfair via the St. Charles Streetcar; Rowan Mayfair and Michael Curry zipped around in a Mercedes convertible purchased from a dealership on St. Charles Avenue.

Readers of both series get a thorough indoctrination in Crescent City lore, both past and present. And for those with playful imaginations, it's an easy mind-hop from New Orleans of the mid-1990s back to 1890 or 1790. For a flashback to the past, simply stroll through the quieter, downriver end of the French Quarter on a foggy evening (carefully averting your eyes from Canal Street's towering, intolerably modern skyscrapers), picnic on a sunny day in Audubon Park, or meander the serene, oak-draped streets of the Garden District. But keep a careful watch; when you start mind-traveling through the past, especially in Anne Rice's world, you never know who your companions might be.

2

The Creole Connection: The French Quarter and Downtown

Surrounded by skyscrapers, concrete-and-steel highways, and the mad rush of twentieth-century life, the French Quarter, or Vieux Carré, steadfastly retains its nineteenth-century aura, despite the ubiquitous tourist shops, panhandlers, and runaways that speak all too poignantly of modern priorities, or lack thereof. By day, visitors can drink their fill of weathered-yet-enduring antebellum and Reconstruction architecture, antique shopping along Royal Street, and spicy Creole and Cajun cuisine (Creole is "city cooking"; Cajun the spicier country variety).

After sunset, temptations range from the wild throngs of Bourbon Street to the calmer pace of Café du Monde, where *beignets* (French donuts topped by heaping drifts of powdered sugar) and café au lait (half coffee, half milk) are available twenty-four hours a day, and frequently served with a side of jazz, courtesy of the street musicians always hovering around Jackson Square.

The Quarter is the oldest part of the city of New Orleans, still following the ninety-six-square-block, perfect-grid pattern laid out in 1721 by Adrien de Pauger. This area of approximately one square mile contains so much mental, visual, and physical stimulation that many tourists never venture out of its confines. About 7,000 people call the French

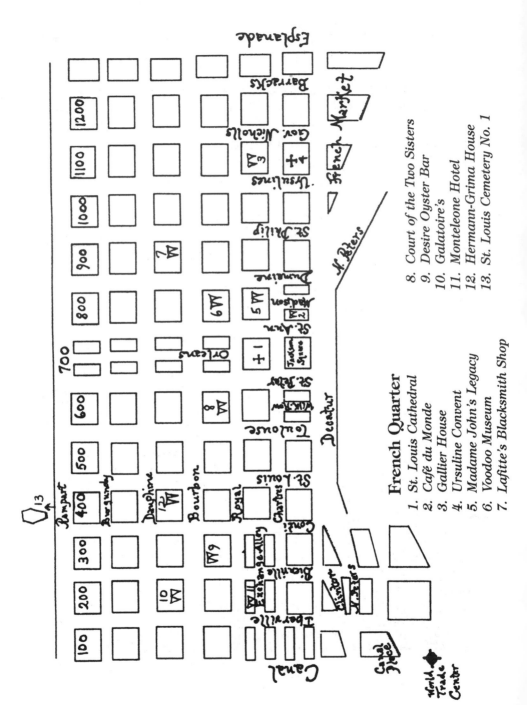

French Quarter

1. St. Louis Cathedral
2. Café du Monde
3. Gallier House
4. Ursuline Convent
5. Madame John's Legacy
6. Voodoo Museum
7. Lafitte's Blacksmith Shop
8. Court of the Two Sisters
9. Desire Oyster Bar
10. Galatoire's
11. Monteleone Hotel
12. Hermann-Grima House
13. St. Louis Cemetery No. 1

Quarter home, staunchly loyal to their neighborhood yet exuberantly welcoming to those with the right attitude—i.e., *"Laissez les bon temps roulez!"* ("Let the good times roll!").

The French Quarter perspective hangs on the easygoing philosophy that magic of any sort rarely occurs before noon. New Orleans is one of only two American cities—Las Vegas is the other—with no closing laws. Entertainment of all varieties continues 'round the clock, dwindling in intensity only in the hours just before sunrise and through midmorning. Get up at dawn and you'll encounter starkly deserted streets, scattered "go-cups" lining Bourbon Street, and buildings caressed by a rainbow of pastels, painted with gentle strokes by a quality of sunlight unlike that anywhere else in the world, with the possible exception of Venice. So awaken early if you must, see the sunrise and enjoy the hush, then take a nap to get ready for the evening. As radiantly beautiful as its early mornings can be, the French Quarter, as certainly Lestat and Louis would attest, is best seen by moonlight, when the fog

The Mississippi River from the decks of the Natchez steamboat, with the Crescent City Connection bridge (Lestat's "Dixie Gates") visible in the background.

seeps in and streetlights cast a spectral glow on rain-slicked streets, turning ordinary passageways into gateways through time, paved in gossamer silver.

The Riverfront

The heart of New Orleans is **Jackson Square**, which fronts St. Louis Cathedral and is bounded by Decatur, Chartres, St. Peter, and St. Ann streets. On Decatur, lining the riverside portion of the square, horse- and mule-drawn carriages line the street, their drivers eager to take visitors on a nostalgic, slow-paced journey through the Quarter. The clop-clop-clop of hooves on brick and slate streets is as much a part of the Quarter's ambiance as the beguiling rhythms of jazz and blues, and the slightly off-key calliope of the paddle-wheeler *Natchez*, announcing its twice-daily departures from the dock behind Jax Brewery with tinny interpretations of "Dixie" and "When the Saints Come Marching In."

Jackson Square, now an oasis of grassy serenity amid the vibrant hubbub of the Quarter, boasts a far less serene past, including use as a military parade ground. Hundreds, if not thousands, of criminals have been dragged from the jails to this spot, then flogged, shot, or hung in public executions that served as entertainment for colonists with the stomach to endure the blood and stench. Rice repeatedly uses Jackson Square as a rendezvous site; notably, it's where Lestat first comes face-to-face with Raglan James, the title villain of *Body Thief*. Rice's first mention of the square is in *Interview* via Louis, who naturally refers to it by its French sobriquet of Place d'Armes. Lasher, the demon spirit of the *Mayfair Witches* series, also appears in Jackson Square, materializing before the shocked eyes of the doctor in the opening chapter of *Witching*.

The centerpiece of the square is the equestrian statue of Major General Andrew Jackson, hero of the Battle of New Orleans. The bronze statue, by sculptor Clark Mills, was unveiled in February 1856 and is the world's first equestrian statute where more than one of the horse's hooves are unsupported. Union general Benjamin Butler further

Jackson Square, the heart of the Vieux Carré, was called the Plaza d'Armas during Spanish rule, 1762–1803.

endeared himself to an already hate-filled populace when, during the Civil War occupation, he had this out-of-context quote by Jackson engraved on the statue's base: "The Union must and shall be preserved." Not exactly balm to the wounded psyche of the South. Oddly, that message was the monument's only identification until late in the twentieth century—no other words, not even Andrew Jackson's name, marked the statue until August 1982, when the general's name was finally inscribed on the granite base.

The lovely cast-iron fence surrounding the square was designed by Louis H. Pilié, city surveyor, and constructed in 1851. The fountain on the Chartres Street side of the square, although it blends in perfectly with its nineteenth-century surroundings, was actually erected in 1960, when French president Charles De Gaulle visited New Orleans.

The five structures surrounding Jackson Square represent one of the best-preserved examples of nineteenth-century architecture anywhere in the United States. On Chartres Street facing the square, and dominating the French Quarter skyline, towers the stately **St. Louis Cathedral**, actually the third St. Louis Church to grace this site. The first church, an unimposing wooden structure, was designed in 1724 by Pauger, the original surveyor of the Quarter. The church was named for Louis IX, a thirteenth-century French king who fought in two Crusades. The Good Friday fire of 1788 destroyed this first house of worship, as well as some 850 other structures—a majority of the Quarter went up in flames that day.

A second St. Louis Church was dedicated on Christmas Eve 1794, and the structure was enlarged and substantially rebuilt from 1849 to 1851 by architect J. N. B. de Pouilly, who also designed many of the remarkable tombs found in New Orleans cemeteries. In 1964, Pope John Paul VI raised St. Louis Cathedral to the status of minor basilica. It is at St. Louis Church, about halfway through *Interview*, that Louis commits his most heinous murder—indulging his blood lust via the throat of a priest on the cathedral's communion railing, immediately in front of the altar. The history of St. Louis Cathedral is discussed in further detail in chapter 5.

The garden behind the church, on Royal Street between Pirates Alley and Père Antoine Alley, is officially called **Cathedral Garden**. Many, however, still refer to it affectionately as St. Anthony's Square, in honor of Antonio de Sedella, the most beloved priest in the history of New Orleans. Redubbed Père Antoine by his French-speaking parishioners, the priest served colonists from 1785 to 1790 and again from 1795 until his death in the 1820s. In the center of the garden, facing Royal and Orleans streets, stands a striking statue called the Sacred Heart of Jesus, arms reaching skyward. At night, the floodlights surrounding the statue throw an enormous, eerie shadow on the rear wall of the cathedral, an eye-catching, ghostly reminder of the city's Catholic heritage. Ironically, Congo Square, the heart of the eighteenth- and nineteenth-century voodoo culture, lurks at the opposite end of Orleans Street, just outside the Quarter.

The spires of St. Louis Cathedral have dominated Jackson Square since the mid-nineteenth century.

Closer to the Royal Street gate of Cathedral Garden is a monument erected during the reign of Napoleon, honoring thirty French marines who died while helping others during a yellow fever epidemic. The garden, like most New Orleans sites, has its sinister side—during the nineteenth century, bloody duels were frequently fought here, as well as under the "Dueling Oaks" in what is now City Park (formerly the Allard Plantation).

Pirates Alley, to the left of the cathedral between Chartres and Royal streets, is a quaint, frequently photographed pedestrian walkway paved with slate. Its name derives from its supposed use as a meeting place for the seafaring rogues, despite the irritating fact that pirates had pretty much gone out of fashion, and departed the city, by the time the alley opened. (It's so annoying when reality messes up a good story.) The street's most famous building is at 624 Pirates Alley, a butter-yellow building known as **William Faulkner House**. The famed Southern novelist, winner of the 1949 Nobel Prize, wrote his first novel, *Soldiers' Pay*, while renting an apartment in this house. During his stay in New Orleans, Faulkner contributed to the *New Orleans Times-Picayune* and the literary magazine *The Double Dealer*. Faulkner House is part of the LaBranche complex of eleven buildings, the most famous of which is at the riverside downtown corner of Royal and St. Peter streets.

The two buildings flanking the cathedral have witnessed some of New Orleans's most historically significant moments. Construction on the **Presbytère** (751 Chartres), on the right (downriver) as one faces the cathedral, was started in 1795. Both the Cabildo and the Presbytère were designed by architect Don Gilberto Guillemard, and both were designated as National Historic Landmarks in 1970. Two earlier, smaller buildings on this site were destroyed in the fires of 1788 and 1794.

The structure was called the Casa Curial by the Spanish, but in modern times has regained its French title of Presbytère. It originally was intended as a rectory for the priests of St. Louis Cathedral, but has never served that function. The Presbytère has been a part of the Louisiana State Museum complex since the early twentieth century, and houses changing historical exhibits. Permanent exhibits include *Uptown New Orleans: Historic Jefferson City*; *On Louisiana Waters*; *In the Eye of the Beholder: Treasures of the State Museum*; *Zachary Taylor: The Louisiana President*; and a Louisiana portrait gallery.

Flanking St. Louis Cathedral to the left (upriver) is the **Cabildo** (701 Chartres), named for the governing council that met here during Spanish rule. Construction began in 1795, the same year as for the Presbytère, but the Cabildo wasn't completed until after the Louisiana Purchase of 1803. Papers closing that mammoth real-estate transfer were signed in the Sala Capitular on the second floor of the then-unfinished

Romantic, spooky Pirates Alley runs along the upriver side of St. Louis Cathedral and Cathedral Garden, connecting Chartres and Royal streets.

Cabildo, and the Marquis de Lafayette used it as his home-away-from-home on a weeklong visit in 1825.

The building was financed by Don Andrés Almonester y Roxas, father of Micaela de Pontalba. A French prison and criminal courtroom sat on this site in the early 1700s, and portions of the previous building's brick walls were used in building the present Cabildo. During the nineteenth century, the building served as the city hall for the First Municipality when New Orleans was officially divided into three separate

The Cabildo, which partially burned in 1988, has been gloriously restored. The second-floor gallery offers spectacular views of Jackson Square.

sectors. The Cabildo also saw service as a criminal courtroom and prison. Through 1914, the prison in the building was used as a jail for the police station that occupied the first floor.

Years ending in "88" haven't been kind to French Quarter buildings; two centuries after the 1788 fire that destroyed most of the city (including the Cabildo that stood in this spot from 1769), a 1988 fire seriously damaged the present-day Cabildo's roof and top floor, and the building was closed. It reopened, gloriously restored, in February 1994. It has been part of the Louisiana State Museum since 1911 and now houses a $1.5 million multicultural exhibit about the history of New Orleans and Louisiana, from the first explorations through Reconstruction. A second-floor gallery display boasts weaponry dating back to the 1770s, and additional Cabildo treasures include Napoleon's death mask and a rosary once owned by Marie Antoinette. For photography buffs, both the Presbytère and Cabildo provide spectacular second-floor views of Jackson Square.

Lining St. Ann and St. Peter streets along the sides of Jackson Square are the red-brick **Pontalba Buildings**, named for the vivacious and clever Micaela Almonester de Pontalba, who financed and oversaw their construction between 1849 and 1851. Her initials—"A" for Almonester and "P" for Pontalba—can still be seen in the ornate ironwork adorning the balconies. The New York–made cast-iron galleries, in fact, were the first of their kind known to have been used in New Orleans. Both Pontalba Buildings were named National Historic Landmarks in 1974.

The headstrong Micaela married her cousin and moved to Paris while still a teenager, then returned to New Orleans after a scandalous divorce and the death of her father-in-law, some claim by Micaela's own hands. Legend has it that the elder Pontalba objected to the divorce and, during a nasty argument with his daughter-in-law, shot and wounded her. Micaela then wrestled the gun from him and shot him in the head. An equally lurid version has the baron shooting her, then turning the gun on himself, not realizing that Micaela wasn't quite dead. Whatever the exact circumstances, Micaela recovered, divorced her hubby, and returned a baroness to her native New Orleans.

The twin Pontalba buildings, designed by renowned local architects James Gallier Sr. and Henry Howard, are sometimes called the oldest apartment buildings in the United States. In fact, they each consist of sixteen separate row houses, with twelve on each side facing Jackson Square and two each facing Decatur and Chartres streets. They are referred to as the "Upper" and "Lower" Pontalbas, with respect to their relationship to the flow of the river.

The Upper Pontalba is to the left, or upriver, as one faces the square; the Lower Pontalba is to the right, or downriver. Following European custom, the buildings have room for commercial endeavors on the ground floors and living quarters on the upper levels. Today, the

The Lower Pontalba Building, completed in 1851, flanks the downriver side of Jackson Square.

ground-floor establishments are mostly small restaurants and specialty shops.

In the 1720s, the Chartres Street corner of the Upper Pontalba site was an officers' barracks, which was later used as a temporary church, warehouse, and governmental residence. Barracks also occupied the remainder of the block from 1738 to 1759. Don Almonester's widow constructed a mansion on the Decatur Street corner in 1811, but that and all the other buildings were demolished to make way for the current structure. Famous Swedish songstress Jenny Lind stayed in the

Upper Pontalba in 1851 during her New Orleans visit. Since 1930, the Upper Pontalba Building has been owned by the City of New Orleans.

The Lower Pontalba includes the **1850 House**, at 523 St. Ann, which is overseen by the Louisiana State Museum to give visitors an authentic look into an antebellum Creole household. The 1850 House, named for the year it was built, is entered by a narrow side passageway that leads to a curving staircase, leading to the living quarters above the downstairs shops. Decorated in the lavish Victorian style, the house is filled with grand touches—nary an inch seems unadorned by velvet, lace, gold leaf, or tapestry. Only the most privileged among New Orleans's elite could afford to live in one of Micaela de Pontalba's row houses; in the 1850s, she was charging as much as $300 per month in rent.

The Chartres Street corner of the Lower Pontalba was the site of the French governor's house from 1727 to 1738, and those who lived here included city founder Jean Baptiste le Moyne, sieur de Bienville. Barracks, matching those on the opposite side of the square, occupied the remainder of the block from 1738 to 1759. The Lower Pontalba was bequeathed to the Louisiana State Museum in 1927.

The **Louisiana Office of Tourism**, at 529 St. Ann, should be an early destination for any New Orleans visitor. Here you can get a wide variety of free maps and literature on various attractions, as well as information on tours, restaurants (including menus), and accommodations.

Café du Monde, part of the **French Market** complex, is a "must stop" for every visitor and an equally popular hangout for locals, especially in the wee hours. Located at 800 Decatur, between Jackson Square and the river, Café du Monde serves coffee, *beignets*, rich conversation, and an endless supply of street entertainment. In *Body Thief*, Lestat and Raglan James go to the café after meeting at Jackson Square; they can't get into the square because the gates are chained after sunset, which Lestat refers to as "a dreadful annoyance." Rowan and Michael also visit the café, in *Witching*.

Rice faithfully renders the restaurant's interior as "extremely noisy but warm," and comments on the stickiness of the tables—but with that many people and that much powdered sugar, it's a wonder patrons don't get permanently stuck to their chairs. In fact, it's a good thing Lestat

Café du Monde by lamplight, as it would have been seen by Lestat and Raglan James in *Body Thief.*

doesn't "eat" in the human sense, because with his penchant for wearing black, he'd never escape Café du Monde looking his dapper best. Word to the wise: If *beignets* are in your future, wear white or off-white. And under no circumstances attempt what I did on my last trip—eating one while *driving*, unless you enjoy looking as though you've been attacked by a vicious bag of flour.

The French Market itself was built on a spot once used by Indians for bartering, or so the tradition claims. The Spanish established a marketplace on the site in 1791, but those first buildings no longer exist. The *Halle des Boucheries* (Butcher's Market) on the upriver corner of Decatur and Dumaine is the oldest French Market building still standing, constructed in 1813 and refurbished in 1975. The remainder of the French Market complex was built later in the nineteenth century. The matching stucco-covered buildings are painted a pale amber color, capped by red tile roofs and brightened by green-and-white trim on the shutters and doors. The green is a light, almost mint color with a slight hint of blue—called Paris green, this color is a favorite among French Quarter decorators and can be seen on dozens of jalousies (shutters) and cast-iron lace balconies in the city.

In *Body Thief*, Lestat describes his townhouse as a four-story, pre–Civil War building with a view of the river and the "twin bridges" (the Crescent City Connection, which he calls the Dixie Gates), near Café du Monde and Jackson Square. This depiction matches the corner of Decatur and Dumaine, where one can still get a glimpse of the Mississippi and its striking double bridge, leading to Algiers and the West Bank, from behind the French Market.

Breaking off of Decatur, downriver from the French Market buildings, are two short blocks called **French Market Place**. This street, now site of the Farmer's Market and open-air Flea Market, was called **Gallatin Street** in the mid-1800s (1840–70) and probably was the roughest, nastiest block in the United States, if not the planet. Even policemen avoided it judiciously, so rife was Gallatin Street with murderers, thieves, rapists, and various other fiends. One visiting writer compared Gallatin to "the Sodom and Gomorrah of old. . . . Every known human vice was indulged in, with the exception of gambling; it was not necessary to gamble to get the clientele's money. . . . Gallatin had its own law, bad as it was." Humans weren't the only creatures at risk here; vicious animal fights were often staged for entertainment, with dog-versus-rat battles especially popular.

One of the foul riverfront bars lining Gallatin Street featured a festive mortuary theme, complete with bartenders attired as undertakers, coffin-shaped liquor bottles, and generously spiked drinks. The back wall was designed to emulate the cemeteries' "oven tombs." In *Witching*, Julien Mayfair frequents the Gallatin Street bars with his sister Katherine, who dresses as a young sailor and covers her hair with a bandage (convincing, since patrons would just assume the "sailor" had been beaten up on the way in).

Another bar/dance hall, the Green Tree, was renowned for the spate of "ill health" that befell its proprietors. One owner, Mary "One-Legged Duffy" Rice (no relation to our favorite author!) was stabbed multiple times and then beaten over the head with her own wooden

leg. The next owner, an Irishman named Paddy Welsh, was found floating in the Mississippi, his head crushed.

Ironically, Gallatin Street was named in honor of one of the country's most upstanding citizens, Albert Gallatin, who served as secretary
of the U.S. Treasury under President Thomas Jefferson. Counties, cities,
rivers, and a national forest were named in Gallatin's honor; the New
Orleans site, however, gained unwanted notoriety that makes it just as
well the name has disappeared from the city's present-day landscape.

At the end of French Market Place, at 400 Esplanade, is the **Old
U.S. Mint**, built in 1835 and renovated in 1856. In 1861, the mint was
seized by Confederate authorities, and for a brief period, Confederate
coins were made here. One loyal Southerner was hanged in front of the
mint in 1862, after New Orleans was under federal occupation, for having torn down the U.S. flag. The building was last used as a mint in
1909, became a federal prison in 1932, and then housed the U.S. Coast
Guard. It was designated a National Historic Landmark in 1975, and in
1978–80 was renovated as part of the Louisiana State Museum.

This fascinating Greek Revival building boasts sensational ongoing Mardi Gras and jazz exhibits. At the top of the stairs leading to the
second floor are several splendid murals devoted to Storyville, including depictions of a "naked dance" in the parlor of Lulu White's Mahogany Hall, which was at 235 Basin Street. Lulu White's is one of many
Storyville establishments mentioned in the *Mayfair Witches* books. A
stained glass window from Mahogany Hall is included in the Mint's jazz
exhibit. Josie Arlington's hall, mentioned in *Witching*, was at 225 Basin
Street, one of more than a dozen "respectable" brothels operating during the Storyville years, 1898–1917.

Also near the river is the historic **Jax Brewery**, a two-building
complex that has been transformed into a neat warren of specialty shops
and restaurants. The Moonwalk (named for influential former mayor
Moon Landrieu), a raised area on Decatur between Jax Brewery and
Café du Monde, offers spectacular views of Mississippi riverboats, Jackson Square, and St. Louis Cathedral. This is the best spot for a twilight
photo of the cathedral, at its most dazzling in those few breathtaking
moments as the sun sets and the streetlights flicker on.

The best way to traverse the riverfront areas of the Quarter is via
the **Riverfront Streetcar**, which runs from Esplanade Avenue all the

way to Julia Street in the Central Business District. The decades-old, bright-red-and-gold streetcars travel the same route as the old French Market line. Hours are 6 A.M. to midnight weekdays, 8 A.M. to midnight weekends.

The Lower Quarter

The Quarter can roughly be divided into "Lower" (downriver from St. Louis Cathedral) and "Upper" (upriver from the church). Aside from the central area around Jackson Square, the French Quarter locale probably most vividly and fondly remembered by Anne Rice fans is the Royal Street townhouse occupied for sixty-five years by Lestat, Louis, and Claudia in *Interview*.

In *Queen*, the character Jesse goes to New Orleans at the behest of the Talamasca, intent on disproving Louis's account of the events in *Interview*. On the contrary, Jesse finds vast evidence that the tale was true, including tax-roll proof that Louis deeded the townhouse to Lestat in 1862. When Jesse explores the house, she finds the forest mural described in *Interview*, as well as a doll, diary, and rosary hidden away in a wall by Claudia. For the record, a 1994 search of tax information revealed no Lestats living in the New Orleans metropolitan area. Pity. In *Body Thief*, Lestat restores the townhouse where he, Louis, and Claudia lived to its nineteenth-century French Creole splendor.

Rice reportedly based her vampire family's fictional abode on **Gallier House**, a feat of literary anachronism since her vampires take up residence there in the late 1790s and the house wasn't started until 1857. Nevertheless, Gallier House, now a museum property of Tulane University, should be high on the list of French Quarter stops for any Rice fan. The house is located at 1118–32 Royal Street. A small parking lot adjoins the property, and visitors should take a peek out there even if they don't have a car—a lovely collection of decorative iron graces one of the lot's brick walls.

Gallier House was built between 1857 and 1860 by architect James Gallier Jr. as his private residence, on land that once was part of the Ursuline Convent grounds. Among Gallier's other architectural triumphs was the French Opera House frequently patronized by Claudia

A mule-drawn carriage passes in front of Gallier House (tallest building in photo).

and her "gentleman parents," as she refers to Louis and Lestat in a diary entry. Gallier lived in the home until his death in 1868, and it was owned by his descendants until 1917. The building is a light charcoal gray with Paris green ironwork. (That Paris green paint, incidentally, would have contained a high, potentially lethal level of arsenic at the time the Galliers lived.)

When Gallier moved into his home, one of the most modern of its era, he brought his wife, four small daughters all under the age of seven, several servants, and the family dog. A built-in doghouse in the courtyard attests to Gallier's attention to detail and his apparent affection for the family canine. In *Body Thief*, Lestat brings his dog Mojo to live in the restored Royal Street house. Mojo, possessed of exceptional intelligence, no doubt would have appreciated Gallier's forethought and consideration. One can almost imagine Mojo poking his inquisitive nose out to greet twentieth-century visitors.

Architect James Gallier Jr., in designing his family home in the French Quarter, took care to include a welcoming spot for the family pooch. The built-in doghouse is in the home's courtyard.

Gallier House's modern conveniences included an attached kitchen with hot and cold running water, which was quite unusual for the time. The kitchen-dining areas contain a plethora of small, intriguing items that give a precise glimpse into the priorities and lifestyle of the mid-1800s—for example, a café au lait server with two spouts, one for the coffee and the other for steamed milk; and an etched-glass "fly-catcher" that drowned the buzzing intruders in a nasty mixture of cobalt poison and sugar water. The etchings on the glass spared the family the

The courtyard of Gallier House, built in 1857.

horror of witnessing the flies' thrashing attempts to flee following their doomed final flights.

When restoration of Gallier House began in the late 1960s, bad taste had triumphed in the form of chartreuse and magenta wall-coverings, which have been replaced by bright, if considerably more soothing, colors appropriate to the antebellum period. The home's furnishings are not original to the house, but match the 1850s time frame. The fireplaces, many of the light fixtures, and all of the plaster molding, however, are original to Gallier House. It's easy to imagine a family of immortals living—okay, existing—here; the interior's murky illumination would not irritate their light-sensitive skin, and the continual creaking and groaning of the cypress-wood floors and stairs add a nicely diabolical touch. Depending on the season of one's visit, the house will be "dressed" for summer in mosquito netting, light curtains, and cotton furniture coverings; for winter with heavy drapes and the reemergence of velvet and brocade chaises and chairs; or in red bows, holly, and ivy for a traditional Louisiana Christmas. In a downstairs corridor lurks a forest-setting mural, similar to the one described in the *Vampire Chronicles* books.

The upstairs living area includes a small "sick room," a practical inclusion in households constantly on alert against yellow fever—Gallier House, after all, was built during New Orleans's deadliest epidemic decade of the nineteenth century. The sick room, where victims were quarantined, features plain walls that were painted, rather than covered in wallpaper, to allow servants (lucky souls) to scrub away any infectious lingerings after the sick person either recovered or died. James Gallier, in fact, died during a yellow fever outbreak, although the cause of death was left blank on his death certificate. In all likelihood, he died of either yellow fever or, as one tour guide speculated, "something so sordid they couldn't write it down."

Also on the second floor is the bathroom, Gallier's crowning achievement in terms of modern convenience. Gallier family members had the joy of bathing in a tub outfitted with hot and cold running water, although they did so infrequently because it was thought that bathing increased one's vulnerability to disease. "Spot bathing" and effusive use of cologne took care of hygiene between the weekly baths. The room also features a water closet with a flushing mechanism, a vast improvement on the local custom of simply tossing the contents of one's chamber pot out the window and into the street below.

Rice fans might affectionately christen one of the upstairs children's rooms "Claudia's Room," as I did. The tiny bedroom, with its serene view of the inner courtyard, is a charming jumble of miniature, adult-styled furniture, curly-haired porcelain dolls having tea around a Lilliputian table, and an exquisite carved-wood bed draped in yards of flowing, romantic mosquito netting. The petite copies of adult furniture were common fixtures in homes of the period—furniture makers constructed small samples of their work and often tossed in the samples as *lagniappe* when homeowners bought the matching regular-sized pieces. From Gallier House's upstairs gallery, surrounding the courtyard, visitors can take a quick visual excursion through time—looking out over the high French Quarter rooftops, one sees almost the identical view that would have greeted the Gallier family or Lestat on a moonlit stroll.

The 1100 block of Royal Street also contains the **LaLaurie House**, so infamous for its atrocious past that for more than a century it has been referred to simply as the Haunted House. The imposing home, at the corner of Royal and Gov. Nicholls Street, was built by Louis Barthelmy de McCarty, who in 1831 gave it to his daughter, Marie Delphine LaLaurie, and her husband. The LaLauries quickly became popular hosts of glittering social events, but also provoked whispers and suspicion because of the emotional and physical condition of their slaves, who were skittish, haggard, and weak.

In 1833, neighbors' misgivings about Delphine LaLaurie increased when a woman witnessed her beating a young Negro slave girl, who then fell, or jumped, from the rooftop to the LaLauries' courtyard three stories below. Madame LaLaurie was investigated, but was punished only with a fine. In April 1834, a fire broke out in the residence. A helpful neighbor reported the blaze, and when volunteer firefighters broke down a locked door, they found seven chained, starving slaves suffocating in smoke-filled cells. The miserable wretches were shackled arm and leg, in painful positions that made it impossible for them to move. A mob demanded vengeance, but the LaLauries escaped to Mandeville across Lake Pontchartrain and then to France, never to return to New Orleans in life. Following her death in December 1842, Delphine LaLaurie's body was secretly returned to the city and buried in St. Louis Cemetery No. 1.

Legends have sprung up continually in the century and a half since the tortured slaves were discovered, including a theory that Delphine buried many of her victims, perhaps not quite dead, in the home's courtyard. Following the Civil War, the residence became the Lower Girls' School, and in the 1880s, it was a music conservatory. It is now once again a private residence, and its occupants seem untroubled by excessive chain-rattling or agonized screams. Still, the Haunted House's deliciously twisted history retains enough fascination in the twentieth century to make some folks jittery about walking near it after dark.

Just one block toward the river from Gallier House and the Haunted House is the **Old Ursuline Convent**, one of the oldest buildings—if not *the* oldest—in the entire Mississippi Valley and one of the few genuine French Colonial structures to have survived all of the Quarter's devastating fires. The convent, at 1112 Chartres Street, was constructed from 1745 to 1752. The Ursuline sisters came to New Orleans in August 1727, the first of their order to immigrate to the "New World" that is now the United States.

The Old Ursuline Convent is the only remaining French Colonial building to have survived the devastating Vieux Carré fire of 1788.

The Ursulines' first convent, at 301 Chartres Street, was started in 1730 and completed in 1734, but improper construction allowed its walls to sink into the unstable, swampy ground. This was also the site of the city's first Charity Hospital, built in the late 1730s with money bequeathed by a dying sailor who worked for the Company of the Indies. A hurricane destroyed Charity Hospital in 1779, and a second Charity Hospital burned in 1810. This second facility could have been the hospital where Louis and Lestat discover Claudia in *Interview*, sick and probably dying in a "long ward of wooden beds, each with a child beneath a narrow white blanket, one candle at the end of the ward."

The Ursulines were industrious and determined in their good deeds, but were not terribly impressed by their New Orleans neighbors. One sister wrote in 1728 that "the devil here has a very large empire, but this does not discourage us from the hope of destroying him." And that was years before Lestat's arrival!

The Old Ursuline Convent has played home to a wide swath of Louisiana society—convent girls, Indian students, and Louisiana state legislators. It now serves as the archives for the Catholic Archdiocese of New Orleans. Our Lady of Victory Church, at the downriver corner of the convent complex, was built in 1845 as the Chapel of the Arch-bishops. Local legend tells that the heart of every archbishop of the dio-cese has been buried under its altar, but the tale cannot be proved, and church leaders, somewhat understandably, aren't talking. The Ursuline Convent is mentioned about halfway through *Interview*, when Louis finds a distraught Claudia wandering near its grounds.

The Ursuline nuns moved to an uptown location in the early 1800s, and it was from this new location that both Deirdre and Stella Mayfair were expelled in *Witching*.

Directly across the street from the Old Ursuline Convent is an his-toric house worth visiting, although it's not mentioned specifically in Rice's books. The **Beauregard-Keyes House** (also known as the Le Car-pentier House), at 1113 Chartres, is named for General P. G. T. Beau-regard. He is most famous as the Confederate soldier who ordered the Civil War–launching shots at Fort Sumter. After the war, when the Greek Revival raised cottage served as a boardinghouse, General Beau-regard rented rooms there.

The Beauregard-Keyes House, built in 1826, was occupied by novelist Frances Parkinson Keyes from the 1940s to 1970.

Beauregard-Keyes House was built in 1826 for Joseph Le Carpentier, a local auctioneer and grandfather of Paul Charles Morphy, the world-class chess champion who is buried in St. Louis No. 1 Cemetery. The historic home barely escaped demolition in the 1920s, when the owner announced that he intended to raze it and replace it with a macaroni factory. Beauregard's relationship to the house helped save it, and the home is now listed in the National Register of Historic Places.

Novelist Frances Parkinson Keyes bought the home in the 1940s, living and working there until her death in 1970. Using the former slave quarters as a studio, Keyes penned many works about New Orleans and its eccentric characters, including *Dinner at Antoine's* and *Steamboat Gothic*. Keyes, like Anne Rice, loved dolls, and Keyes's doll collection and Victorian dollhouse are especially enchanting attractions at Beauregard-Keyes House. At Christmas each year, local children are invited to bring their own favorite dolls to the Doll's Tea Party at the house.

Another attractive feature of the house is its magnificent adjacent garden. The home's interior is furnished with mostly turn-of-the-century pieces, and the Beauregard Chamber contains items that belonged to the general and his family.

Some say that the general's furniture isn't all that remains; numerous ghostly tales have identified Beauregard as one of several otherworldly occupants that slink through its darkened rooms after the day's

"Iron lace" and quaint streetlights typify the look of today's French Quarter.

tourists have departed. Supposedly, Beauregard's guilt over having "started" the Civil War transcends the centuries, causing the appearance of spectral battles and apparitional cannon fire in the stately rooms.

Other ghosts stem from a more modern "war." In the late 1890s, the French Quarter teemed with Italian immigrants, some purportedly linked to the Mafia. One wealthy Sicilian family, the Giaconas, lived in Beauregard House in 1909, when they were threatened with mayhem unless they paid bribes to the Mafia. The Giaconas wouldn't give in, however, and when mob henchmen broke in one night, the Giaconas turned the tables and fatally shot three of the four intruders. The bad guys left the Giaconas alone after that. The gunfight has reportedly been on "instant replay" ever since that bloody night, with phantom assassins repeating the shootout in a bleak, spooky tableau.

If you're planning on visiting, though, not to worry. None of Beauregard-Keyes House's supposed ghosts have ever been known to tamper with the living; they merely play out their ancient tragedies and leave the tourists to their modern worries (like finding a parking spot in the Quarter).

Closer to the center of the Quarter is **Madame John's Legacy**, at 632 Dumaine Street. This site wrestles with the Ursuline Convent for the title of "Oldest Building in the Mississippi Valley." The current house was built in 1788–89, immediately after the 1788 fire, but an earlier house was built in 1725 on the same site. Some claim this house should get the "oldest" designation because the original building was not completely destroyed by the fire, and portions of the earlier structure remain in the current building. The first house was built for Jean Pascal, a sailor who was killed in the infamous Natchez Massacre in 1729, and his widow remained in the home until 1777.

Whether or not it's the oldest, Madame John's Legacy is certainly one of the most historically important buildings in New Orleans and the South. Its West Indies style echoes that favored by the early plantation dwellers, with wide galleries surrounded by plain wooden colonettes (very small columns), a steeply banked roof, and dormer windows. Madame John's Legacy is owned by the Louisiana State Museum, but is not currently open to the public.

The house's provocative name derives from "'Tite Poulette," a short story by nineteenth-century author George Washington Cable. He

Madame John's Legacy (foreground), on Dumaine Street, is one of the few surviving eighteenth-century buildings in the French Quarter. Exterior scenes for the film version of *Interview* were shot here.

wrote, "This was once the home of a gay young gentleman whose first name happened to be John. . . . As his parents lived with him, his wife would, according to custom, be called Madame John—but he had no wife." When John died, he willed the house to a quadroon servant, Zalli, and her infant, 'Tite Poulette. So the house became known as Madame John's Legacy, even though there was no Madame John.

The house has a brief but memorable scene in the film version of *Interview*, after Louis (in a voice-over) reveals Lestat's "mischievous" practice of sometimes feasting on entire French Quarter families. The next scene shows several coffins being removed from a home and put into horse-drawn hearses; the exterior in that scene is Madame John's Legacy. The house also served as one of Rice's inspirations for Pointe du Lac, Louis's indigo plantation outside New Orleans. Madame John's Legacy was designated a National Historic Landmark in 1970.

Just down the block from Madame John's Legacy is the **New Orleans Historic Voodoo Museum**, at 724 Dumaine between Royal and Bourbon. If you're looking for black candles and incense, *gris-gris* (charms against harmful spells), or a complete voodoo kit, daintily packaged in a black, coffin-shaped box, this is the place. In *Witching*, Stella Mayfair buys voodoo supplies in the Quarter to use in a séance.

The cramped, dim little Voodoo Museum building is appropriately creepy and suffocating (try to go on a cool day), and crammed to overflowing with dusty voodoo artifacts, paintings, and a genuine voodoo altar. In the back room, live snakes peer at visitors from cages lining the

The 700 to 900 blocks of Royal Street were used during the filming of *Interview* in autumn 1993. The street pavement was covered in mud for a genuinely mucky, nineteenth-century look.

The 150-year-old Marsoudet-Caruso House, at 1519 Esplanade Avenue, stood in for Lestat's Prytania Street residence in the film of *Interview*.

floor. The museum conducts a variety of offbeat excursions, including a cemetery tour and nighttime visits to swamp-based voodoo rituals.

Rice clearly has a strong affinity for Dumaine Street, because it shows up frequently in her works. In *Interview*, Rue Dumaine is where Lestat's musician friend lives, and where Lestat himself keeps a townhouse after returning to New Orleans in *Vampire Lestat*. In *Lasher*, Julien Mayfair maintains a flat in Rue Dumaine.

A block and a half away from the Voodoo Museum is **Lafitte's Blacksmith Shop**, at 941 Bourbon Street. The shop's origins are something of a mystery. The building's oldest ownership record dates to 1772, and legend has flamboyant pirate Jean Lafitte operating a smithy here. It now houses a fittingly dark and gloomy bar, which boasts the strongest tequila sunrise I have ever tasted. Patches of stucco have broken away in several places, allowing glimpses at the native brick-and-cypress-plank construction that permeated the Quarter in the eighteenth and nineteenth centuries. In 1970, Lafitte's Blacksmith Shop was named a National Historic Landmark.

At 1132 Bourbon Street is the **Frances Benjamin Johnston House**, home of photographer Frances Johnston from 1940 to 1952. The West Virginia native first won fame in Washington, D.C., photographing presidents and other leaders, then came south on a Carnegie Foundation grant to photograph architecture. This Greek Revival home was built in the early 1800s.

The **Jean Baptiste Thierry House**, at 721 Gov. Nicholls Street, was built in 1814 and may be the oldest surviving New Orleans example of Greek Revival architecture; the architects were Arsène Lacarrière Latour and Henry S. Latrobe. Its first owner, Jean Baptiste Thierry, was editor of *Le Courier de la Louisiane.*

For those interested in the ornate ironwork of the Quarter, one of the most stunning examples is at 515 Royal Street, the **Cornstalk Hotel**. The front fence and gate of this charming hotel feature an 1830s cast-iron confection of ears of corn and morning glories, painted dark green. The fencing was cast in Philadelphia and sent by sea to its New Orleans buyer, Dr. Joseph Secondo Biamenti, who bought the house on this site in 1834. (New Orleans's only other "cornstalk" fence surrounds a Garden District mansion.) The current hotel building dates from about 1850, but earlier structures stood here at least as far back as the 1730s. Judge Francois-Xavier Martin, first chief justice of the Louisiana Supreme Court and author of the state's first history, lived in a house on this lot from 1816 to 1826.

Two blocks farther upriver, closer to St. Louis Cathedral, the 700 to 900 blocks of **Royal Street** were completely shut down and transformed during the filming of *Interview With the Vampire*, in the fall of 1993. Dirt covered the street, and many of the French Quarter exteriors were shot here. Royal Street is one of the main shopping hubs of New Orleans, lined with dozens of antique stores that will delight those whose tastes run toward eighteenth- and nineteenth-century finery. Royal Street's treasures also include galleries of fine art and photography, tiny bookstores, and shops selling everything from lace and crucifixes to nineteenth-century weaponry and limited-edition Disney serigraphs. Rice pays special tribute to Rue Royale in *Interview*, when Louis takes Armand on a tour of the Quarter.

The downriver border of the Quarter, **Esplanade Avenue**, showcases rows of gorgeous, restored antebellum houses, à la those owned by
the "French Mayfairs" in the *Witching* books. In *Lasher*, Mona Mayfair
remembers riding the bus downtown and eating barbecue in a "ram-
shackle building on Esplanade." Indeed, rundown, seedy-looking restaurants and stores stand gate-to-gate with the elegant mansions and
townhouses, and in true New Orleans tradition, no one seems to notice
(or care about) the disparity. Also in *Lasher*, Beatrice Mayfair's home on
Esplanade is described as "rather like a palazzo in Rome or a town house
in Amsterdam." The fictional house is "dark Pompeian red, with a deep
ocher trim."

The **Bringier-Barnett House**, at 606 Esplanade, once was one of
a triplet of identical homes built in 1834 by a local attorney. The **John
Gauche House**, at 704 Esplanade, was built in 1845 in the form of an
Italianate villa and boasts especially fine cast iron.

Though technically outside the Quarter (and not quite within
walking distance from it), the **Marsoudet-Caruso House**, at 1519 Esplanade, at the intersection of Claiborne (Interstate 10), is worth viewing for visitors with cars. The house was used in the filming of *Interview*;
ironically, this historic downtown house "portrays" Lestat's Uptown
house on Prytania Street, where Louis visits him near the end of the
book. The scene takes place in the twentieth century; attentive viewers will notice the sounds and headlights of cars swishing by on an elevated freeway outside one window. That's the giveaway to the locale;
the Garden District and Prytania Street lie fairly distant from the cacophony of I-10.

This home predates the Pontalba Buildings, having been constructed in 1846. Its surroundings are a study in twentieth-century
bleakness—gas stations and convenience stores, with only the graceful
oaks lining the neutral ground to remind visitors of its more dignified
past. It was constructed in an "American" style, with brick exterior and
interior walls and a predominant central hallway. The home retains
many original architectural details, including five marble mantels, plaster rosettes, a bronze chandelier, and a nineteenth-century room layout.

Also on the edge of the Quarter was **St. Joseph's Academy**, on
Ursulines near Esplanade, where Anne Rice spent a few miserable years
as a boarding student in her early teens. In the *Mayfair Witches* books,

she resurrected it as St. Rose de Lima's, an "ugly old brick building" with swings under the pecan trees and a Negro bar across the street. Deirdre Mayfair, who loved to play on the yard swings, is expelled from "St. Ro's" at age sixteen, one of a series of unhappy school experiences for the agonized child, who can't help it that Lasher tends to appear at inappropriate moments and frighten the nuns.

The Upper Quarter

The Upper Quarter runs basically from St. Louis Cathedral to Canal Street, although Iberville is where the Quarter "officially" ends. This section of the old Vieux Carré fairly teems with points of interest to Anne Rice fans.

Upper Royal Street showcases three bank buildings that could easily have been where Louis, Lestat, or the Mayfairs conducted their financial affairs. The **Old Bank of Louisiana**, at 334 Royal at Conti, was designed by James Gallier Jr. and completed in 1826. After the bank was liquidated in 1867, this building served as the Louisiana state capitol, an auction exchange, a concert hall–saloon, a criminal court, and headquarters for an American Legion post. In 1971, it was restored for use by the Tourist and Convention Commission, and later became the Vieux Carré police station.

Banks once stood on three of the four corners at the intersection of Royal and Conti, making it the financial heart of the city. Across the street from the Bank of Louisiana building, at 343 Royal, is the **Old Bank of the United States**, built in 1800 and the oldest extant bank building. This building sports exceptionally well-preserved wrought-iron railings and was home to the Planters Bank from 1811 to 1820 and the Bank of the United States from 1820 to 1836. It also briefly housed the New Orleans Gas Light and Banking Co.

The **Old Louisiana State Bank**, at 403 Royal, preserves its heritage through monograms ("LB") still visible in its wrought-iron railing. This bank opened in 1821, and was designed by Benjamin Latrobe, one of the architects of the U.S. Capitol.

Casa Faurie, at 417 Royal, was built in 1801 for the grandfather of French impressionist painter Edgar Degas. The property was bought in 1805 by the Banque de la Louisiane, and its monogram ("BL") was added to the balcony ironwork. It eventually became a private residence again and was the site of many exorbitant banquets in honor of General Andrew Jackson when he revisited the city in 1828.

The site of the old **Orleans Ballroom** is at 717 Orleans, now the Bourbon Orleans Hotel. John Davis opened the palatial ballroom in 1817, and Davis also operated the Orleans Theatre there for twenty years. During the Marquis de Lafayette's visit in 1826, a grand ball was given for him at the Orleans. The property was eventually sold to an order of black nuns, then the hotel took over in the 1960s. New additions have replaced some sections, but the old Orleans Ballroom remains, in the guise of a business meeting room on the second floor. Davis also was the entrepreneur behind the James Gallier–designed French Opera House at Bourbon and Toulouse streets. The Opera House, much enjoyed by Lestat in *Interview*, was destroyed by fire in the 1920s.

Nearby, at 716 Dauphine at Orleans, is the **Gardette–Le Prete House**, the so-called Sultan's Retreat, another of the Quarter's infamously haunted domiciles. This imposing house was built in 1836 for Joseph Coulon Gardette, a dentist, and purchased in 1839 by Jean Baptist Le Prete, who furnished it in grand Creole style——polished wood floors and crystal chandeliers that almost begged for parties and sophisticated dalliances. After a few years, however, Le Prete's fortunes dwindled and he was forced to rent his home, to a mysterious man of Turkish descent. The tenant claimed to be the "deposed potentate of a distant eastern realm," according to a 1979 *Times-Picayune* article.

Whatever his royal lineage, or lack thereof, "the Sultan," as he was called, surely had unusual tastes and habits. He transformed the stately Creole mansion into an oriental palace, complete with eunuchs serving his every need. The parties ceased, the Sultan's eunuchs guarded the property with wickedly sharp swords and knives, and the gates were chained and locked. No one was invited in, with the exception of the young men and women who arrived to populate the master's "harem."

Someone apparently didn't like being excluded, because in the late 1870s a horrific, blood-soaked slaughter took place within the Sultan's walls. Neighbors noticed blood running beneath the locked gates, and police were called. Breaking in, they found mangled bodies in pools of blood, all murdered in relative silence with axes or swords. Some of the victims were decapitated, and so obscenely scattered that authorities found it difficult to match heads with the correct bodies. The Turk himself was found partially buried in his blood-drenched garden. The culprits never were identified or apprehended.

The La Prete house has endured a colorful history of hauntings in the ensuing century. As recently as the 1950s and 1960s, residents reported hair-raising tales of ghastly, ghostly encounters. A female occupant of the 1950s reported being startled on several occasions by a male figure attired in oriental garb. Undaunted, she continued to live there until she and a friend were terrorized one night by hideous, unearthly screams emanating from no identifiable source. In the late 1960s, another owner reported seeing a male spirit. This woman, upon learning of the house's ... um, *interesting* history, told friends about a gnarly, twisted tree growing near the spot where the Sultan supposedly died. She speculated that perhaps the murdered Turk's tortured spirit infests the tree, writhing and contorting in a grotesque imitation of his death throes.

Several Upper Quarter restaurants provide picturesque rendezvous spots for Rice's characters, notably the **Desire Oyster Bar, Galatoire's** and **The Court of Two Sisters.** In *Witching,* Llewellyn tells Aaron Lightner that he had lunch with Stella Mayfair at The Court of Two Sisters, at 613 Royal. The restaurant, which boasts one of the Quarter's most gorgeous courtyards, was named for two sisters who ran a variety store there in the late 1800s.

Aaron Lightner and Rita Mae Lonigan dine at the Desire Oyster Bar, 300 Bourbon, when Lightner is staying at the Monteleone Hotel, just around the corner. Rice describes the Desire as "a pretty place with ceiling fans and big mirrors and doors open along Bourbon Street." Michael Curry and Rowan Mayfair share a dinner of gumbo, shrimp, and andouille sausage at the Desire, which is part of the glitzy Royal Sonesta Hotel.

Galatoire's, at 209 Bourbon, is another dining spot for Aaron and Llewellyn in *Witching.* The elder Mayfairs take Rowan there after a meeting at Mayfair and Mayfair about the disposition of the Mayfair Legacy. The restaurant was established in 1905 by Jean Galatoire, who took over another restaurant, Victor's, that had been in the same building. The building itself was erected in 1831.

The Desire Oyster Bar, part of the Royal Sonesta Hotel, is a favorite dining spot for many of Rice's characters.

The **Monteleone Hotel**, at 214 Royal, greets visitors with four spectacular crystal chandeliers in its lavish lobby. The hotel, where Aaron Lightner stays on a visit to the city in *Witching*, provides a dramatic, 360-degree rooftop view of the Quarter, the Mississippi, and the city outskirts. One can barely spy the tombs of St. Louis No. 1 to the northwest, offering a hint of what Lestat and Louis must have seen when they soared above the cemetery in *Queen*.

Maison Seignouret, at 520 Royal Street, now occupied by the WDSU television station, was built in 1816 by French wine merchant and furniture maker François Seignouret. The Bordeaux, France, native fought at the Battle of New Orleans. Although he originally came to New Orleans to satisfy discriminating Creole palates yearning for the wine of the homeland, Seignouret is remembered today more for his exquisite furniture creations. All of his pieces were distinguished by his initial, "S," cunningly worked somewhere into the design. Today, an "S" can also be seen in the fan-shaped iron *garde de frise* on the left end of the third-story balcony. Alas, a wooden jalousie often hides this feature from those glancing upward from Royal Street.

The **Historic New Orleans Collection**, at 533 Royal Street, offers enticement to those seeking historical anecdotes and a sense of the past. The group of buildings includes the Williams Gallery, which hosts changing exhibits on local culture and history; the Williams Residence, dating from the late 1800s and decorated with both antiques and contemporary pieces; and Merieult (pronounced "Mary-oo") House, built in 1792 and one of the few homes to survive the 1794 fire. Merieult House features an especially fine cast-iron railing on the balcony above Royal Street. A museum shop offers prints, books, and gift items.

The **Court of Two Lions** house, at 537 Royal, was purchased by Vincent Nolte in 1819 from Jean François Merieult, who built Merieult House at 533 Royal. The book *Anthony Adverse,* and a subsequent 1936 film version starring Mervyn LeRoy, Fredric March, and Olivia de Havilland, were based largely on Nolte's autobiography, *Fifty Years in Both Hemispheres.* On the Toulouse Street side of the house (710 Toulouse) is a high wooden gate flanked by immense pillars, atop which loom the stone lions that give the house its name. The Court of Two Lions house was built in 1798.

The **Pedesclaux-Lemonnier House**, at 640 Royal Street, was built starting in 1795. Its architect, Barthelemy Lafon, had his office in the building in 1805. In the 1870s, the house gained local notoriety as the setting for author George Washington Cable's *Sieur George.* This three-story building is frequently referred to as the "first skyscraper."

At 820 St. Louis Street, between Dauphine and Bourbon, is the **Hermann-Grima House**, constructed in 1831 and a wonderfully restored example of Georgian architecture. The house is not mentioned in any of the *Mayfair Witches* or *Vampire Chronicles* books, but was Rice's inspiration for the Lermontant family's home in her historic novel *The Feast of All Saints.*

Wealthy merchant Samuel Hermann Sr. purchased the site on which the home stands in May 1823, and the Hermanns lived there until 1844, when they moved due to financial problems. On first arriving in Louisiana, Hermann, a German immigrant, lived in the area near

Baton Rouge called the German Coast. He married a French-German Catholic widow, Emeronthe Brou.

The Hermanns moved downriver to New Orleans sometime before 1816, and in the early 1820s, they moved into an older house at 820 St. Louis Street. This earlier structure was demolished in 1831 to make way for the Hermanns' grand new house, suitably spacious for a family with six children. Samuel Hermann commissioned architect-builder William Brand to design his family's French Quarter home in a distinctly non-Creole style. Brand, while following Hermann's edict for American architecture similar to that found in Philadelphia or Boston, wisely retained a few Creole touches that made the New Orleans climate more bearable—notably, the custom of an enclosed courtyard; as a result, Hermann-Grima House boasts one of the largest courtyards in the Vieux Carré. The formal, austere facade of the home, with its double arched doorways framed by Ionic columns, is softened only by the addition of a graceful wrought-iron second-floor balcony.

The home's interior includes a wide central hallway, another major departure from the Creole homes that eschewed hallways altogether (one room simply led into another). The Hermann house's spacious rooms, more on a scale with River Road plantation houses than a Vieux Carré mansion, easily accommodated the hundreds of guests invited to the Hermanns' spectacular parties and receptions.

When Hermann's fortunes crumbled in the financial chaos of the 1830s, particularly the Panic of 1837, the family was forced to leave its opulent house. In 1844, attorney-notary Felix Grima bought the mansion, and it stayed in his family throughout the War Between the States.

Today, the home is open to the public, offering a rare glimpse of an American outpost amid the predominantly Creole architecture of the French Quarter. On Thursdays from May through October, open-hearth Creole cooking (and tasting!) demonstrations are given in the home's restored nineteenth-century kitchen. The building was named a National Historic Landmark in 1974.

The sumptuous St. Louis Hotel opened at Royal and St. Louis streets in 1838, on land now occupied by the **Omni Royal Orleans** at 621 St. Louis Street. In *Witching*, Rémy, Katherine, and Julien Mayfair enjoyed sojourns at the St. Louis Hotel when visiting New Orleans from the plantation at Riverbend, in the period before the First Street house was constructed uptown. Work on the St. Louis Hotel, which cost an astronomical (for the period) $1.5 million, began in 1835. It was designed by Jacques Nicolas de Pouilly and his brother, Joseph Isadore de Pouilly. The hotel was completed in 1838 and named for the patron saint of the city.

The St. Louis, a popular vacation spot for wealthy planters and slave owners, also housed the auction exchange and exquisite ballrooms, which quickly became the primary competition for the Orleans Ballroom. Slave auctions frequently took place beneath the lofty, 88-foot-high dome in the lobby. The St. Louis Hotel was damaged extensively in an 1841 fire, but was rebuilt and remained popular until the late 1800s. After the rebuilding, the hotel took up the entire block of St. Louis between Royal and St. Charles.

The venerable old hotel eventually succumbed to neglect and disintegration, and in 1915, after being unoccupied for many years, the hotel suffered its final indignity when a hurricane tore the roof off. Rats scurried through the ruins in terrifying profusion, and residents feared an outbreak of bubonic plague. Bats fluttered among the rafters, and enterprising neighbors kept their mules tethered in the former lobby. The St. Louis finally was demolished, and the site held an undistinguished parking lot until 1960, when the Royal Orleans was built. A painting in the lobby of the "Royal O," as locals affectionately call it, pays homage to the original St. Louis Hotel.

Today, another **St. Louis Hotel** presides over the Quarter, at 730 Bienville Street. This modern hostelry was the inspiration for the "new Spanish hotel" mentioned in *Interview*. It is here that Louis and Lestat put down stakes, so to speak, during their first few days in the Quarter after leaving Pointe du Lac. This is the setting for the distressing scene in which Louis and Lestat prey on two prostitutes, and it is here that they bring Claudia and transform the five-year-old girl into a vampire.

Exchange Alley, which dissects the blocks between Royal and Chartres from Canal to Conti streets, is an interesting remnant of nineteenth-century days. This throughway, originally called Exchange Place, once ran all the way from Canal to the Cabildo. A tiny original section of Exchange Place, from St. Peter to Pirates Alley, is now called Cabildo Alley.

The riverside downtown corner of St. Peter and Royal is New Orleans's equivalent of the Lincoln Memorial in Washington—the most

The St. Louis Hotel served as Rice's inspiration for the "Spanish Hotel" where Lestat and Louis live before moving to the Royal Street townhouse.

photographed, most sketched and painted site in the city. The principal draw is the **LaBranche Building** complex, actually eleven separate buildings, sporting some of the Quarter's most fanciful ironwork. The site includes land that once housed a French colonial prison. The three-story brick houses were built in 1840 by Melasie Trepagnier LaBranche, widow of Jean Baptiste LaBranche. The buildings at 622 and 624 Pirates Alley sport narrow wrought-iron balconies, while the others at 621–39 St. Peter Street and 708 Royal Street feature fancier cast-iron details added after 1850.

    The Inn on Bourbon, at 541 Bourbon at Toulouse, now marks the site of the famed 1,800-seat French Opera House. One section of the curb still curves inward; this was to allow room for the horse-drawn carriages that pulled up bearing gentlemen and ladies on their way to the opera.

At 616 St. Peter at Chartres, just off Jackson Square, is the **Orue-Pontalba House**, which was started in 1789 for a Spanish official. The house was damaged in the 1794 fire and rebuilt from 1795 to 1791. Marcelino Hernandez, a Canary Island native who had moved to New Orleans, made the wrought-iron balconies. The building was reconstructed from 1962 to 1963 for **Le Petit Théâtre du Vieux Carré**. The building was designated an Orleans Parish Landmark in 1963.

The **Avart-Peretti House**, at 632 St. Peter Street, was built in 1842 by J. N. B. de Pouilly and Ernest Godchaux. Originally a two-story dwelling, the house acquired the third story when it was added as a studio for famed artist Achille Peretti, who lived here from 1906 to 1923. Playwright Tennessee Williams lived here in 1946–47, during which time he wrote *A Streetcar Named Desire*. The play's title was supposedly inspired by the nearby Royal Street streetcar that ran at that time. The building received Orleans Parish Landmark status in 1987.

Also in the Upper Quarter is the grimly intriguing **Musée Conti Wax Museum**, at 917 Conti Street. The more unsavory aspects of the city's history are depicted through a series of amazingly realistic tableaux, including a voodoo dance led by Marie Laveau, terrifying deeds of infamous ghosts and vampires, and heroic actions by Andrew Jackson and Jean Lafitte. Napoleon Bonaparte even makes an appearance, shown sitting in a bathtub supposedly discussing the Louisiana Purchase.

Several interesting historical spots line the upper section of Chartres Street, including the **New Orleans Pharmacy Museum** at 514 Chartres. The house now occupied by the museum was designed by J. N. B. de Pouilly and was built for Louis J. Dufilho, America's first licensed pharmacist. Here visitors can get an idea of the sorts of concoctions used to treat infirmities during New Orleans's past—old prescriptions and heinous-looking instruments, *gris-gris* potions and herbal remedies. The building has been a museum since the 1930s.

Just down the street at 500 Chartres at St. Louis is **Napoleon House**, built in 1814 for Mayor Nicholas Girod. The mayor, apparently an ardent admirer of Napoleon Bonaparte, wanted to rescue the French general from exile on St. Helena and bring him to New Orleans. Jean Lafitte's cohort (or brother, according to some historians), Dominique You, was to have led the rescue attempt, but Napoleon had the ungracious audacity to die before the daring feat could be accomplished.

Napoleon House, built in 1814 for Mayor Nicholas Girod.

Today a popular restaurant and bar, Napoleon House sports its original tile roof and an interesting octagonal cupola.

Closer to Canal Street, at 241 Chartres, is the **Boyer Antiques and Doll Shop**, which played an important role in the filming of *Interview With the Vampire*. Doll artisan Karl Boyer, the shop's proprietor, crafted the dolls used in the movie, including a grim-looking blond creation that is much fancied by little Claudia. She admires the doll so much, in fact, that she kills the movie's doll maker rather than do anything so ordinary as pay for it. Boyer's porcelain and cloth "offspring" cost anywhere from about $30 for small contemporary dolls to $1,000 or more for antique collectibles. The movie company, in addition to using Boyer's dolls, filmed inside the tiny red-brick shop, where hundreds of little eyes stare out expectantly from antique glass-and-wood cases.

The riverside 300 block of Chartres Street was the site of both the first Ursuline Convent and the first Charity Hospital. The hospital, built in the late 1730s, was constructed with money bequeathed by a former sailor for the Company of the Indies. A hurricane destroyed the building in 1779, and a second Charity Hospital burned in 1810.

Just outside the boundaries of the French Quarter is **St. Louis Cemetery No. 1**, at 400 Basin Street between Conti and St. Louis. The cemetery, established in 1789, is the oldest extant burial ground in New Orleans and the entire Mississippi River Valley and is still in use today. St. Louis No. 1 shows up repeatedly in Rice's works. This important historic site is discussed further in chapter 4.

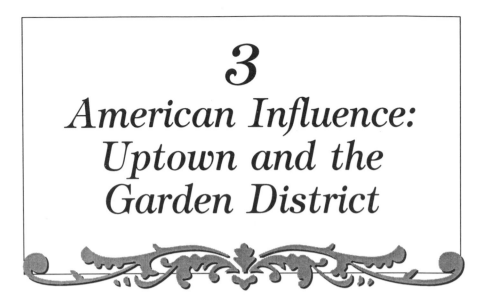

3

American Influence:
Uptown and the
Garden District

In the same way the French Quarter is central to *Interview* and Rice's other *Vampire Chronicles* books, the Garden District is the geographical heart of the *Mayfair Witches series*. It is here that Anne Rice and her family have lived for years (although at this writing, there is speculation that a move farther uptown may be imminent), and here that the Mayfair clan builds its "legacy" home—the nineteenth-century townhouse at the corner of Chestnut and First that is inherited by the designated witch. When the Rices moved back to New Orleans from San Francisco, Anne was entranced by the handsome Greek Revival–Italianate townhouse and felt "called" to buy it. She already had started *Witching*, set in another house on nearby Philip Street, but the First Street house captured her imagination, and she rewrote the story to accommodate her atmospheric new dwelling.

Rice, well-known for her generosity to her fans, has never tried to hide from them. In fact, through the 1993–94 edition, the Rices at 1239 First Street were listed in the New Orleans white pages (although the New Orleans phone company spelled her name wrong, as Ann without the "e"—for shame!). Even without a specific address, savvy fans could pinpoint the house's exact location through careful reading of *Witching*,

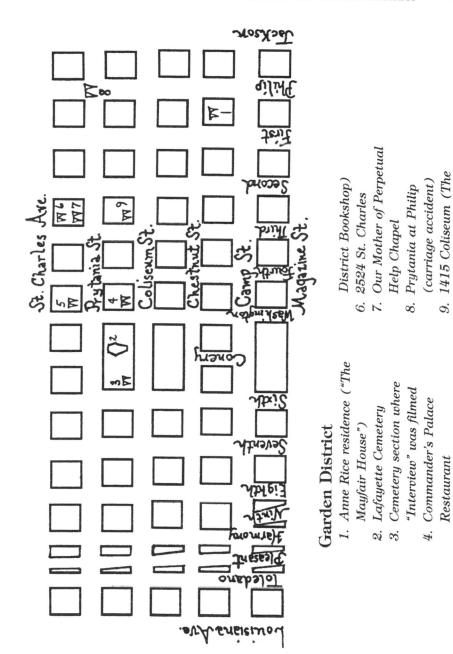

Garden District

1. Anne Rice residence ("The Mayfair House")
2. Lafayette Cemetery
3. Cemetery section where "Interview" was filmed
4. Commander's Palace Restaurant
5. The Rink (Garden District Bookshop)
6. 2524 St. Charles
7. Our Mother of Perpetual Help Chapel
8. Prytania at Philip (carriage accident)
9. 1415 Coliseum (The "White House")

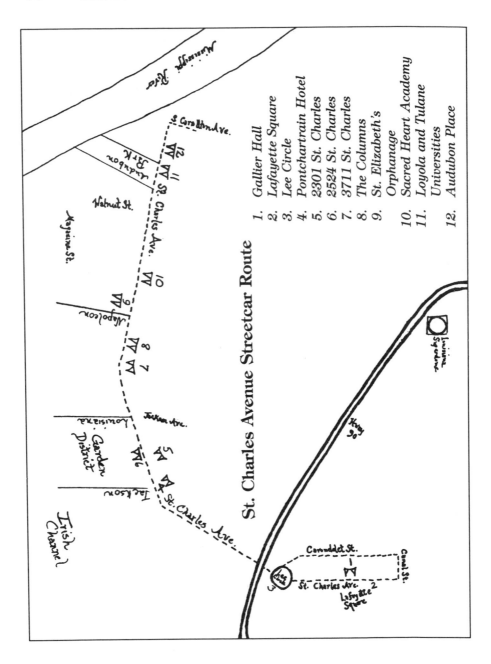

St. Charles Avenue Streetcar Route

1. Gallier Hall
2. Lafayette Square
3. Lee Circle
4. Pontchartrain Hotel
5. 2301 St. Charles
6. 2524 St. Charles
7. 3711 St. Charles
8. The Columns
9. St. Elizabeth's
    Orphanage
10. Sacred Heart Academy
11. Loyola and Tulane
    Universities
12. Audubon Place

in which it is identified as the "riverside downtown corner." The house, historically called the Brevard-Clapp House and also nicknamed Rosegate, is so well-known to New Orleanians that it's impossible to stand in front of it for more than a few minutes without encountering camera-laden Anne Rice fans. They confer in hushed tones and point as subtly as they can at that famous "keyhole" doorway where the Mayfairs traditionally had their photos taken, or the side porch where Deirdre Mayfair waited out her final days. (Deirdre's fictional porch was screened, to let in the river breeze; the real-life counterpart is enclosed by glass.) The strikingly lovely residence also captures the attention of Garden District visitors who have no idea who lives there, drawn merely by its classic architectural lines and photogenic tangle of tropical greenery.

The lush foliage pushing through the First Street fence makes it impossible to view more than a tantalizing sliver of the gardens beyond—the pool where Michael nearly drowned, the oak tree Deirdre loved to climb, the graves of Lasher and Emaleth beneath it. Although all those events were fictional, the settings were real. For the Rice reader, it's impossible to see these sites without thinking of their significance and consequently suppressing a shudder or two. And even in bright sunlight, this particular corner is blanketed in an impenetrable, ominous haze of darkness—the strongest rays cannot fully pierce the gloom.

So it is this section of New Orleans that holds the most allure for many Anne Rice fans. The First Street house in the Garden District possesses a double whammy of attraction, as both the home of their favorite author and her most famous setting. The nearby Irish Channel and Uptown sections of the city also play important roles in Rice's *Mayfair Witches* series, as well as supporting parts in the *Vampire Chronicles*.

This chapter begins with an overview of the American migration uptown, then moves into detailed descriptions of the Garden District and the Irish Channel; the second half includes a trek along Canal Street on the edge of the Central Business District (CBD) and a tour of Uptown via the city's "rolling museum," the St. Charles Streetcar, which is a National Historic Landmark. A trip on the streetcar highlights many of the sites mentioned in Rice's books and also is a quaint, relatively relaxing way to get an overview of the "new" city on the upriver side of Canal Street. The word *uptown*, by the way, is capitalized when referring to the Uptown section of the city, lowercased when used as a directional reference (as in traveling uptown on the streetcar).

The Movement Upriver

The Americans who surged into New Orleans following 1803's Louisiana Purchase quickly established their own society. Shunned by the Creoles of the French Quarter, they began settling upriver of Canal Street, in the area now known as the Central Business District (CBD). As the population grew, it expanded still farther upriver, swallowing plantation land in a frenzy of urbanization.

The first area settled by the Americans was Faubourg St. Marie, which had been the plantation of Bertrand Gravier. Following the fire of 1788, Gravier had his land adjoining the Quarter subdivided into city blocks to allow expansion beyond the disaster-prone Vieux Carré. Gravier's land ran along the Mississippi from Iberville to present-day Howard Avenue. Iberville is still the "official" uptown boundary of the Quarter, but for practical purposes most people consider Canal Street as the line of division. This also was true in the nineteenth century; the hostilities between the French and Spanish Creoles and the Americans were so tense that the median of Canal Street became known as the "neutral ground," a nickname that has stuck for nearly 200 years and now encompasses all New Orleans medians.

Americans stubbornly adhered to the northeastern styles of architecture to which they were accustomed, no matter how impractical for New Orleans resources and climate. The Americans' penchant for steeply pitched roofs indicated that perhaps they expected snowfall at any moment; that this hot, humid weather was merely a brief meteorological anomaly. They also built family rooms barely above street level and probably spent a good deal of time bailing out their precious belongings, while the dry Creoles smugly waited out the storms in their second-floor parlors and bedrooms. Georgian row houses were popular in the earliest American sections of the city, as evidenced in the restored example at Julia Row in the CBD.

In 1806, Madame Marguerite Delord-Sarpy subdivided her plantation land, which was just above Faubourg St. Marie. The narrow wedge of land ran roughly from Howard Avenue uptown to Felicity, and from the river to what is now Lee Circle. Barthelemy Lafon, deputy surveyor of Orleans Parish, proposed a new Faubourg Annonciation for the new area. His plans called for a grand canal, a circular park called Place du Tivoli (now Lee Circle), a coliseum, and a *prytanée*, or classical school. At the center of Lafon's Place de l'Annonciation would be a soaring Catholic cathedral. Lafon's plan was brilliant, amounting to a true metropolis with classically modeled elements similar to Washington, D.C., but it flopped. The only major element that survived was Lafon's grid pattern of streets, with larger lots than those in Faubourg St. Marie. Eventually, the proposed Faubourg Annonciation became what is now called the Lower Garden District, with Annunciation and Prytania (after the proposed *prytanée*) streets as remnants of Lafon's grandiose plan.

Expansion continued upriver beginning in the 1820s and throughout the heyday of the 1850s. Plantations once owned by the Ursuline nuns, the Panis family, and the Livaudais family eventually coalesced into the Faubourg, then City, of Lafayette, which thrived for nineteen years (1833–52) and gave New Orleans a run for its money as the area's most prosperous port. Lafayette, named for the French patriot who had visited New Orleans in 1825, ran upriver from Felicity Street to Harmony Street, and from the Mississippi River to the undrained marshes that lay along what is now Claiborne Avenue. The predominant developer in this era of rampant speculation was Samuel Jarvis Peters, a Canadian by birth who arrived in New Orleans in 1821 and helped establish the Whig Party in 1834.

Peters's most intense political rival was Democrat Bernard de Marigny, who beat Peters for a spot in the state legislature in 1822. Marigny, incidentally, was the developer of the land downriver of the French Quarter during this same period, in what is still called Faubourg Marigny. He also introduced the game of craps to the United States and was so fond of it that he named a street after the popular gambling diversion. However, the street's name was later changed to Burgundy (already its French Quarter designation), to alleviate the embarrassment felt by patrons of the four churches located on Craps Street.

Peters eventually got his revenge on his rival, but through land rather than politics. Madame Livaudais, who owned the plantation that would become a good portion of Lafayette, was a Marigny by birth,

Bernard's sister. In 1832, a decade after his political defeat, Peters and three partners bought the Livaudais plantation for $490,000. By creating his own faubourg on land once owned by a Marigny, Peters considered his old political score settled, and indeed, a portion of his suburb would become one of America's most acclaimed residential areas—the Garden District.

Maps of the old Faubourg Lafayette reveal an interesting irregularity in the otherwise evenly spaced grid pattern laid out by surveyor Benjamin Buisson. The blocks between Sixth and Washington, all the way from the river to St. Georges Street (now La Salle), are nearly twice the width of the other sections. This is due to the original land deal—although she was living in Paris at the time of the sale, Madame Livaudais apparently thought she might one day return to New Orleans, and she retained the plot of land containing her house and garden, near Levee Street and the Mississippi River. To maintain uniformity, Buisson drew all the blocks behind Madame Livaudais's the same width as hers; city planners wisely chose one of these extra-wide sections for the city cemeteries, Lafayette Nos. 1 and 2. St. Joseph No. 1, which opened in 1854 next to Lafayette No. 2, is also located in one of these wider blocks.

Madame Livaudais's grand house never was completed, although portions of it saw less dignified uses as a public ballroom, a flophouse for vagrants, and a plaster factory before its 1863 demolition. And, of course, it was called the Haunted House of Lafayette for many years, although the identity of the supposed haunter never was clear. The "back area" of the new faubourg, away from the river and bordering Nayades Street (now St. Charles Avenue), was designated the residential district. The street names followed the same pattern as those in Philadelphia— north-south streets were numbered, and comfortingly Anglo-Saxon names adorned the east-west thoroughfares. Original boundaries of the residential area extended from Felicity to Louisiana, and from Magazine to Dryades (now Carondelet). Today's Garden District boundaries are generally considered to be Jackson and Louisiana (downtown and uptown, respectively), and Magazine and St. Charles (riverside and lakeside).

Lafayette's riverfront section, below Magazine Street, teemed with manufacturing, industry, stench, and noise. Slaughterhouses clustered at the riverfront mouth of St. Mary's Street, in the area called Bull's Head. The carnage attracted so many scavengers that a local baseball team renamed itself the Buzzards. Other enterprises contributing to the din included tallow factories, steam-driven cotton presses, a sugar refinery, and a bustling slave market. Flatboats, which made one-way trips down the river from Kentucky and Indiana, propelled much of the area's commerce—by 1834, in fact, Lafayette had surpassed New Orleans as the busiest flatboat port on the Mississippi. These powerless boats floated downriver, driven only by the strong currents, then were broken up for lumber upon arrival at Lafayette. The lumber formed the foundation for many a Lafayette outhouse and residence, and a "Flatboat Church" was built on Felicity Street.

By the 1840s, German and Irish immigrants began flooding into the area, with some 11,000 Germans and 20,000 Irish living in Lafayette by 1850. The area around Adele and Tchoupitoulas streets was wholly Irish, and the entire riverfront sector became known as the Irish Channel, a nickname that remains today, although today's local residents are mostly black and Hispanic. The Germans were more prosperous than the Irish, typically building homes for themselves in addition to one or more to use as "rent houses." The Irish, usually renters living six or eight to a room, became a paid servant class that was treated worse than the slaves. What with overcrowding and a decided lack of hygienic amenities, it should come as no surprise that the worst yellow fever epidemic in New Orleans history, in 1853, began in the Irish Channel.

Although business was thriving along the Lafayette wharves, civic improvements clearly were not a priority—in 1836, three years after incorporation, the only civic building was the jail. Paving was nonexistent except for the occasional flatboat-plank road, which barely kept the mud and muck at bay. There was no gas lighting until the 1840s, and oil cost too much for most of the poor immigrants to use. Crime was rampant, with prostitutes and pickpockets prowling the dark wharves.

Lafayette's fortunes spiraled quickly downward in the city's second decade. The flatboat industry was dying, victim of the new steamboat era, and New Orleans rebounded in authority as the primary port. Development away from the river came to a virtual standstill, saving the Garden District from the slum conditions that marked the riverfront. By

1852, when Lafayette was swallowed whole by New Orleans, it was more than $500,000 in debt. Lafayette's population was more than 12,000 at that time, with another 1,500 slaves.

The Garden District and Lower Garden District

The Garden District area initially had attracted scant attention, and few of the plots had sold by the mid-1840s. Still, the area was attractive and abundantly fertile; in 1816, the river had broken the levee at the McCarty plantation several miles upriver, submerging land all the way to New Orleans. Along with water, the flood deposited a layer of silt so rich it would grow just about anything. This profuse fertility continues today; neglect a New Orleans yard for long and it soon will be entirely covered in bougainvillea and wildflowers.

The mid-nineteenth-century Garden District atmosphere was far from bucolic, however, considering the noise and odors from the riverfront wafting through the air, and livestock including horses, mules, and goats running loose in the streets. The goats, at least, contributed one civic duty—they kept the grass cropped in Lafayette Cemetery. Some things simply could not be tolerated, however—in 1841, a law was passed prohibiting the keeping of bears in the city of Lafayette.

Garden District development picked up in the late 1840s and boomed in the 1850s, fueled by an influx of businessmen who worked in New Orleans but preferred a more pastoral environment for their homes and families. The area's architecture is remarkably diverse but achieves an aesthetic harmony that many claim is unequaled in the South, or just about anywhere for that matter. The Irish Channel's popular "shotgun cottages," so called because of their floor plans—one room behind another with a long hallway from front door to back, through which a fired bullet could fly unimpeded—gave way to more opulent versions in the Garden District.

The austere Greek Revival style, with many variations, was the most popular Garden District motif, appearing as late as the 1890s. Practical raised cottages, with the living quarters above a basement, also were common, and many homes sported Italianate features such as large windows, a more expansive scale than typical Greek Revival, and extensive ornamentation. One nearly universal element in Garden District homes is the construction of covered riverside galleries (or porches), so positioned to catch the refreshing river breezes. The appellation "Garden District" harkens back to the British custom of calling a property's entire yard area the "garden."

The Garden District's beauty has been well-chronicled and has attracted more than its share of literary residents. Walt Whitman lived on Washington Street in the 1840s, and transplanted Northerner George Washington Cable lived on Annunciation Square and in a series of Garden District homes. One illustrious gathering at Cable's Eighth Street raised cottage (still standing, at No. 1313, between Chestnut and Coliseum) included Cable, Mark Twain, Charles Dudley Warner of *Harper's Magazine*, Lafcadio Hearn, and Joel Chandler Harris.

Twain paid tribute to the District in *Life on the Mississippi*, writing: "Those [homes] in the wealthy quarter are spacious; painted snowy white, usually, and generally have wide verandas, or double-verandas, supported by ornamental columns. These mansions stand in the center of large grounds and rise, garlanded with roses, out of the midst of swelling masses of shining green foliage and many-colored blossoms. No houses could well be in better harmony with their surroundings, or more pleasing to the eye." In *Witching*, Rice devotes a large section to evoking the Caribbean atmosphere of her home city, in particular the Garden District.

Today, many of Twain's "snowy white" houses have been painted soft pastels—peach, buttercup, mint, lavender, and pink—and the profusion of merry hues merely adds to the feeling of being completely surrounded by blossoming vegetation. Gallery ceilings often sport a cheerful sky-blue coat of paint, perhaps to evoke a rain-freshened sky. It strains imagination to conceive of the rank riverfront scent that so perturbed early residents; present-day visitors to the Garden District will be engulfed, instead, by the sweet fragrance of olive, jasmine, and dozens of floral varieties. Rice utterly captures the area's ambiance in *Taltos*, when she describes it as "a speaking twilight, a city so wooded still that the creatures of the air sang the songs of dusk."

Rice's house, the primary residential setting for her *Mayfair Witches* series, is at **1239 First Street**, on the riverside downtown corner at Chestnut. From St. Charles Avenue walking toward the river, the house is in the fourth block on the left. Anyone who has read the *Mayfair Witches* series needn't fret about accidentally passing it by—the townhouse looks exactly as Rice describes it, a Greek Revival–Italianate mixture, washed a deep violet-gray color, with dark green shutters and black ironwork. Before they even catch sight of the crape myrtles along First Street, where the vengeful Lasher stood guard over his witches, fans will recognize this, unmistakably, as the Mayfair house. The house is just two blocks inland from Magazine Street, the traditional border between the working-class Irish Channel and the wealthy Garden District.

The bounteous, almost junglelike greenery surrounding the house contributes to its otherworldly demeanor. Gnarly, enormous oak trees extend their branches almost to the ironwork of the upstairs gallery, giving the impression that they're reaching for, or trying to protect, the home and its occupants. Usually in the city, oak branches have been pruned to extend toward the street, forming a canopy of leaves over cars and pedestrians; here, it's just the opposite. The roots of the oaks along First Street poke through the sidewalk, turning the already uneven bricks into treacherous territory (if you're walking here, be sure to look down, or you'll end up with scraped knees and an embarrassed face). The trees sometimes perform their own feats of witchcraft—after rainstorms, fitful little gusts of wind from the river capture the leftover droplets on leaves, blowing them off in a soft kiss of rain that can be felt only under the oak boughs. Step out from under the leafy haven and the magical "rainfall" instantly ceases.

The front-door lanterns at "First Street," as the house is called by the Mayfairs and Rice fans, always seem to be lit, perhaps to cast a welcoming glow, perhaps simply to dispel a few of the menacing shadows.

Living in the Garden District never has been inexpensive. The First Street house, built by wholesale merchant Albert Brevard, was given a tax assessment value of $13,500 in the late 1850s, and at that time tax judgments tended to be extremely low, nowhere approaching market value. The Rices reportedly paid in the ballpark of $1 million for the house in early 1989. The three-story, 11,000-square-foot townhouse was built in 1857, the same year James Gallier Jr. built his private French Quarter residence that would one day play home to a family of fictitious vampires. Coincidentally, Gallier also was the architect for many Garden District dwellings, but not this one.

1239 First Street, the home of Anne Rice and her Mayfair Witches.

Architect James Calrow—in Rice's books, First Street's architect is Darcy Monahan, who becomes a Mayfair by marriage—and builder Charles Pride included many modern touches in the Brevard house, including mahogany washstands with marble tops and silver-plated fittings in all the main bedrooms. Hot and cold running water were common in Garden District homes by the 1850s, an area in which the French Quarter lagged behind. When Gallier installed running water in the upstairs bathroom at his Royal Street home, he was perhaps emulating specifications for his wealthy Garden District patrons. The convenience of running water had its price, however—the visual symmetry of the Garden District was marred somewhat by the cisterns in every yard. These necessary but homely water catchers sometimes rose as high as two stories, giving the District a paradoxical "mansion-and-brewery" look, in the words of Mark Twain.

First Street's Greek Revival gravity is lightened somewhat by the Egyptian "keyhole" doorway and the Italianate mélange of column styles on the galleries—Doric (plain) at the corners, Ionic (down-turned curlicues at the top) on the first floor, and Corinthian (the most ornate type) on the second floor. About 25 percent of the original Brevard floor plan was devoted to working space and living quarters for servants. The third-floor room used by Julien Mayfair in the *Mayfair Witches* books was probably originally servants' quarters.

Brevard, unlike many of his Garden District neighbors, owned no slaves, but that most likely was more of an economic than a humanistic decision on his part—employing German and Irish immigrants was more cost-effective than owning slaves. The Irish, especially, faced formidable cultural prejudices and generally were less skilled than the Germans, and hence quickly became the dominant serving class, competing with blacks for work and engendering a distrust among the two groups that can still be detected. The Irish also had the misfortune to be Catholic in an overwhelmingly Protestant suburb. By the time St. Mary's Assumption Catholic Church was built for the immigrant population, the Irish refused to worship with their German neighbors and insisted on having their own church. So St. Alphonsus was built right across the street.

The Brevard house was eventually purchased by Emory Clapp, who in 1869 added a large hexagonal library to the home. The house's cast-iron balconies and fence bear a distinctive rose pattern, lending it the nickname of Rosegate, at least before it was known as "Anne Rice's house" or "the Mayfair house," depending on whom you talk to. The property now includes two guest houses.

In the next block of First Street, toward Magazine, is the **Payne-Strachan House**, where Confederate president Jefferson Davis died. This Greek Revival house at 1134 First Street at Camp was built in the late 1840s by Jacob U. Payne and remained in his family until the 1930s. A granite marker outside the house, courtesy of the Ladies'

Confederate Memorial Association, marks it as the site where Davis died.

Payne, a successful cotton planter, originally was from Kentucky. His showplace Garden District home features double galleries with six Corinthian columns above and six Ionic ones below, distinctly classical elements softened by the Creole touch of black cast-iron railings on both levels. The architect is unknown, and Payne may well have designed the home himself and brought plantation slaves to town to build it.

During the Civil War, Union forces forced the Paynes to leave their Garden District home and return to their country plantation. The Payne house was occupied by none other than the universally detested General Benjamin Butler. The Paynes, compelled to leave with little notice, had to leave behind many of their fine furnishings and decorations to suffer the whims of the Yankees. Jacob Payne did manage to bury some of the family silver under the garden rosebushes. When they returned after the war, Payne recovered the silver but found that much of his furniture had apparently been swapped for that from other Garden District households. One night at a postwar dinner party, a guest made a startling announcement: "I hate to say this, but we are sitting on my chairs and eating off my table." The Paynes, unlike the Yankees, promptly paid the guest for their "new" dining room suite.

Although emotionally and financially difficult, Reconstruction was not relentlessly grim, and one of the great social events of the 1870s—the debut of Varina Ann (Winnie) Davis, daughter of Jefferson Davis—took place at the Payne House. The Davis family were frequent guests of Payne's daughter, Caroline, and her husband, Louisiana Supreme Court justice Charles E. Fenner. The Fenners had inherited the home when Caroline's parents died soon after the war. Winnie Davis's father, the man whom many also regarded as the "Father of the Confederacy," died in the Fenners' downstairs guest room in December 1889. For years afterward (and occasionally still), Southern loyalists and Civil War buffs rang the front doorbell wondering if they could see the room where Davis died.

Four blocks away, back toward St. Charles and uptown by two blocks, is another house mentioned prominently in *Witching*. Irish Channel native Michael Curry particularly admires the massive residence at **1415 Third Street** at Coliseum; it fascinated him when, as a youth, he fled the indigence of home by ambling through the affluent Garden District. Just as described by Rice, the house is a glistening stark white, with ivory railings all around, one of the few local abodes to retain the "snowy" look so admired by Twain. On one recent day, even the cars parked out front conformed to the all-white edict. The yard is fairly bare compared to some Garden District surroundings, allowing strollers a clear view of the fancy riverside galleries.

The house was built by Virginia native Walter Robinson, a prominent figure in both banking and real estate. He was president of the Merchants and Traders Bank, and he also traded extensively in cotton and tobacco. Building on his palatial Garden District home began before the Civil War, but was not completed until 1865, and Robinson didn't move in until 1867. Architect Henry Howard expanded the traditional three-bay Greek Revival style to five bays, plus an octagonal bay on the right (river) side for use as a dining room. Howard also was the architect of several River Road and bayou plantations, notably Nottaway, the largest plantation home in the South, and Madewood, which influenced Rice in her "construction" of Fontevrault, the plantation owned by the bayou-country Mayfairs.

The other Garden District locale most prominently mentioned in the *Mayfair Witches* series is **Lafayette Cemetery No. 1**, which is discussed extensively in chapter 4. The cemetery occupies the entire extrawide block bordered by Prytania, Washington, Coliseum, and Sixth streets. This cemetery was the primary burial ground for the city of Lafayette beginning in 1833. Among those buried here are developer Samuel Jarvis Peters and the fictional Mayfairs, whose twelve-vault tomb just off the center aisle is described as having been the final resting place for family members since 1861. Lafayette No. 1 has been restored and maintained largely through the efforts of Save Our Cemeteries, and was listed on the National Register of Historic Places in 1972.

Directly across the street from Lafayette No. 1 is **Commander's Palace Restaurant**, on the downtown lakeside corner of Washington and Coliseum. The restaurant was established in 1890 and, according to a plaque adorning it, "dedicated in 1944 to dining in the grand manor."

The "white house" at Third and Coliseum, much admired by Michael Curry in *Witching*.

The Victorian-style building, originally constructed as a lodging house, is painted a bright teal blue offset by milky white trim, with fluttering blue-and-white-striped awnings dangling over the sidewalks. The Mayfairs enjoy dining here following family funerals, gazing out over the windows at the whitewashed walls and tombs of Lafayette No. 1. In New Orleans, one Mayfair explains to a discomfited visitor, the dead are never really left behind. And don't *all* major cities have fine restaurants with lovely cemetery views?

Commander's Palace Restaurant, Washington at Coliseum.

Prytania Street, which runs parallel to St. Charles Avenue one block to the south (toward the river), is where Lestat lives when he returns to New Orleans toward the end of *Interview*. He clearly likes being near the cemetery, which is described as a mere block from "the finest of his houses." Catty-corner to the cemetery, at the downtown lakeside corner of Prytania and Coliseum, is **The Rink**, a shopping mall whimsically carved out of a popular nineteenth-century skating rink. Rice fans should definitely pay a visit here; the mall houses the **Garden District Book Shop**, which offers limited-edition and signed copies of her books. Rice frequently appears at signings at her neighborhood bookstore, which is owned by Britton Trice. When Trice offered special editions of *Taltos*, he reported receiving orders from as far away as Australia. The Rink also features a bright, charming **PJ's Coffee & Tea** shop, where humidity-zapped visitors can refresh themselves with spiced tea or iced coffee.

The oldest house in the Garden District, called **Toby's Corner**, is farther downtown on Prytania, at No. 2340 (corner of First). The Greek Revival, raised-cottage structure was built in 1838, by an unknown architect, for Philadelphia native Thomas Toby.

The **Louise S. McGehee School**, in the same block at 2343 Prytania, was constructed in 1872 for Bradish Johnson, a prominent sugar planter, and turned into a girls' school in 1929. The building, of "free Renaissance" design, is attributed to James Freret and was rumored to cost the exorbitant sum of $100,000. Its four sets of fluted Corinthian columns along the first-floor facade add a classical element to the stately building. As far as early records indicate, this is most likely the *least* haunted building in New Orleans—it is one of the few structures built as a private home that has seen no marriages, births, or deaths within its walls.

Louise Schaumburg McGehee opened her first school for young ladies in 1912, in a small cottage on Louisiana Avenue (near St. Charles). The school moved in 1913 to larger quarters at 1439 Louisiana Avenue, then in 1929 purchased the Johnson house and moved it to the present location on Prytania.

Just a half-block downtown from the Louise McGehee School is the foliage-covered corner of Philip and Prytania, where the character Victor is killed in a carriage accident in *Witching*.

At No. 2423 Prytania is the **John Adams House**, named for the merchant who purchased this section of the Livaudais Plantation in 1860. The **Gilmour-Parker House**, at 2520 Prytania, was built in 1853 for cotton merchant Thomas Corse Gilmour. John M. Parker Jr., whose sons bought the house in 1882, was governor of Louisiana from 1920 to 1924.

Also along this section of Prytania is **Our Mother of Perpetual Help Chapel**, at No. 2523 (at Third). The chapel, built in 1856 as a private residence, earns numerous mentions in the Mayfair books, first in *Witching* as "the little chapel for the rich over there in the Garden

District." The parish chapel supposedly opened at the urging of wealthy families who did not want to attend St. Alphonsus or St. Mary's, after the third parish church, Notre Dame on Jackson Avenue, was torn down in the 1920s. The Mayfairs usually attend mass at Our Mother of Perpetual Help, but in the late 1890s begin using St. Alphonsus in the Irish Channel for special occasions such as baptisms and weddings.

Services still take place at Our Mother of Perpetual Help; visitors should take care not to disturb worshipers during masses. However, the

Our Mother of Perpetual Help Chapel on Prytania, where Rice's Mayfairs sometimes worship.

property's gates are left hospitably unlocked, allowing visitors a quiet turn around the exquisitely maintained grounds or a quick peep through the glass front doors at the chapel's magnificent, somber interior. The building is painted a pale tawny-buff trimmed in white, enhanced by forest-green ironwork and columns. Two towering magnolia trees frame the stately front gate. The chapel is in the same city block as 2524 St. Charles, where Anne Rice lived as a child. That house is described later in this chapter, in the St. Charles Streetcar section.

Just across Prytania from Our Mother of Perpetual Help is another lovely nineteenth-century home, with especially beautiful oaks and brick pavement out front. Along the home's Third Street curb, five matching bronze carriage rings stand as mute reminders of days when horse-drawn buggies conveyed the cream of society to Garden District soirees.

Two blocks uptown on Prytania (heading back toward the cemetery), at No. 1448 Fourth, is **Colonel Short's Villa**, an Italianate–Greek Revival mansion built in 1859 by architect Henry Howard. Colonel Short's Villa was seized by Federal troops during the Civil War, but was returned to the owner in 1865. The wrought-iron fence surrounding the villa features a motif of interwoven cornstalks and morning glories, similar to the fence outside the Cornstalk Hotel in the French Quarter. The cast iron was constructed by Wood and Miltenberger, the New Orleans branch of a Philadelphia foundry. Nearby at 1604 Fourth is the **Alfred Grima House**, built in 1857 in Greek Revival style.

The **Alexander Harris House**, at 2127 Prytania, is a classic Greek Revival raised cottage built the same year as Rice's townhouse, 1857, for cotton merchant Alexander Harris. James H. Calrow, who designed Rice's house, also was the architect for this house, in collaboration with William K. Day. The home features especially lovely columns, topped by cast-iron Corinthian capitals. This fine nineteenth-century home has been recognized by both the Orleans Parish Landmarks Commission (1984) and the New Orleans Historic District Landmarks Commission (1985).

Still farther uptown (just outside the Garden District) is **Touro Infirmary**, at the intersection of Prytania and Aline, designed by the architectural firm of Favrot and Livaudais. Many Mayfairs are treated through the years at this hospital, erected in 1906, notably Ancient Evelyn in *Taltos* and the doomed Cee-Cee Mayfair (Mona's mother) in

Lasher. Touro Infirmary is only a few blocks from 3711 St. Charles, where the "Uptown Mayfairs" reside. That house is described as part of the St. Charles Streetcar tour later in this chapter.

Many beautiful homes line the downtown border of the Garden District, Jackson Avenue. The **Warren House**, at 1531 Jackson, was built in 1860 by James Gallier Jr. and Richard Easterbrook. The Greek Revival structure features lovely ironwork galleries on both the upper and lower floors. The Greek Revival **Henry Sullivan Buckner House**, at 1410 Jackson, is one of the area's largest homes. In fact, from 1923 to 1983, it housed an entire school, Soulé College.

The **Hattie Thorn House**, at 1435 Jackson, is an Italianate raised villa built in 1883 by architect William Fitzner. In the same block, the **William Martin Perkins House** at 1411 Jackson was constructed in 1850–51 and designed by architect Lewis Reynolds. The asymmetrical facade served as an architectural "bridge" between the Greek Revival and Italianate styles. In 1965, Perkins House was bought by neighboring Trinity Church and later named Canon Turner Hall, honoring Canon William Turner, church rector from 1945 to 1968. It was named a New Orleans Historic District Landmark in 1987. **Trinity Church**, at 1329 Jackson, was built in 1852–54 and named a landmark in 1986. At 1305 Jackson Avenue is **Augustus Tardy House**, a Greek Revival–Italianate mixture built in 1869. This house also was sold to Trinity Church, in 1959, and received landmark status in 1986.

The **George O. Sweet House**, at 1236 Jackson, was constructed in Italianate style in 1874 by architect Henry Howard. The **Manuel Goldsmith House**, at 1122 Jackson, was built in Greek Revival style from 1859 to 1860 and designed by Henry Howard and Albert Diettel. In the 1890s, the Goldsmith House was bought by Leon Godchaux, who founded one of Canal Street's most illustrious department stores.

The Garden District section of Magazine Street includes the unusual **Mayer-Seidel Houses** at Nos. 2331–33. This double house was built in 1860 as a rental property for Louis Mayer, whose own residence was next door. The cast-iron fencing surrounding the homes matches that of the neighboring **Louis Mayer House**, at 2323 Magazine. Both properties were honored by the New Orleans Historic District Landmarks Commission in 1987.

The somewhat spooky-looking **John Turpin House**, at 2319 Magazine, was built in 1853–54 for architect John Turpin, who at that time was a partner of James Gallier Jr. The house bears a strong resemblance to Gallier's own house in the French Quarter, built three years later and fictitiously occupied by a trio of vampires. Farther down Magazine, at No. 3000, is the **Protestant Orphans Home**, a magnificent Romanesque Revival building designed in 1887 by architect Thomas Sully. The orphanage stopped operating in 1972; offices are now housed in the building, which received landmark status in 1979.

Also at this end of the Garden District, at 2328 Coliseum, is **The Manse**, a Greek Revival townhouse designed in 1859 by architect William Freret for the widow of a prominent insurance agent. The Prytania Street Presbyterian Church bought the house in 1871 for use as a rectory, and the downtown-side bay was added as the minister's library. The building was given landmark status in 1990.

The **Clarke House**, at 1620 Eighth Street, is a typical example of early Garden District architecture, designed in 1845 by James Gallier Sr. The house, which originally stood on St. Charles Avenue, was built for Jefferson Parish judge Joseph Calvitt Clarke, when the city of Lafayette was the parish seat. The home was moved to Eighth Street in 1869. In 1985, the Clarke House became the Swiss consulate, and it was designated a New Orleans Historic District Landmark the same year. Also on Eighth is the **Byerly-McGraw House**, at No. 1437. It was built in the Second Empire style in the early 1870s and features an unusual (for the period) mansard roof. This house also has been moved, from its original location on Prytania Street.

The **George Washington Cable House**, at 1313 Eighth Street, was constructed in 1874 for the acclaimed writer. Cable's novels are famed for their colorful portraits of nineteenth-century Louisiana life. In 1962, the Cable House was recognized as a National Historic Landmark. Another famed local writer, Kate Chopin, author of *The Awakening*, lived at **1413 Louisiana Avenue** from 1876 to 1879. The double house was built in 1871 for a local sugar broker. In 1974, the Chopin House was bought and restored by the Louisiana branch of the National Society of the Colonial Dames, and it was designated an Orleans Parish Landmark in 1987.

The area between the Central Business District and the Garden District has in recent years become known as the Lower Garden District; this part of town was laid out in 1806 by architect-surveyor Barthelemy Lafon. Apparently fond of the classics, Lafon dubbed many of the streets with names straight out of Greek legend—Nayades (now St. Charles), Apollo (now Carondelet), etc. Nine streets were christened after the muses: Calliope, Clio, Erato, Thalia, Melpomene, Terpsichore, Euterpe, Polymnia, and Urania. The names have lost some of their romance through the years; Clio, for instance, is often referred to as "CL10," because of the way it appears on some street signs (no dot on the "i").

The Lower Garden District area, bordered by Annunciation Street, Jackson Avenue, Prytania Street, and Erato Street, was named an official historic district in 1976.

At 1507 Magazine Street is the former **St. Vincent's Orphan Asylum**, a red-brick complex built in 1864 for the Sisters of Charity of St. Vincent de Paul. The Magazine Street side's gorgeous cast-iron gallery was added in the 1880s.

The Lower Garden District section of Camp Street also contains many significant historic structures. The **Archibald Bouleware House**, at 1531 Camp Street, was built in 1854. The brick house, which was designated a landmark in 1976, contains many unusual features—for example, Corinthian columns on both front galleries, and an arched iron trellis in the front garden area. The **E. T. Robinson House**, at 1456 Camp Street, was built in the Italianate style in the late 1850s. The building originally held Sophie Bell Wright's Home Institute–English and Classical School for Young Ladies and Children. The **Coliseum Place Baptist Church**, at 1376 Camp Street, was constructed of red brick in the Gothic Revival style in 1854. The tower steeple was destroyed by Hurricane Betsy in 1965 and never replaced.

At 1420 Euterpe Street is the **John Thornhill House**, built in 1847 and named a local landmark in 1976. In 1863, at the height of the War Between the States, it was occupied by Federal forces and used as headquarters for the Freedman's Bureau. The bureau, in turn, opened New Orleans University, the city's first school for blacks. Following the war, the home was returned to its owner, commission merchant John Thornhill, and his heirs lived there until the mid–twentieth century. Just down the street at No. 1524 Euterpe is the **Captain Robert C. Young House,** built in the late 1840s or early 1850s by the captain. The house includes a side gallery, detached kitchen, and service building. The Young House was given landmark status in 1985.

The **Coliseum Theater,** at 1233 Coliseum Street in the shadow of Interstate 10, was used in the film version of *Interview.* Louis, waxing poetic about the glories of cinematic dawns, is shown emerging from the theater following a showing of *Tequila Sunrise.* Some extraordinarily attentive moviegoers spotted an anachronistic boo-boo—Louis's voice-over says he's talking about the spring of 1988, but *Tequila Sunrise* didn't hit theaters until fall of that year. Several affronted gaffe-spotters pointed out this seasonal slip in the March 1995 issue of *Premiere* magazine. In 1993, Morrison Productions converted the renovated art deco building into a state-of-the-art video production center.

Several noteworthy nineteenth- and early-twentieth-century homes stand in the 1700 block of Coliseum Street, including the **William Garrison House** at No. 1717 and the **Henry Morton Stanley House** at No. 1729. The Garrison House was built in the 1850s, with side bays added later. The Stanley House was built in the 1830s for local jeweler William Goodrich and originally stood at 904 Orange Street on Annunciation Square. It was moved to Coliseum Street in 1981. The home is named for a runaway Welsh cabin boy who was befriended and unofficially adopted by Henry Hope Stanley and his wife. They named the child Henry Morton Stanley, and he grew up to have an illustrious and adventurous life—serving in the Civil War in the Confederate army and becoming a journalist. In Africa, on assignment for an American newspaper, he found the missing Dr. David Livingston and greeted him with the much-repeated question, "Dr. Livingston, I presume?" The British citizen eventually earned a knighthood from his native country.

The **Hugh Wilson House,** at 1741 Coliseum Street, was built in 1847 for commission merchant Hugh Wilson. With the exception of a brief period in the 1860s when it was owned by others, the Wilson family resided in this house until 1910. It features a simple, almost stark front gallery with Ionic columns above and Doric below. The Wilson house earned landmark status in 1976. Just down the block at No. 1749

The Coliseum Theater in the Lower Garden District, where a scene from *Interview* was filmed.

is the **Grace King House**, built in 1847 for banker-merchant Frederick Rodewald. Respected Louisiana historian and writer Grace King lived here from about 1905 until she died in 1932.

In the next block, at 1805 Coliseum, is the **Flower-Morrison House**, a Greek Revival–Italianate raised cottage that has served as the abode for two New Orleans mayors—Walter Chew Flower, who moved here in 1886 and was mayor from 1896 to 1900, and de Lesseps Story Morrison, who moved here about 1950 and was mayor from 1946 to

1961. This interesting home was named an Orleans Parish Landmark in 1976.

The 1300 block of Felicity Street also is a treasure trove of fascinating architecture. The **John T. Moore Jr. House**, at 1309 Felicity, was built in 1880 on grounds owned by businessman John T. Moore. Moore's son-in-law, apparently much loved by, or an especially zealous admirer of, his father-in-law, took the name John T. Moore Jr. The house originally was designed by James Freret and was restored by architect Moise Goldstein in 1954 when he moved there. At 1328 Felicity is an imposing brick Italianate villa, the **John Augustus Blaffer House**, built in 1869.

At 1322 Felicity is the **John McGinty House**, another Italianate structure built in 1870 and designated a landmark in 1976. The home features unusual gallery ornamentation—wood columns on the first floor and lacy ironwork on the second. **Felicity United Methodist Church**, at 1226 Felicity, was built in the Gothic Revival style around 1888. Its tower steeples were destroyed by a 1915 hurricane and never rebuilt.

St. Anna's Asylum, at 1823 Prytania Street, may have served as Rice's inspiration for the "St. Ann's Asylum" mentioned in *Witching*; it's where the unhappy Antha is committed after running away and becoming a writer in New York. The real St. Anna's was originally opened "for the Relief of Destitute Females and Their Helpless Children of All Religious Denominations." A nondenominational organization of Christian women was formed in 1850 for this purpose, and the Prytania Street site was donated in 1853 by Dr. William Newton Mercer. The society gratefully named the asylum in memory of Mercer's daughter, Anna.

Nearby at 1780 Prytania is **Eagle Hall**, which was built in 1851 at the border of Faubourgs Annunciation and Nuns, the dividing line between New Orleans and the city of Lafayette. In 1862, Eagle Hall was occupied by the popular Lafayette Volkstheater (Peoples Theater). It also was the site for German political meetings during and after the Civil War, and a grocery store in the late 1800s. In the 1940s, it was the home of Hinderer's Iron Works. Eagle Hall was designated an Orleans Parish Landmark in 1976.

The Irish Channel

The exact confines of the Irish Channel are difficult to define (ask five people and expect five different answers, along with a vivid, detailed history of the area!). The area near Adele Street and the river held the highest concentration of Irish immigrants starting in the 1840s, and remains the heart of the Channel. Magazine Street and the river historically mark the Channel's north-south boundaries, and most present-day sources put the east-west borders basically at Howard Avenue and Louisiana Avenue. The working-class riverfront Channel was home to thousands of Irish and German immigrants, and although its ethnic makeup has changed through the years, its tough demeanor has not. Shrewd visitors will not wander its streets alone or after dark. The safest way to see the old Irish Channel, unfortunately, is in a car with the windows rolled up and the doors locked, or simply through photographs.

In *Interview*, Claudia asks Lestat and Louis to take her "through the Faubourg St. Marie to the riverfront places where the immigrants lived," where the child vampire preys on a single family, killing one at a time. Although it is not named as such, Rice probably refers to the Channel in this passage. The Irish Channel plays a much more prominent role in the Mayfair series, though, as the childhood home of Michael Curry and site of the two proud parish churches, St. Mary's Assumption and St. Alphonsus. Like many of the Irish who settled in Lafayette, Michael Curry's ancestors had fled the potato famines in their native country, only to be dumped into the "wet grave" of Louisiana. In Ireland, they faced hunger; in New Orleans, they fought yellow fever cholera, and other pestilence, not to mention the social scorn of being from the "wrong side" of Magazine Street, a sort of emotional and cultural equivalent to the Berlin Wall.

Michael's family is described as having lived in the same double cottage on **Annunciation Street** for three generations. To this day, one can see row after row of "double shotguns" lining Annunciation and the other streets of the Channel. Many of these structures have been beautifully restored, but often sit side by side with rat-infested ruins that reek of poverty and apathy. As a child, Michael frequently slips across Magazine Street to wander through the quiet Garden District streets, a few blocks and a world away from the physical and spiritual squalor of the Channel.

Double-shotgun houses along Annunciation Street, the Irish Channel thoroughfare where *Witching's* hero, Michael Curry, grows up.

Magazine Street still contains the rowdy bars frequented by a couple of Rice's Irish Channel characters, although the clubs now share block space with rows of exclusive antique shops, where security concerns dictate that shoppers must ring to gain admittance. One store in particular, **Bush Antiques** at 2109 Magazine Street near Jackson, will be of special interest to Rice fans—Bush auctioned off many of the props and furnishings used in the film version of *Interview*. Most of the items sold within two days, but a bed constructed especially for the film remains, tucked in an upstairs niche with a newspaper story about the filming hanging above it. Proprietors say they don't plan to sell the bed. From the corner of Jackson and Magazine, looking downtown and toward the river, one can glimpse the tower of St. Mary's Church and also the Crescent City Connection bridge, Lestat's "Dixie Gates."

In the next block of Magazine, at No. 2241 (corner of Philip), is the imposing **Leitz-Egan Funeral Home**, one of Rice's inspirations for Lonigan & Sons, the Mayfair family morticians.

St. Mary's Assumption and **St. Alphonsus**, the great German and Irish parish churches, face each other in the 2000 block of Constance, between St. Andrew and Josephine. This is one block toward the river from Magazine and two blocks downtown from Jackson. St. Mary's was founded in 1843 by the German-speaking Catholics of Lafayette; the small original church has been moved to St. Joseph Cemetery uptown. Construction began on the current German Baroque structure in 1858, and the church was dedicated in 1860.

The Irish immigrant population, staunch in its refusal to worship with the Germans, built its church, St. Alphonsus, right across the street. Construction began in 1855, with the dedication in 1857. So although the St. Mary's congregation predates that of St. Alphonsus, the Irish actually beat the Germans in building their great parish church. Another church, Notre Dame de Bon Secours, served the French-speaking population from a nearby Jackson Avenue location for many years until being demolished in the 1920s. The same parish priests served all three churches. St. Mary's and St. Alphonsus, as well as other notable New Orleans churches, are discussed in more detail in chapter 5.

Redemptorist School, attended by Anne Rice, Michael Curry, and several members of the Mayfair family (after their expulsion from more exclusive private schools), stood just to the left of St. Alphonsus. The former school building, along with the St. Mary's rectory and several other church buildings, has been turned into public housing. The gym building, constructed with money raised by the children of Redemptorist Parish (including Anne and her fictional counterpart Michael Curry), is on the riverside uptown corner of Constance and Josephine. Anne was distraught to discover that although boys *and* girls raised money for the gymnasium, girls could use it only after the boys finished their activities. The building is now painted a peach color with darker melon trim, with window frames and shutters of Paris green.

Many mid- to late-nineteenth-century homes and other buildings also grace the Irish Channel. The **Isaac Bogart House**, at 1020 Fourth Street, was built in Greek Revival Style in 1849–50, and received landmark status in 1989. The **Nathaniel R. Cotton House**, at 3232 Laurel Street, was built in a simple variation of the Greek Revival style about

1838. In the late 1870s, the ground floor was converted to a grocery, and the building was used as a store until the 1960s. It was named a New Orleans Historic District Landmark in 1986.

The **Mary Ann Grigson House**, at 436 Seventh Street, is one of the oldest remaining buildings in the former city of Lafayette. It was built in about 1835 for Grigson. The simple wood-frame house features front and rear galleries supported by boxed columns. The Grigson House earned landmark status in 1981.

The Central Business District

The Central Business District, identified by New Orleanians and street signs as the "CBD," extends from Canal Street uptown, basically to just beyond Lee Circle (near today's Interstate 10 overpass). Originally the Faubourg St. Marie (quickly changed to Faubourg St. Mary in most people's pronunciation), this area first was subdivided in the 1780s, with blocks carved out of plantation land owned by Don Beltran (also known as Bertrand) Gravier. Americans arriving after the Louisiana Purchase found the Creoles of the Vieux Carré unwelcoming, at best, and quickly started building their own city on the other side of the "neutral ground," Canal Street.

One of the most imposing CBD buildings is the **U.S. Custom House**, at 423 Canal Street near the riverfront. The massive mid-nineteenth-century building occupies an entire city square, bounded by Canal, Decatur, North Peters, and Iberville streets. Alexander Thompson Wood served as architect for the Custom House, which was started in 1848 and built of granite and brick. The grand second-floor Marble Hall, 125 feet by 95 feet and 54 feet high, features fourteen Corinthian columns. The Custom House, which took thirty-three years to build and cost about $4 million, served as a prison for captured Confederates during the city's Civil War occupation, no doubt to the consummate horror of General P. G. T. Beauregard, the brilliant Confederate officer who had served as the Custom House's first superintendent of construction. From the late 1800s until 1915, the building was used as a post office. In 1974, it was named a National Historic Landmark.

Nearer the river is the enormous **Canal Place** high-rise shopping center, which includes the Canal Place Cinema, where a private New

Orleans premiere of *Interview With the Vampire* was held in early November 1994. Anne Rice hosted the festivities for some 500 invited friends and relatives. Attendees were treated to popcorn, candy, soft drinks, and distinctive souvenirs—rubber rats signed by the hostess.

The **Montgomery Buildings**, at 500–504 Canal and 510–12 Canal, were built in the 1860s for William W. Montgomery, president of the Bank of Louisiana. The massive Italianate buildings were designated as local landmarks in 1979.

At 622 Canal is the **Merchants Mutual Insurance Company Building**, which features a quartet of unusual twisted columns on the front facade. Architect William Freret designed the building, which was built in 1859 and named a local landmark in 1981.

Both the **D. H. Holmes** site and the **Maison Blanche** department store on Canal are mentioned in Rice's works. The D. H. Holmes building, at 819 Canal, was built in 1849 by merchant Daniel Henry Holmes. The Gothic Revival–style facade has been remodeled significantly through the years. In 1994, work began on converting the landmark building into a hotel, the Chateau Sonesta. In the same block is the **William Newton Mercer House**, at 824 Canal. James Gallier Jr. was the architect on the house, built in 1844. The half-octagonal, three-story wing on the Carondelet Street side was added in the 1880s. Mercer House was named a local landmark in 1980. Maison Blanche, at 900–921 Canal Street, was built in 1906–9, replacing an earlier store on the same spot. The French Renaissance-style architecture was designed by Stone Brothers. The thirteen-story facade is covered with white enameled terra cotta. Maison Blanche was recognized as a local landmark in 1980.

The **Saenger Theatre**, at 1111 Canal between Basin and Rampart, was constructed in 1925–27 for the Saenger Amusement Company of Shreveport. The Saenger was famed for its interior ceiling, which through "movie magic" was covered with moving clouds and sparkling stars for each performance. Dozens of marble statues and a Florentine-garden motif adorned the lobby, which featured imposing black marble columns and white marble staircases. The Saenger is still used, housing Broadway touring productions and musical performers.

On Carondelet, the street where the imaginary Mayfairs had their law firm, are several interesting 1920s buildings. The **Hibernia National Bank Building**, at 313 Carondelet, was built in 1920–21 and reigned as

The historic Maison Blanche department store on Canal Street.

New Orleans's tallest building for four decades. Architects Charles Allen Favrot and Louis Livaudais spent some $3 million on the handsome structure, which combines Greek, Roman, and Renaissance components. The twenty-three-story building is capped by a circular colonnade and beacon. It was designated a local landmark in 1980. Another bank building, the **National American Bank Building**, soars twenty-nine stories at 200 Carondelet. It was built just prior to the Depression, in 1928–29, in American Art Deco style, designed by architect Moise Goldstein. An octagonal tower rises from the twenty-fourth through twenty-ninth floors.

Saenger Theatre, built at the beginning of the twentienth century on Canal Street.

The **New Orleans Cotton Exchange Building**, at 231–37 Carondelet, was built in 1920–21 and designed by the firm of Favrot and Livaudais (which also created the Hibernia National Bank during the same time period). In 1977, it was designated a National Historic Landmark, and now houses business offices.

The **Old Post Office**, at 600 Camp Street, cost $2.5 million to build in 1914. Twenty-five-foot sculptures perch at each corner of the Italian Renaissance building, which served as a post office until 1962 and now houses the U.S. Fifth Circuit Court of Appeals. It was designated an Orleans Parish Landmark in 1984.

Confederate Memorial Hall, at 929 Camp Street near Lee Circle, opened in 1891 and is the state's oldest museum. Architect Thomas Sully, who designed many of the Victorian-era homes along St. Charles Avenue, devised the exterior to blend with the Howard Memorial Library next door. On May 29, 1893, the remains of Confederate president Jefferson Davis lay in state in the hall. It is currently operated as the Confederate Museum by the Louisiana Historical Association and was designated a New Orleans landmark in 1977.

Right next door, and visible from the St. Charles Streetcar circling Lee Circle, is the red-brick **Howard Memorial Library** at 615 Howard Avenue. Built in 1888, it sports the distinctive "Richardsonian Romanesque" style of Henry Hobson Richardson, whose architectural firm designed it two years after his death. Most of the interior and part of the roof were destroyed in a World War II-era fire, possibly set by arsonists. The Howard Library was honored as a New Orleans landmark in 1977.

The thirteen row houses at 600–648 Julia Street, known as **Julia Row**, were built in 1832–33 and served for many years as home to some of the American sector's most prominent citizens. Several of the red-brick houses have been restored in recent years, showcasing their graceful ironwork, fanlights, and sidelights. The nonprofit **Preservation Resource Center**, at 604 Julia Street, was instrumental in saving Julia Row and several other historic structures in the Warehouse District. Julia Row was designated an Orleans Parish Landmark in 1984.

The **Board of Trade Plaza**, at 316 Magazine Street, is a modern building (built in 1968) using historic elements—the cast-iron columns, arches, and lintels from the St. James Hotel, which previously had held that spot since 1859 as part of the **Banks' Arcade**. The only buildings remaining of the once block-long Banks' Arcade are at 336 Magazine Street. The massive three-story structure, built in 1833, was the heart of business and social dealings in the mid-1800s. The first floor contained offices and the John Hewlett restaurants, the second housed the Washington Guards and billiards rooms, and the third was a gentlemen's hotel (presumably for those too exhausted by the activity to go home). The entire assemblage, topped by a glass arcade, could house as many as 5,000 people at one time for public events. In 1835, a committee met there to plan assistance for the Texas Revolution. In 1941, the remaining Banks' Arcade buildings were restored.

Closer to the river on Tchoupitoulas Street, at No. 923, is **Leeds Foundry**, an unusual neo-Gothic masonry structure built in the mid-1850s by James Gallier Jr. and John Turpin. The cast-iron Gothic details on the building's facade probably were produced in the foundry, which was the second-largest ironworks in the South before the Civil War. The foundry manufactured cannons and other military supplies during the first days of the Confederacy.

A Streetcar Named St. Charles

By far the most comfortable and charming way to get acquainted with Uptown New Orleans, all the way from Canal Street to Carrollton Avenue, is via the nostalgic St. Charles Streetcar, the oldest continuously

The St. Charles Streetcar line runs twenty-four hours a day, seven days a week along the oak-lined avenue.

running street-railway system in the country. The thirty-five olive-green cars operating today run along the thirteen-mile tracks of the old New Orleans and Carrollton Railroad, which in 1835 started commuting between New Orleans and the then-independent suburb of Carrollton. In *Witching*, Julien Mayfair often rides his chestnut mare along the same route, and we are told that after he died, "four different witnesses claimed to have seen his ghost riding through the mist on St. Charles Avenue."

The streetcar runs twenty-four hours a day, and a round trip (fare must be paid both ways) takes about an hour and a half. Because the streetcar is still a much-used public transit, it's best to avoid traveling during rush hours on weekdays. The after-school crowd hits about 3:15 P.M. weekdays, with uniform-clad kids crowding the cars and filling the air with giggles and spitballs. Also, the streetcar is not the way to go if you're in a hurry—frequent stops, as well as pauses for streetlights and automobiles crossing St. Charles or Carondelet, conspire to keep speeds in the 15- to 20-mile-per-hour range. The streetcars also sometimes pause to wait while a prone person is removed from the tracks, most often a sleeping vagrant or someone overcome by the heat; committing suicide by streetcar would be virtually impossible, given the snail's pace of the cars.

The current cars were built in North Carolina in the 1920s and retain many features of that earlier era—glossy wooden seats, and windows that actually open and close, a blessing since the cars are not heated or air-conditioned. Visitors should remember that these are *streetcars*, not trolleys or cable cars (calling them trolleys will immediately label you a tourist). The difference is in the mechanics of movement— trolleys are connected cars pulled by a locomotive of some sort, and cable cars, such as those in San Francisco, are operated by underground pull-cables. Streetcars, such as those in New Orleans, are powered by electric overhead cables.

The streetcar takes passengers through the Central Business District, then into a miles-long stretch lined by elegant mansions and hundred-year-old oak trees, past Audubon Park and Tulane and Loyola universities. The streetcar tracks follow St. Charles Avenue, which in turn imitates the natural bends of the river. At Carrollton Avenue, the streetcar makes a sharp right turn and travels on another few blocks. If you hop off at the Carrollton turn, however, you can cross the street for a fabulous view of the river (this is a great spot for a picnic). The sharp bow in the Mississippi just a little farther upriver gave this area its original name—**Riverbend**, possibly inspiring Rice's name for the eighteenth-century Mayfairs' fictional plantation, La Victoire at Riverbend, which eventually was drowned by the river's raging torrents.

The following streetcar tour directs your attention to points of interest on both sides of St. Charles, with the assumption that you begin your journey at either Carondelet and Canal (the final boarding point for streetcars headed downtown), or around the corner at St. Charles and Common, the first stop for cars headed uptown. The Carondelet stop is where passengers traveling downtown end their journey; it's usually easier to get a seat here than if you wait and catch the streetcar around the corner at St. Charles and Common on its way back uptown.

You'll notice that most of the street names change on the uptown side of Canal Street, from the original French designations of the Quarter to the American appellations in the CBD and Uptown. Starting at the lakeside boundary of the Quarter, Rampart remains Rampart, Burgundy becomes O'Keefe, Dauphine becomes Baronne, Bourbon becomes Carondelet, Royal becomes St. Charles, Chartres becomes Camp, Decatur becomes Magazine, and North Peters becomes Tchoupitoulas.

The streetcar-tour sights are designated as being to either your left or your right, assuming you're traveling uptown. Boarding at Carondelet and Canal, glance around at the tall modern buildings and try to imagine which was the inspiration for Mayfair and Mayfair, the family law firm with thirtieth-floor offices at this corner. The streetcar will pull onto Canal for one long block, then turn uptown onto St. Charles. At the corner of St. Charles and Canal, at No. 115 on the left, is the old **Crescent Billiard Hall**, built in 1826. It was the site of the Merchants Hotel in the 1850s before being converted to the Billiard Hall in 1865. In the 1870s, architect Henry Howard oversaw extensive renovations, both interior and exterior. In 1980, the building was designed a CBD Historic District Landmark.

Kolb's Restaurant, at 121–25 St. Charles, on the right, served the New Orleans community from the 1890s through the 1990s, but closed recently. The 125–27 section was built sometime prior to 1844, and the

121–23 section was built before 1853. The fancy cast-iron galleries probably were added after both buildings had been completed. Kolb's, originally a saloon, opened in 1898.

The first major intersection after the streetcar stop at St. Charles and Common is **Poydras Street**; look to your left and you'll get a glimpse of the entrance to **Riverwalk Mall** and the **Louisiana Superdome**, home of the New Orleans Saints football team. In the next block on the right, at 543 St. Charles, is the city's most acclaimed remaining example of Greek Revival architecture. Famed architect James Gallier Sr. oversaw the building of **Gallier Hall**, which was constructed of granite and marble between 1845 and 1850. The tensions between the Americans and Creoles had come to a head in 1836, resulting in a division of New Orleans into three separate municipalities, each having its own aldermen. A single mayor and a citywide board of aldermen served the city at large. The Vieux Carré became the First Municipality, the American sector above Canal the Second, and the rest of the city was lumped into the Third. Gallier Hall originally served as city hall for the First Municipality, then in 1852, when the three sections were again consolidated, it became city hall for all of New Orleans. It remained the seat of city government until 1957, when the new city hall was built. The bodies of Jefferson Davis, P. G. T. Beauregard, and many city mayors have lain in state in its classically formal parlor. Gallier Hall is now used primarily for official receptions.

Directly across St. Charles from Gallier Hall, on your left, is **Lafayette Square**, which was the Americans' answer to a central city park such as the Creoles had with their Plaza de Armas. Lafayette Square was laid out in 1788 as part of the Faubourg St. Marie. The formally landscaped park's focal point is a bronze statue of Henry Clay, a nineteenth-century U.S. senator and frequent New Orleans visitor. Clay's likeness was originally erected at St. Charles and Canal in 1860, and the statue was moved uptown to Lafayette Square in 1901. Another statue, of John McDonogh, also adorns the park. McDonogh, a nineteenth-century Algiers businessman, was a major benefactor of the New Orleans public schools. Some local traditions contend that McDonogh was one of Micaela Almonester's many lovelorn suitors, although Micaela would have been a child of nine or ten during the supposed courtship. Micaela later went on to fame as Madame de Pontalba, builder of the Pontalba Buildings lining Jackson Square.

The next few blocks of St. Charles form the border of the **Warehouse District**, a section of late-nineteenth-century buildings that have been renovated and converted to galleries, shopping areas, restaurants, apartments, and offices.

The streetcar will make a right turn, then a left and another quick right, to circumvent **Lee Circle** before heading on uptown. Lee Circle was part of Barthelmy Lafon's failed Faubourg Annunciation plans; it originally was dubbed Place du Tivoli after the Southern Italian city. In the center of the circle, a 7,000-pound bronze statue of General Robert E. Lee stands proudly atop a sixty-foot-tall fluted white-marble column. Lee is facing defiantly north; locals explain that Lee would *never* have turned his back on those sneaky Yankees. A public library once stood on the perimeter of Lee Circle; it was here that young Anne Rice and her *Witching* hero, Michael Curry, got their literary nourishment of Dickens (their shared favorite) and other authors.

As the streetcar edges around the circle to the right, you'll see the **K&B Plaza**, built on land where the public library once stood. The K&B building is decorated with sculptures by contemporary artists, including Henry Moore, Isamu Noguchi, and George Segal. The lobby of the building, which is headquarters to the K&B Drugstore chain, contains additional sculptures and paintings.

Just past the I-10 overpass, between Clio and Erato streets, is the circa-1916 **Jerusalem Temple**, which features a gorgeous, detailed tile mosaic on its St. Charles side. Another two blocks uptown is the corner of **Melpomene and St. Charles** (once called Nayades Street). This spot is mentioned in *Interview*, when Lestat is seen killing on Nayades and subsequent rumors connect him with a "haunted house" near this intersection.

The next several blocks run through what is now called the Lower Garden District. Many of the Greek Revival mansions lining St. Charles in this sector have been transformed into businesses and restaurants. Two special spots loom in the 2000 block of St. Charles, between St. Andrew and Josephine. On the left is **Restaurant de la Tour Eiffel**, at No. 2040, an eccentric edifice that may cause mouths to drop open in amazement at the sight. This glass-and-steel conglomeration contains the reassembled interior of a restaurant that actually operated inside Paris's Eiffel Tower from 1936 to 1981. Those who ate at the Paris site included Pablo Picasso, Marc Chagall, Charlie Chaplin, Maurice Chevalier, Brigitte Bardot, and Charles de Gaulle.

The Tour Eiffel building is now owned by **The Pontchartrain Hotel** and is used as a catering facility for special events. The Pontchartrain, at 2031 St. Charles on your right, is a gracious hostelry that will be of particular interest to Rice fans. The eleven-story Pontchartrain, permeated with old-world charm and exquisite attention to service, boasts more than one hundred rooms and is now operated by Grand Heritage Hotels. It was built in 1927 by E. Lysle Aschaffenburg, who operated it until the mid-1980s, and it was named for Count Pontchartrain of the court of Louis XVI. If you visit, ask someone to point out the whimsical drawings included in the lobby's faux marble wall design—with help, you'll detect a skillfully disguised donkey, dancing girls, and in tribute to the area's favorite cuisine, crawfish and shrimp.

In *Witching*, Michael Curry remembers visiting the Pontchartrain's world-class restaurant as a child. He recalls the **Caribbean Room** as "a near silent, eerie world of candlelight, white tablecloths, and waiters who looked like ghosts, or better yet, they looked like the vampires in the horror movies, with their black jackets and stiff white shirts." I am happy to report that Michael Dietrich, current Caribbean Room maitre d' and a treasure trove of information about the hotel, looks more like one of the hotel's movie-star guests than a ghost or vampire. The Caribbean Room specializes in grand Creole cuisine, which savvy diners will cap with a slice of the restaurant's irresistible, one-of-a-kind Mile-High Pie.

It's also in the Pontchartrain that Rowan Mayfair and Michael Curry stay on their arrival in New Orleans, in a suite with a baby grand piano, overlooking St. Charles Avenue. That lushly decorated suite does indeed exist; it's called the Mary Martin Suite and is Room No. 403. The hotel names its suites after celebrities who have stayed there, including Richard Burton, Yul Brynner, Tennessee Williams, Walt Disney, Helen Hayes, and Rod Serling. Napoleon also has a suite named in his honor (although he never actually paid a visit, unless it was a ghostly one, since the hotel wasn't built until this century). The Anne Rice

The Pontchartrain Hotel towers over St. Charles Avenue at the downriver boundary of the Garden District.

Suite, No. 303, is one floor directly below Mary Martin's. Tom Cruise, who doesn't yet have his own suite, rented the hotel's penthouse during Mardi Gras a few years ago, before returning to New Orleans in 1993 as the star of *Interview*.

Rice describes with precision the Pontchartrain's distinctive blue awnings, glass doors, narrow lobby, and cozy coffee shop (the delightful Cafe Pontchartrain, a popular breakfast spot for the city's movers and shakers). In *Witching*, Michael Curry also remembers Smith's Drugstore, next door to the hotel, which has now been resurrected as Smith's

The elegant Caribbean Room restaurant at the Pontchartrain Hotel.

Record Center. Just down the block, at the St. Andrew corner, is the boarded-up Mercedes-Benz dealership where Rowan and Michael shop in *Witching*.

One block beyond the Pontchartrain, at 2139 St. Charles on the right, is the **Williams Super Market**, historically called the P. T. Phillips Grocery. It was built in 1860, with Henry Howard and Henry Thiberge serving as architects. The Italianate facade fronting St. Charles has been obscured by the modern sign. The building was named a landmark in 1978. The next major intersection, **Jackson Avenue**, marks the downtown border of the Garden District. In *Taltos*, the Talamasca's Aaron Lightner is killed near this corner, after leaving the Pontchartrain.

In the next block on the right, at the corner of Philip Street, is **2301 St. Charles**, where Rice's parents lived when she was born. (There is a jog in Philip at St. Charles—you may notice a Philip Street sign on the left, then it's another short block to where the street picks up on the other side of St. Charles.) Stan Rice stayed at 2301 St. Charles when

2301 St. Charles at Philip, where Anne Rice's parents lived when she was born.

he and Anne, as teenagers, visited New Orleans from Texas; Anne's childhood home had been turned into a boardinghouse.

When the Rices returned to New Orleans in 1988, the house had fallen to near ruins. Happily, it has now been meticulously restored, painted a glowing peach with dark teal shutters and black ironwork. The only sinister note emanates from the immense black oak trees guarding Philip Street next to the house; their twisting roots extend out over the curb and thrust through the pavement, as if guarding the property from harmful intent. If you wonder why the city doesn't keep the sidewalks in better repair, remember that in New Orleans it's against the law to hurt an oak tree, and roots would have to be cut to make the sidewalks even.

Another two blocks uptown on the left is **2524 St. Charles**, where Anne's family moved while she was still a little girl. The home was built for Antoine Mandeville de Marigny, the youngest son of Samuel Peters's rival Bernard de Marigny, and also was owned by priests at one time. The center-hall raised cottage, on the riverside downtown corner of St.

Charles and Third, is painted butter-yellow with white trim, accented with dark green shutters and ironwork. Voluminous lace curtains fill the large windows, and the polished wooden door features sparkling leaded-glass panes. Decades-old oaks and magnolias grace the front garden. It was from this house that Anne made her daily journeys through the Garden District to attend Redemptorist School in the Irish Channel, fueling her dreams to one day live in a Garden District mansion of her own.

About four blocks uptown on the right, in the 2900 block of St. Charles, is **Christ Church Cathedral**, constructed in 1887 and the center of the New Orleans Episcopal community. New Yorker Lawrence Valk was the architect. At 3029 St. Charles (corner of Seventh) on the right is the elaborate **Watson Van Benthuysen–Elms** mansion, built of stone in 1869 by Van Benthuysen, who served as treasurer of the Confederate States of America.

At the uptown border of the Garden District, on the left at 3338 St. Charles at Louisiana, is the **Bultman Funeral Home**. This extremely

2524 St. Charles, where Rice's family moved when she was a child.

palatial funeral home was built in the 1930s from sections of three wood-frame houses that dated from the 1850s. The Bultman family no longer operates the business. Just across Louisiana, on the right, is a K&B Drugstore, probably the same one referred to in the Mayfair books, this being the closest K&B to the First Street house.

Traveling another four blocks uptown, look to the right and you'll see **3711 St. Charles** at Amelia (lakeside uptown corner), the residence of the "Uptown Mayfairs," including Mona until she moves into the First Street house in *Taltos*. Anne Rice bought and restored this house in the early 1990s, but has since sold it. In the 1993–94 New Orleans telephone directory, evidence of her (or someone's) sense of humor shone through in a listing for one Mona Mayfair at that address. The Italianate mansion, which was built in 1881 and designed by German architect William Fitzner, is painted a bright melon-peach, with white trim and black ironwork. Sky-blue ceilings crown both the upstairs and downstairs galleries, which feature fluted Doric columns. In the Mayfair books, it's originally called the "big pink house," but attains its present peach color when renovated.

Rice fans in the mood for an adventurous jaunt might want to explore by retracing the long walk taken by Ancient Evelyn in *Lasher*, which she began at 3711 St. Charles and ended at 1239 First Street. The walk takes about thirty minutes at a fairly fast clip. Ancient Evelyn crosses from 3711 to the other side of St. Charles at Amelia, then crosses Amelia and Antonine on her way downtown. The cafe described as "Patrick's restaurant" in the book could be the Que Sera Restaurant & Bar, which sits at that corner. As you pass the restaurant, you'll glimpse Touro Infirmary on Prytania across a row of vacant lots on your right. Continue downtown on St. Charles, past the business section at Louisiana and into several blocks occupied by apartments and banks. At Connery, look to the right and you'll see the tombs of Lafayette Cemetery peeking over the high whitewashed brick walls.

At Washington, Ancient Evelyn turns right into the Garden District. She takes mental note of the florist at the corner (Peter A. Chopin Florist) and the white shingled Queen Anne house on the lakeside downtown corner (No. 2727), the only house left standing at the in-

3711 St. Charles, the home of the "Uptown Mayfairs" in the *Mayfair Witches* series.

tersection. It may not have long; as of this writing the house appeared dilapidated and a For Sale sign was planted in the yard. As she enters the Garden District, Evelyn's walk takes her past The Rink, Lafayette Cemetery, and Commander's Palace as she makes her way to Chestnut Street, where she crosses Washington and continues downtown (turning left) to the First Street house.

Back to the streetcar route: In the next block after 3711 St. Charles is **The Columns Hotel**, at 3811 between Peniston and General Taylor. The hotel, which is listed in the National Register of Historic Places, was built in 1883 for cigar magnate Simon Hernsheim at a cost of $40,000. Its architect, Thomas Sully, designed dozens of Victorian-era homes along St. Charles, many of which still stand a century later. The hotel's massive white columns were among several additions and

The Victorian-era Columns Hotel on St. Charles Avenue.

alterations to the house made after a powerfully destructive 1915 hurricane.

The Columns' Victorian Lounge is a popular local hangout, and the veranda is a lovely place to sip a cool drink in the early evening, listening for the pleasant screech of the next streetcar along the avenue. The hotel's nineteenth-century ambiance has made it a favorite location for movie scenes, including the interiors for *Pretty Baby*, the 1978 Louis Malle film, set in Storyville and starring Brooke Shields and Susan Sarandon. The current owners, Claire and Jacques Creppel, have resurrected a Victorian aura of warmth and hospitality. In 1992, Anne Rice hosted one of her famous Halloween parties at the house.

Two more Thomas Sully–designed homes are in the next two blocks of St. Charles. At **3932 St. Charles**, on the left, is Grant House, an 1887 Queen Anne, and at **4010 St. Charles**, also on the left, is the gingerbread palace the architect built for his own family.

Looking left at **Napoleon Avenue** toward Prytania, you can get a glimpse of the old **St. Elizabeth's Home** (1314 Napoleon), a 47,000-square-foot former orphanage capable of sleeping 300. The Rices purchased St. Elizabeth's in 1993. The couple bought the three-building complex from the Daughters of Charity of St. Vincent de Paul, which closed the orphanage in 1989. St. Elizabeth's occupies the equivalent of two city blocks, bordered by Napoleon, Prytania, Perrier, and Jena. The original three-story white masonry structure, in the center of the complex facing Napoleon, was built in 1865 as a school and in 1871 became a girls' orphanage. The taller, red-brick wing buildings were added in the 1880s, the left one (on Perrier) in 1884 and the right one (on Prytania) in 1883. The Prytania Street wing includes a private chapel on the second floor, with radiant stained-glass windows that soar two stories high.

The orphanage complex, which is on the National Register of Historic Landmarks, constitutes New Orleans's largest collection of French Second Empire architecture. Rice has announced plans to open a doll

St. Elizabeth's Home, a nineteenth-century former orphanage, takes up an entire city block but is nearly obscured by the thick trees and foliage surrounding it. Anne and Stan Rice purchased the landmark property in 1994.

museum on the ground floor in the Prytania Street wing. Her doll collection includes hundreds of both contemporary and antique examples of the art of doll making. The Rices also have said they plan to live at St. Elizabeth's with their extended families, and renovations will create a writing studio for Anne and a painting studio for Stan. The Rices have announced no plans to sell the First Street house.

St. Elizabeth's appears in *Witching*, when nine-year-old Deirdre Mayfair runs away to the orphanage. Deirdre, plagued by Lasher, tells the startled sisters that she is "cursed" and "possessed of the devil." Rice has said that St. Elizabeth's also plays a starring role in the fifth *Vampire Chronicles* book.

Continuing past Napoleon uptown on St. Charles, on the right at No. 4521 is the beautiful **Academy of the Sacred Heart** Catholic girls' school, an elite private institution built in 1899. The school was founded in 1887 by the Society of the Sacred Heart, a teaching order established in 1800 by Saint Madeleine Sophie Barat. The academy's

The Prytania Street wing of St. Elizabeth's includes a private chapel, with two-story stained glass windows visible from the street.

French name, Sacré Coeur, is announced on the iron gates fronting the St. Charles perimeter.

The school also goes by the nickname The Rosary. Sacred Heart's first St. Charles Avenue home was in a house built in 1847 by John Calhoun, a real estate auctioneer and politician. In 1851, the estate became the final home of Garden District developer Samuel J. Peters, who died there in 1855. Three more owners lived in the home before the Society purchased it in 1887, and in 1900 the present building was constructed to accommodate a rapidly growing enrollment demand. Additions were completed in 1906 and 1913, and the school still occupies two full blocks from St. Charles back to Baronne. Newer buildings have been added on the rear block.

In the Mayfair books, Sacred Heart is one of several schools that Deirdre briefly attends prior to (yet another) expulsion, and the 1990s Mayfair witch, thirteen-year-old Mona, also attends the Uptown school.

Two more blocks past the school, on the right at the corner of Bordeaux, is the **W. P. Brown House** at 4717 St. Charles. This Romanesque Revival landmark was built from 1902 to 1905 at a staggering cost of $250,000. Brown rose from working as a clerk in a country store to cornering the New Orleans cotton market, and had the house built as a wedding gift for his wife.

The **Latter Memorial Library** at 5120 St. Charles, on the left, is one of the few Uptown mansions open to the public—built in 1907 as a private home, it is now a branch of the New Orleans public library system. The downstairs reading rooms are a wonderful spot to relax and enjoy the historic milieu. In the 1920s, film star Marguerite Clark lived in this house; it was donated to the city in 1947.

At 5300 St. Charles, on your left, is the **De La Salle High School**, which in autumn 1993 attracted hundreds of vampire wanna-bes to an extras casting call for *Interview With the Vampire*. Two of the city's most eminent universities sit side by side between 6300 and 7000 St. Charles, on the right. The red-brick, Tudor/Gothic-style **Loyola University** at 6363 St. Charles, a Catholic university operated by the Society of Jesus, has an enrollment of more than 5,000 students on its fourteen-acre campus. Loyola was formed in 1911, when the Jesuit College of the Immaculate Conception, established downtown in 1840, merged with Loyola Academy, a prep school that had been on the present site since

1904. Rice characters who attend Loyola include Carlotta Mayfair, who graduates from its famed law school. (Carlotta also went to Sacred Heart.) **Holy Name Church**, part of the Loyola campus, was the preferred church for Gifford and Alicia, two of the Uptown Mayfairs.

Right next door, at 6400 St. Charles, is **Tulane University**. Tulane is a private, nonsectarian school that was founded downtown in 1834 as the Medical College of Louisiana. It became the University of Louisiana in 1847 and took its present name in 1883 after a bequest by Paul Tulane. The school moved to the neo-Romanesque buildings fronting St. Charles in 1894 and currently has enrollment of more than 13,000 and a campus covering 110 acres of Uptown New Orleans.

A few steps uptown from Tulane is **Audubon Place**, New Orleans's only remaining gated community—you have to get past the security guards to gain admittance to the street, which features twenty-eight magnificent homes and a broad median lined with palm trees. During the filming of *Interview*, Tom Cruise and his wife, Nicole Kidman, lived at No. 3 Audubon Place, and Kidman was frequently spotted jogging in Audubon Park. Residents, apparently offended by the presence of "movie people," later voted to allow no future rentals of Audubon Place properties.

No. 2 Audubon Place, on the lakeside uptown corner of St. Charles (and visible from the public sidewalk) is the **Zemurray House**, a 1907 mansion that was built for Sam Zemurray, president of United Fruit Company. The home now serves as the official residence for the Tulane University president.

Directly across St. Charles from the two universities, on the left, is **Audubon Park**, site of many an early-morning horseback ride by Julien Mayfair. For those who would like to re-create Julien's equine romps, public stables are still located in the park, at the Magazine Street entrance. The wedge-shaped park, a remarkable oasis of serenity (and squirrel capital of the universe) amid the city's commotion, spans 400 acres, from St. Charles all the way to the Mississippi River, and was named for naturalist John James Audubon. A riverboat shuttle, also named for him, transports passengers from the New Orleans Zoo, in the riverfront section of the park, downriver to the Aquarium of the Americas near the Quarter. Audubon Park originally was part of the Étienne de Boré sugarcane plantation. Boré, the city's first mayor, energized the sugar industry in 1794, when he invented a method for granulation. The Boré land was bought by the city in 1871 and originally was named New City Park.

Most of the land uptown from the universities and Audubon Park originally was part of Carrollton, an independent community until 1874. The streetcar turns right at Carrollton Avenue and continues for several blocks before reversing its route to go back downtown. The streetcars don't actually turn around; instead, conductor stations are located at both ends of each car, and the seats are ingeniously constructed to face either way (the seat backs roll from side to side) and are simply reversed for the downtown jaunt.

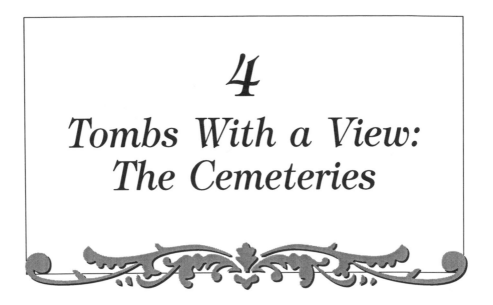

4

Tombs With a View:
The Cemeteries

In New Orleans, one can't escape the dead for long.

It's *possible* not to include a burial site on a tour of the city, but if you miss the cemeteries, you bypass the very essence of New Orleans—the "live life *now*" attitude that might not be so prevalent if the specter of death wasn't so ominously, yet somehow comfortingly, present. Visitors confining themselves to the strict boundaries of the French Quarter might not see a cemetery—but only if they don't stray as far as Rampart Street, the lakeside boundary, from which the imposing walls and sky-reaching society tombs of St. Louis Cemetery No. 1 are clearly visible.

Even those timid souls who would rather not include graveyards on their holiday jaunts (most likely not the folks reading this book!) would have to exert some serious effort to avoid them. On the way into New Orleans via Interstate 10, tombs from the dozen or so cemeteries clustered at the end of the Canal Street inevitably elicit gasps from unprepared tourists: "Fred, *what* is that?!" Cabbies will chuckle and begin the explanation.

New Orleans, dredged out of swampland and surrounded by water, is the large-scale equivalent of a bowl—a natural basin that, until the present-day drainage system was started in the late 1890s, had no flush valve. The water came hard and often, and it had nowhere to go. The city is an average of six feet below sea level, and given its extraordinarily high water table, below-ground burials met with limited success. Eighteenth-century mourners might have loved ones' funeral services interrupted by the unsettling sight of a just-buried coffin floating right back to the surface. They tried filling coffins with rocks; they tried drilling holes to let the water immediately seep in and weigh them down. Finally, they gave up on traditional methods and started using the above-ground tombs that are still favored today.

In what other American city would a museum, in this case the Cabildo on Jackson Square, devote an entire room of exhibits to disease, death, mourning, cemeteries, and hospitals? Such was the savage immediacy of death and its cohorts in the Crescent City, which for much of the antebellum period had the highest death rate of any American city. As early as 1810, the City Council had passed a law forbidding the ringing of funeral bells between July 1 and December 1 each year. The somber tolling of the bells, which rang through the Vieux Carré with distressing frequency, was deemed too depressing and bad for business. This may have set a precedent for modern city government with regard to seemingly insurmountable problems: Just ignore them, and hope they'll disappear.

It would be nearly a century after that optimistic ordinance before yellow fever finally departed New Orleans. The worst years occurred in the decade before the Civil War. Between 1851 and 1855, with epidemics in four of the five years, 73 of every 1,000 New Orleanians died. Mortality rates could reach as high as 60 percent of those who contracted the prevalent diseases, which included not only yellow fever (also called Bronze John and the saffron scourge, for the yellowish tint its victims' skin acquired), but also cholera, smallpox, and malaria.

An English lady visiting New Orleans in 1849 expressed her amazement at local burial customs, in this graphic excerpt culled from the archives for the Cabildo exhibit: "New Orleans has several peculiarities of its own ... for instance, the cellars and graves are above ground ... the dead are buried in sepulchral houses, which are termed here ovens! ... There was something very melancholy in the appearance of the cemetery. ... The damp swamp of the unwholesome looking ground, the low, flat, gloomy enclosure with its cold and somber houses of death and the carelessness and neglect visible I thought, in general, made it a very mournful spectacle."

A reporter for the *New Orleans Daily Crescent* gave this graphic description of a yellow fever graveyard in August 1853, the worst month of the worst plague year: "At the gates, the winds brought intimation of the corruption lurking within. Not a puff was not laden with the rank atmosphere from rotting corpses. Inside they were piled by 50s, exposed to the heat of the sun, swollen with corruption, bursting their coffin lids ... what a feast of horrors. Inside, corpses piled in pyramids and without the gates, old and withered crones and fat huxter women ... dispensing ice creams and confections, and brushing away ... the green bottleflies that hovered on their merchandise and that anon buzzed away to drink dainty inhalations from the green and festering corpses." The popular saying during the 1853 outbreak was that pretty soon, people would have to start digging their own graves. Some 12,000 people— about one in every ten residents—died that year of yellow fever alone.

Death was such a preoccupation for antebellum New Orleanians that the newspapers actually printed helpful advice on topics such as "How to Tell Whether a Person Is Dead or Alive." The method: "Apply the flame of a candle to the tip of one of the great toes of the supposed corpse, and a blister will immediately arise. If the vitality is gone, this will be full of air, and will burst with some noise if the flame be applied to it a few seconds longer. Though very few are actually buried alive, many more may be abandoned as dead while life is still in them, and then die from being handled and exposed as corpses are. The test, therefore, should be applied as soon as life is supposed to be extinct, and before an undertaker is called in."

This determination apparently was often more necessary than one would imagine: In 1875, the *New Orleans Bulletin* reported the story of a smallpox victim who, being carted to the cemetery in the "charity wagon," revived from his state of supposed death and got in a fight with the wagon driver. The driver, insisting that the man was legally dead, finally smothered him in an attempt to subdue him back to a deceased state, and subsequently was charged with the crime of murdering a dead man.

Nineteenth-century writer Lafcadio Hearn would have no doubt been astounded at the twentieth-century popularity enjoyed by New

Orleans cemeteries—present-day tourists rank them right behind jazz and the French Quarter in terms of seductive charm. Hearn viewed them with a considerably more jaded eye. Following the 1878 yellow fever epidemic, he wrote: "They are hideous Golgothas, these old intramural cemeteries of ours. In other cities the cemeteries are beautiful with all that the art of the gardeners and the sculptor can give. There horror is masked and hidden. Here it stares at us with empty sockets."

From an airplane or the elevation of the freeway, it's easy to understand how the cemeteries got their nickname: cities of the dead. The whitewashed vaults, often topped with angels, lambs, or other statuary, mixed with the lushness of the Louisiana landscape, combine to create a picturesque miniature mirror of an eighteenth- or nineteenth-century village.

There are dozens of cemeteries in and around New Orleans—more than forty are documented and described in exquisite detail in *New Orleans Architecture, Vol. 3: The Cemeteries*, published in 1974 by The Friends of the Cabildo. The two cemeteries most often referred to in Rice's books are St. Louis No. 1, just outside the Quarter, and Lafayette No. 1, in the Garden District. Luckily for Rice fans, these also happen to be the graveyards where the most tours are offered.

Wise visitors will take heed of the advice given by experienced tour guides (and New Orleans police): Never go into a New Orleans cemetery alone, and certainly not at dusk (sorry, they're closed at night). They're undeniably alluring for those of us into this sort of thing, but they also present an abundance of hiding places for purse snatchers and those with nastier conduct on their minds. Lestat might have been perfectly safe; the rest of us, lacking fangs and preternatural strength or the ability to fly, need the reassurance of a group.

Understandably, though, Rice fans might not get enough of St. Louis No. 1 or Lafayette No. 1 in one short visit. The recommended remedy is to take a guided tour (a list is provided in chapter 7). Then, if you just haven't had your fill or taken quite enough pictures, find out when that same tour will be in the cemetery on another day. Most tour guides, if you explain that you've already paid once and just want another look around, won't object to your hovering nearby on a second tour. Do not, however, intrude on a tour without having taken it al-

ready as a paying customer. This is considered the height of rude behavior, and guides and the legitimate customers will (rightly) make you
feel like swamp scum if you try it.

St. Peter Street Cemetery

When the city was founded in 1718, its first burial grounds were along
the banks of the Mississippi and in the levee separating New Orleans
from Old Muddy. Levee burials were both impractical, raising the un-
pleasant prospect of "unburial" when flooding occurred, and danger-
ous—the constant digging weakened the levee, the only protection the
city had from an often raging river. When royal military engineer Adrien
de Pauger laid out the streets of the Vieux Carré in 1721, he designated
a cemetery site bounded by present-day Toulouse, Rampart, St. Peter,
and Burgundy streets. Burials at St. Peter Street Cemetery were below-
ground; ditches were dug surrounding the square, and dirt from the
ditches was used to raise the ground level. A wooden palisade enclosed
the site. Obviously, this artificial restructuring of the ground couldn't
continue for long, not with a fast-growing, disease-prone population, and
New Orleanians had to rethink their traditions to the current above-
ground arrangement.

But St. Peter Street Cemetery stood its ground, so to speak, for the
better part of the eighteenth century. It was so close to residential property that, in the mid-1740s, cemetery neighbors complained about having to endure the sight (and stench) of tombstones while taking the
evening breeze from their galleries. A five-foot brick wall, built with the
money of the rich and the sweat of the poor, was constructed around
the cemetery and dedicated on All Saints' Day, November 1, 1743. People brought flowers to honor the deceased, as was the old European custom on All Saints' Day. This probably was the first such "celebration of
the dead" in New Orleans, an All Saints' Day custom that continued
well into the twentieth century and is still practiced by some families.

Undoubtedly the single worst year in New Orleans history, 1788,
saw frequent catastrophes, beginning with the overflowing of the Mississippi, which completely covered the city in several feet of water. The
Good Friday fire burned most of the town to the ground, and as if that

weren't enough calamity for one year, a series of epidemics substantially diminished the population. St. Peter Cemetery, which was by this time completely filled, was unceremoniously covered over with lime, in the futile hope that this would prevent further outbreaks of disease.

Today, not a single tombstone remains to mark the site of St. Peter Cemetery. Although this first official New Orleans cemetery was closed in 1788, burials continued there for several years, and some of the older remains and monuments may have been transferred to the new cemetery, St. Louis No. 1. The St. Peter Cemetery land was subdivided for building lots in 1800. Interestingly, Pauger, designer of the first cemetery, was not buried there, but in the foundation beneath the St. Louis Church, which he also designed.

St. Louis No. 1

Even the most jaded tour guides whisper when they take groups through St. Louis Cemetery No. 1, located at 400 Basin Street between Conti and St. Louis, just one block from the lakeside edge of the French Quarter. No matter how sunlit the day, St. Louis No. 1 exudes a nearly palpable air of the sacred and the immortal, of dark emotions and fleeting, furtive shadows. If a guide or visitor says something funny, the ensuing laughter echoes uneasily, almost obscenely, off the walls of cracked, weathered tombs, some with their tops broken open, others sporting resilient tropical weeds flourishing along the sides and out of fractures in the masonry.

Established by royal decree in August 1789, St. Louis No. 1 is the oldest existing cemetery in New Orleans and the Mississippi River Valley and is still used today, though fairly infrequently. Cemeteries in New Orleans are either city- or church-owned; St. Louis No. 1 is owned and administered by the Catholic Archdiocese of New Orleans. One of the earliest decipherable epitaphs is that of one Nannette F. de Bailly, dated September 24, 1800.

St. Louis No. 1 earns an early mention in Rice's work, in the first chapter of *Interview*, when Louis refers to it as his brother's burial place. Near the end of *Queen*, Louis and Lestat visit the cemetery and find the "grave" of Louis himself, located "down the narrow corridor between the

St. Louis Cemetery No. 1, the city's oldest extant "City of the Dead." In *Interview*, Lestat and Louis visit the tomb of Louis's brother here.

oldest, the most venerable tombs; tombs that went back to the oldest time of the colony." "Louis de Pointe du Lac, 1766-1794," states the inscription on the obviously empty crypt.

A few pages later, the two vampires soar above the cemetery, viewing it as a "tiny sprawling toy of itself with little bits of white scattered all over under the dark trees." That view can be experienced today from any number of high-rise hotels skirting the edge of the Quarter. The Monteleone Hotel, which is mentioned in several of Rice's works, boasts an especially striking rooftop panorama of the old Quarter.

Most of the earliest inscriptions have long since disappeared from the tombs of St. Louis No. 1, victims of time, neglect, and the persistently inhospitable climate. One early engraving, copied by a *Daily Picayune* reporter on All Saints' Day 1903, reads: "*Ci git un malheureuse qui fut victim de son imprudence. Vers une larme sur sa tombe, et un 'De Profundis' s'il vout plait, pour son âme. Il n'avait que 27 ans, 1798.*" Translation: "Here lies a poor unfortunate who was a victim of his own imprudence. Drop a tear on his tomb and say, if you please, the psalm 'Out of the depths I have cried unto Thee, O Lord,' for his soul. He was only 27 years old, 1798."

Today, the paths of St. Louis No. 1 are treacherous and overgrown, sometimes ending in abrupt dead-end alleys. The first families to use the cemetery simply wandered in, found an open spot at random, and erected their tombs with little regard for tidiness or symmetry. The result is a twisting, eerie maze that can quickly turn from charming to terrifying. Don't go in near closing hour without knowing *exactly* where the entrance is at all times; it's amazingly easy to get disoriented, and one wouldn't want to get locked in. Many of the families whose ancestors are buried here have moved away or died out, leaving no one to tend the graves. Nowhere in New Orleans are decay and desolation so evident as at St. Louis No. 1.

The cemetery now occupies roughly one large city block; it once extended at least one more block closer to the river (nearly to Rampart), and several additional blocks on either side of its current walls. Supposedly, as the original cemetery was eaten up by development and streets cut through its borders, all displaced remains were exhumed and reinterred within the current walls. Tour guides will tell you, though, that it's highly likely that the folks living all around St. Louis No. 1 are resting just a few feet or so above those in a far more permanent sleep.

At the front of the cemetery, to the left of the entry gates on Basin Street, are the famous wall vaults, or "oven" tombs (so nicknamed for their resemblance to the ovens used for baking bread). These community tombs, for those with no family or society tomb (tombs purchased by benevolent societies and organizations, and maintained for their members), were put to use repeatedly. Remains from previous burials were simply pushed to the back of the extra-long chambers to make room for new occupants. Some of the lower oven tombs at St. Louis No. 1 have sunk so deeply into the ground that it is now impossible to open them; their occupants, at least, can rest easy that they will not be disturbed to make way for new tenants.

At the rear of the cemetery was a section for Protestant burials; within it was a tiny parcel set aside for blacks. The Protestant section blocked an extension of Tremé Street, so many of these remains were moved in the 1830s to the new Girod Street Cemetery. What remains now of the Protestant area of St. Louis No. 1 is a forsaken, depressing strip of land that even the tours don't bother with. Girod Street Cemetery, in the American sector across Canal Street from the Vieux Carré, also fell victim to "progress" and was closed in 1957. Part of the Louisiana Superdome now sits on part of the site; one is tempted to speculate on the effect this has had on the New Orleans Saints' record in the NFL.

Architecturally, St. Louis No. 1 and other New Orleans cemeteries reflect the abiding tastes of the time. Tombs range from the fairly modest to the incredibly ornate, with miniature Greek and Roman temples sharing space with simple stepped-top tombs constructed of slave-crafted brick and covered in plaster. In St. Louis No. 1, the stepped-top style is most prevalent. The most visually arresting tomb in the cemetery is that of the Italian Mutual Benevolent Society, founded in 1848 by Joseph A. Barelli. A woman holding a cross tops the tomb, towering goddesslike over the cemetery, visible from every corner and from outside the walls. The marble, circular tomb contains nearly 250 vaults, with a basement receptacle guarded by an iron door. Niches in the outer walls hold statues representing "Italia" and "Charity." The tomb cost the enormous (at least for the time) sum of $40,000, and was dedicated in 1857. Pietro Gualdi, its architect, was the first person buried in it. Barelli, the president and founder of the society, was the second, leading to its not-quite-tongue-in-cheek designation as the "hex tomb."

Another distinctive feature of New Orleans cemeteries is the use of intricate, often ornate ironwork, echoing that seen adorning the Spanish-style dwellings of the French Quarter. Many tombs are completely surrounded by small ironwork fences, which too often display disheartening signs of decay, vandalism, or neglect. Single or multiple iron crosses decorate the tops of some crypts.

Many tombs feature marble slabs on the front, bearing simple inscriptions (usually limited to the name of the deceased, with accompa-

Iron adornments such as crosses mark many of the tombs in St. Louis No. 1.

nying birth and death dates). The slabs were bolted into place for easy removal when another family burial was required. Ever practical, New Orleanians "recycle" their family tombs over and over—some bear witness to ten, fifteen, even twenty or more burials in one two-vault tomb. The methodology is simple and efficient: New burials are placed in the upper chamber. When another person dies, the decaying casket is removed from the upper chamber, and what's left of the human remains are placed in the lower chamber. Law prevents opening a tomb less than one year and one day from the previous entombment, in the interest of disease prevention. Some of the more elaborate tombs, such as the multivault society tombs, are constructed with the vaults facing inward, at a slight downward incline. Remains eventually slide down into the central *caveau* (a French word meaning "cellar" or "vault"), making room for future burials.

In addition to the fictitious Pointe de Lac family, those buried at St. Louis No. 1 include world chess champion Paul Morphy (1837–84); Étienne de Boré (1741–1820), first appointed mayor of New Orleans; his grandson, historian Charles Gayarré (1805–1895); Blaise Cenas (1776–1812), the first U.S. Postmaster of New Orleans; and Bernard de Marigny (1785–1868), who made several fortunes through land speculation and died a near pauper because of his penchant for gambling. Homer Plessy, who fought for racial desegregation in the landmark Supreme Court case *Plessy vs. Ferguson*, died in 1925 at age sixty-three and is buried in St. Louis No. 1. Plessy's loss in the 1896 case led to another half century of court-sanctioned, legalized segregation.

St. Louis No. 1 is also the final respite for "voodoo queen" Marie Laveau, whose crypt bears hundreds of rusty-colored chalk Xs. Marking an X on Marie's tomb supposedly ensures believers that their wishes will be granted (no word on success rates). Visitors also leave little gifts to Marie—beans, Mardi Gras beads, candles, bones that may or may not have belonged to animals (believe what you wish!). The tomb of Marie Laveau was restored in 1983 by the New Orleans Archdiocesan Cemeteries organization. A plaque marking the crypt reads: "Marie Laveau. This Greek Revival tomb is reputed burial place of this notorious 'voodoo queen.' A mystic cult, voodooism, of African origin, was brought to [sic] city from Santo Domingo and flourished in [sic] 19th century. Marie Laveau was the most widely known of many practitioners of the cult." Only in New Orleans, one suspects, would the Catholic Church erect a marker pointing out the burial site of voodoo royalty.

Marie's life would have been fascinating even without her involvement in voodoo—she was a free woman of color, born either in New Orleans or Saint-Domingue (Haiti) around 1794, possibly to a white father and black mother. In 1819, Marie married Jacques Paris, a free black man, in a Roman Catholic ceremony officiated by the beloved Père Antoine. In 1826, Paris died, and Marie took up with another free black, Christophe Glapion. Her daughter, called Marie Junior, was born in 1827 to uncertain paternity. In any case, the elder Marie's relationship with Glapion was never legitimized by the Catholic Church, but Marie had borne fifteen children by the time she died in 1881.

Marie, a hairdresser by trade, began practicing voodoo in the same year her husband died, and remained active in the hybrid cult-religion until her old age. A March 1869 *New Orleans Times* account describes a voodoo ritual involving both blacks and whites:

> The rites having been commenced, an elderly turbaned female dressed in yellow and red (Marie Laveau), ascended a sort of dais and chanted a wild sort of fetish song, to which the others kept up an accompaniment with their voices and with a drum-like beat of their hands and feet. At the same time, they commenced to move in a circle while gradually increasing the time.
>
> As the motion increased in intensity the flowers and other ornaments disappeared from their hair, and their dresses were torn open, and each one conducted herself like a bacchante. . . . In the midst of the Saturnalia of witches, the pythoness of this extraordinary dance and revel was a young girl. . . . In this awful state of nudity she continued her ever-increasing frantic movements until reason itself abandoned its earthly tenement. In a convulsive fit she finally fell, foaming at the mouth like one possessed, and it was only then that the mad carnival found a pause.

Some suspect, fear, or hope (depending on one's outlook) that Marie has never really left New Orleans; that her ghost, along with that of her daughter, haunts the area around the "voodoo crypt" at St. Louis Cemetery No. 1. tour guides tell of a Depression-era vagrant who fell asleep atop a tomb in the cemetery and was awakened to the sound of drums and chanting. Stumbling upon the tomb of Marie Laveau, he encountered the ghosts of dancing, naked men and women, led by a tall woman wrapped in the coils of a huge snake. Bodies have supposedly been found near the tomb. Some people never learn, however—as recently as 1994, tour guides told of college kids who, undaunted (or perhaps simply clueless about the legends of Marie's ghost), have climbed the cemetery walls to snooze on flat-topped tombs during Mardi Gras.

Near St. Louis No. 1, at 401 N. Rampart Street, is the old Mortuary Chapel, built in 1826 as a burial church for yellow fever victims. The oldest surviving church in the city, it is now called **Our Lady of Guadalupe** and is the official chapel of the New Orleans police and fire departments. This chapel is discussed further in chapter 5. Looking toward Canal Street from St. Louis No. 1, visitors will see block after block of low-income housing in the section known as Tremé. This once was the site of Storyville, the district where prostitution was permitted, if not precisely legal, from 1897 to 1917.

Lafayette No. 1

Lafayette No. 1 Cemetery, one of the Garden District's most picturesque spots, is situated at 1400 Washington between Prytania and Coliseum streets. It can be briefly glimpsed from St. Charles Avenue between Sixth and Washington streets. Its main gates, guarded by two ancient, fierce-looking oak trees, are directly opposite Commander's Palace Restaurant on Washington Street. Lafayette, a city cemetery, has been rescued largely through the efforts of Save Our Cemeteries, a nonprofit group dedicated to the preservation and restoration of New Orleans's historic burial grounds.

Once neglected and overgrown much as St. Louis No. 1 is still, Lafayette now boasts mostly clear walkways and an overall aura of care, although signs of vandalism and neglect appear intermittently. Cast-iron fences were popular here, but cast iron disintegrates quickly once rusted; it must be kept painted and meticulously maintained. Some tombs are adorned with sturdier wrought iron, easy to pick out because of its relative simplicity. The iron "lace" found on the buildings of the French Quarter is predominantly cast iron, often imported from foundries in Pennsylvania. Wrought iron usually was imported from Spain. Small chunks of broken-off fence material sometimes can be found lying near tombs, although most of the loose ironwork has been carried off by overly enthusiastic souvenir seekers. The rule for considerate visitors: Take pictures, not relics. A sign at Lafayette's Washington Street gate

The Washington Avenue gates of Lafayette Cemetery No. 1 in the Garden District.

also admonishes the athletically inclined, "Please do not climb on the tombs."

Lafayette plays a supporting role in both the *Vampire Chronicles* and *Mayfair Witches* books, but is probably most closely associated with the Mayfairs, who, Rice tells us, have buried their dead here since 1861, in a twelve-vault family tomb just off the main aisle. In reality, tombs that large usually were society tombs, administered by various professional, social, and ethnic groups. Lafayette is also prominently mentioned in the *Vampire Chronicle* books, especially *Interview* and *Lestat*. In *Interview*, Rice mentions it as the place where Lestat hides his valuables, and in *Lestat*, she describes Lafayette as being a block from the "finest of his houses," near Prytania and Sixth. In *Interview*, Claudia asks to be taken to the cemetery to "roam the high marble tombs in search of those desperate men who, having no place else to sleep, spend what little they have on a bottle of wine, and crawl into a rotting vault."

The "faux granite" tomb built in Lafayette No. 1 for the filming of *Interview*. The tomb looks terrific in the movie, but is obviously out of place among the "real thing."

Near the spot described by Rice as the Mayfair burial site, just to the right of the crossroads formed by the two main aisles, are two tombs that might have served as her inspiration: the Jefferson Fire Company No. 22 tomb, with more than twelve vaults and a cast-iron railing, and the Lafayette Hook & Ladder Fire Company twelve-vault tomb, located directly across the center aisle.

Just *try* dissuading an Anne Rice fan of the notion that Mayfairs aren't really buried here. While I was on a Save Our Cemeteries tour researching *Haunted City*, a woman who wasn't with our group interrupted the guide with this question: "May I ask you, where is the tomb of the Mayfairs? I'm reading *The Witching Hour* and wonder where the family tomb is."

The guide, obviously not a Rice fan, responded: "How do you spell that name? I don't think I've ever heard of it, and I'm in here two or three times a week." The Mayfair seeker patiently spelled it out, M-A-Y-F-A-I-R. One of our group members cautiously ventured that Anne Rice's books are fiction, after all, and perhaps the Mayfairs are a *fictional* family. "Oh, no!" exclaimed the fan. "They're an old, established New Orleans family. . . . She [Rice] interweaves that with fiction, but some of the stories and things she tells about the Mayfairs are true, I know they are." The guide finally gave up. "Well, I don't know of any Mayfair tomb. You peek around and let us know, okay?" When last seen, the hapless fan was still searching.

On another occasion, I decided to test the "Anne Rice quotient" of visitors to Lafayette. I chose a sunny afternoon, made sure the cemetery was well-populated with tour groups so that I wasn't easy prey to whomever (or *what*ever) might be lurking among the crypts, and staked out a plot of grass under a magnolia tree, near the juncture of the two main aisles. In my hand was my tattered paperback copy of *The Witching Hour*. Within a one-hour time span, eight people had wandered over to chat with me, all of them Rice fans checking out the Garden District sites in her books. None of them seemed to expect to find an actual Mayfair tomb, however.

The oven tombs at Lafayette were used by a wide social spectrum—whites, blacks, free people, and slaves. Since this is a city-owned cemetery, religious preference was never a consideration for burial here. Dozens of the yellow fever victims were buried here, including many children.

Lafayette No. 1 was first established as the municipal cemetery for the city of Lafayette, which in turn sprang from land that once belonged to the Livaudais Plantation. City surveyor Benjamin Buisson planned the cemetery, on land purchased from Cornelius Hurst for $6,000 in 1832. The cemetery was officially opened in 1833.

Buried here are the city of Lafayette's German and Irish immigrants, thousands of whom swelled the suburb's population from the 1840s to the 1860s. Many Germans had tired of the skirmishes and unsuccessful revolutions that constantly played havoc with the borders of their homeland, and the Irish were plagued by famine and poverty. Lafayette Cemetery was laid out in four quadrants along two wide main aisles. The huge, graceful trees that once lined those center aisles were destroyed in a hurricane, and young magnolias were planted in 1970 to take their place. Oak trees growing along the surrounding streets shade the walled perimeter.

Most of the tombs in the cemetery date from roughly 1830 to 1860 and boast neoclassical architecture much the same as that in the Vieux Carré—plastered-over brick, sometimes faced with marble. As in St. Louis No. 1, an occasional open tomb can be seen, its plaster broken

Both St. Louis No. 1 and Lafayette No. 1 (pictured) feature walls of "oven tombs," recycled for multiple occupants through the centuries.

out by decay or vandals, leaving visitors to wonder nervously about the state of the entombed remains. An undertaker in *The Witching Hour* describes his distaste at opening tombs in the cemetery, with "so many ruined graves with rotting coffins plainly visible, even with the bones showing." A vampire seeking sanctuary wouldn't have to search long to find a daytime hiding place here. Some families built up the turf so that they could have in-ground burial, but those plots are scarce, and often almost entirely obscured by tangled weeds and grass.

Anne Rice and her fans are not alone in succumbing to Lafayette Cemetery's seductive, if somewhat peculiar, powers. In 1980, a Texas-based vice president of Neiman-Marcus and his fiancée chose Lafayette No. 1 as the site for their wedding—on Friday, June 13. The bride, groom, and guests, all clad in formal black, were transported from the airport in four ebony limousines. A lone trumpeter played "Summertime" as the nuptials commenced in one of the cemetery's main aisles. The wedding couple, both previously married, said the unique site was chosen, in part, in an effort to "bury the past."

A pensive angel guards a tomb at Lafayette No. 1.

Those entombed at Lafayette include Samuel Jarvis Peters, a major Garden District developer and "father of the New Orleans Public School System," and Confederate general Harry T. Hays. In the lakeside uptown "quadrant" is the Karstendick tomb, unique to Lafayette in that it is constructed entirely of cast iron. The street-side corner of the riverside uptown quadrant (nearest the corner of Coliseum and Sixth streets) was used during the filming of the movie version of *Interview* in the fall of 1993. Warner Bros.' set designers constructed a faux marble tomb, painted a pale grayish-green color and speckled with paint to give it an archaic appearance. At last check,

Vandals and neglect have taken their toll on much of the ornate statuary adorning New Orleans cemeteries, such as the headless angel sitting forlornly beside a Lafayette No. 1 tomb.

remnants of the fake tomb remained, near the matching Griswold, Palfrey, Dupuy, and Ginder tombs. Archdiocese officials refused permission to film in St. Louis No. 1, which is older and more prominent in the *Vampire Chronicles* series. So director Neil Jordan and crew had to settle for city-owned Lafayette, which was blanketed with extra security to protect publicity-shy star Tom Cruise.

Open tombs, just perfect for a visiting vampire, are not uncommon in most of New Orleans's cemeteries.

St. Joseph Nos. 1 and 2

St. Joseph No. 1 Cemetery, located in the 2200 block of Washington Street, across St. Charles from the Garden District, opened in 1854, operated by the St. Joseph German Orphan Asylum Association. In 1873, permission was given by the city council to expand it, creating St. Joseph No. 2. Their location, in a distinctly "nontourist" part of town, has rendered these cemeteries largely ignored except by the families of the deceased.

Rice's Mayfair family has a twelve-vault tomb, such as the one pictured second from left, at Lafayette Cemetery.

Although they boast the same intricacies of architecture and iron-work as St. Louis No. 1 and Lafayette No. 1, these two burial grounds are surrounded by unphotogenic chain-link fence, with aisles paved not in romantically tangled grass, pebbles, or even weeds but in unyielding, pragmatic-but-ugly concrete. They are, however, quite well maintained by the archdiocesan cemetery group.

Despite its drawbacks, however, St. Joseph No. 1 is likely to lure Anne Rice fans for a couple of reasons. Her mother, Katherine Connel O'Brien, is buried there, in the Connel family plot. In the 1994 Life-time documentary *Anne Rice: Birth of a Vampire*, the author is shown visiting her mother's grave, which appears to be above-ground in built-up turf. The St. Joseph cemeteries contain hundreds of this type of plot, called a coping, and sometimes built as much as three feet higher than the sidewalk. St. Joseph No. 1 also serves as the burial site for the Currys, Michael's family in the *Mayfair Witches* series.

St. Joseph No. 1 is now the home for the original chapel of St. Mary's Assumption congregation. The frame building, constructed in

St. Joseph Cemetery No. 1, where Anne Rice's mother and the *Mayfair Witches'* Curry family are buried.

1844 for the German settlers of the Irish Channel, seated eighty and was moved in 1862 when the much larger St. Mary's Assumption Church was built. The little St. Mary's chapel is one of the oldest buildings in Uptown New Orleans.

St. Joseph No. 2 contains a miniature Gothic chapel, once the tomb of the Redemptorist fathers, but now owned by a private family.

If your appetite for cemetery "culture" has been stirred by visits to St. Louis No. 1, Lafayette No. 1, or the St. Josephs, several other New Orleans graveyards are worth a (temporary!) stop. At Metairie Road and City Park Avenue, where Canal Street ends, more than a dozen cemeteries cluster in an astonishing, stark reminder of the fragility of life and finality of death. Streetcars designated "Cemeteries" used to transport mourners or visitors directly to this area, and some city buses traveling northwest on Canal Street still bear that unsettling label, albeit in neat twentieth-century electronic letters.

Cypress Grove

The Cypress Grove Cemeteries were founded as a special burial place for the volunteer firemen of New Orleans, who helped save the city during its many catastrophic blazes. Cypress Grove No. 1 is at the end of Canal Street (120 City Park Avenue); Cypress Grove No. 2, near Greenwood Cemetery, survived a mere nine years before being closed to make way for street expansion. Founded in 1840, Cypress Grove is commonly known as Firemen's Cemetery.

One of Cypress Grove's most interesting sights is the memorial to Irad Ferry, a leading businessman and fireman of Mississippi Fire Co. No. 2. Ferry died in a Camp Street fire on New Year's Day 1837. He was buried at Girod Street Cemetery, but a memorial monument was erected at Cypress Grove. Designed by J. N. B. de Pouilly, renowned architect of some of New Orleans's finest tombs and monuments, the Ferry memorial includes both a tomb and a visually striking "broken" Doric column, symbolizing a life cut short.

In addition to Ferry's, three other memorial tombs were built at the entrance to Cypress Grove. The Perseverance Fire Co. No. 13 memorial tomb, topped by a small classical dome held aloft by eight columns, was constructed in 1840. The twin Philadelphia Fire Engine Co. No. 14 and Eagle Fire Co. No. 7 tombs also were built in the 1840s. Two prominent Protestant ministers of the 1820s and 1830s are entombed with Eagle Fire Co.—the Reverend Theodore Clapp and the Reverend Sylvester Larned.

In 1841, remains of firemen who had been buried at other cemeteries throughout the city were moved to Cypress Grove. Hence, those stately, dignified fire company tombs at, for instance, Lafayette, are now empty. Some have suggested reselling the vaults within those tombs to raise funds for cemetery upkeep, although it is uncertain if many present-day New Orleanians would want to be entombed in a deserted fireman's crypt. When Girod Street Cemetery (in what is today's Central Business District) began to deteriorate, Cypress Grove became the primary burial ground for many of the local Protestant families.

Those buried at Cypress Grove include James H. Caldwell, builder of the first American Theatre and the first St. Charles Theatre and founder of New Orleans Gas Light Company. Former New Orleans mayor Charles L. Leeds, a foundryman, is buried (fittingly enough) in a cast-iron tomb at Cypress Grove. Also entombed here is Maunsell White, who fought at the Battle of New Orleans and invented Maunsell White Peppersauce, a popular condiment of the nineteenth century. The unusual Soon On Tong Association "receiving tomb," built in 1904, was used to temporarily hold remains of Chinese citizens until they could be shipped home for burial. The tomb includes a small fireplace, which was used to burn ceremonial offerings brought by mourners.

In addition to its many splendid tombs, Cypress Grove harbors dozens of glorious trees, magnolias and moss-hung oaks that offer shade and an almost rural charm.

Greenwood Cemetery

Greenwood, at Canal Boulevard and City Park Avenue, is one of the cluster of cemeteries near the foot of Canal Street. Greenwood was founded in 1852 and features small (six-by-nine-foot) lots that allow more than 20,000 lots total. Five attractive memorials, bounded by beautiful lawns, greet visitors; aside from this distinction, however, Greenwood is starkly utilitarian.

The five memorials are the Confederate Monument, the Firemen's Monument, the Elks tomb, and the tombs of Michael McKay and John Fitzpatrick. The Confederate Monument marks a mass grave of some 600 Confederate soldiers whose remains were gathered by the Ladies Benevolent Association of Louisiana. Busts of Generals Stonewall Jackson, Robert E. Lee, Leonidas Polk, and Albert Sidney Johnston embellish the monument. Erected in 1874, this was the first Civil War memorial in New Orleans.

The tomb of the Benevolent and Protective Order of Elks features a grassy mound topped by the bronze figure of a wise, watchful elk, caught eternally gazing across Greenwood's wide field of crypts. The Doric-style tomb, erected in 1912, holds eighteen vaults protected by heavy bronze doors. Near the Elks tomb are the tombs of Michael McKay and John Fitzpatrick, both of whom served as president of the Firemen's Charitable and Benevolent Association.

The neo-Gothic Firemen's Monument, forty-six feet high, features the six-foot marble figure of a diligent, mustached volunteer fireman. Hose poised for action, he stands under a group of austere Gothic arches, looking for all the world as if he's just waiting for the next alarm. The names of twenty-three volunteer fire companies are engraved into the monument's eighteen-foot-square granite base. The Firemen's Monument was erected in the 1870s in honor of the volunteer firemen who had lost their lives in service. Until the paid fire department was organized in 1891, the city's dedicated volunteer units were all that kept New Orleans from dissolving into a huge pile of ash.

Greenwood also holds the society tomb of the New Orleans Typographical Society, established in 1855 as the area's first labor union; and a monument to the memory of A. D. Crossman, who as city mayor from 1846 to 1854 saw New Orleans through some of its worst yellow fever epidemics.

Several tombs in Greenwood, built on the banks of the Metairie Bayou, tilt slightly to one side or another, the result of inadequate foundations built on unstable, spongy ground.

Lafayette No. 2

Lafayette No. 2, located adjacent to the St. Joseph Cemeteries, is bounded by Washington Avenue and Sixth, Saratoga, and Loyola streets. This cemetery was probably opened in the 1850s, but it wasn't until after the city of Lafayette was incorporated into New Orleans that authorities ordered the first survey of the property, in 1865. As if the view really mattered, the 96 "corner lots," each 12 by 12 feet, were more expensive (at $150 each) than the 384 interior lots, which, at 12 feet by 5 feet 6 inches, went for a mere $50 each. A small section of the Sixth Street frontage was designated for the "colored population."

Several large society tombs were also erected here, including the eighty-vault Butchers' Association tomb, built in 1868, and the French Society of Jefferson tomb, built in 1872. However, the sad state of the surrounding neighborhood has bled into Lafayette No. 2, and even the most lavish tombs have become dilapidated and vine-choked. In the early seventies, vaults along Washington Avenue were unceremoniously demolished.

Metairie Cemetery

Metairie Cemetery, located at Metairie Road and Pontchartrain Boulevard, just across Interstate 10 in the suburb of Metairie, boasts a unique distinction: It is the only American cemetery built on the grounds of a converted racetrack. Its oval shape and curving thoroughfares attest to its original purpose. From the air, it looks precisely like a small city built on a racetrack, which, in a way, is exactly what it is; the residents just don't get out much. The 150-acre cemetery contains more than 7,000 tombs and plots, with both above- and below-ground arrangements. The town of Metairie, whose name roughly translates to "small farms," was settled by French colonists.

Metairie Cemetery flaunts a distinctly modern aura, and its precision and cleanliness discourage a traditionally spooky atmosphere (as is abundantly prevalent at the St. Louis and Lafayette cemeteries). Metairie is meticulously maintained, largely because of a law passed in 1908 after much lobbying by the Metairie Cemetery Association. This legislation gives cemetery corporations the ability to take tombs and plots into trust for perpetual maintenance, thus relieving the family of constant repairs and upkeep. The cemetery's wide aisles, lagoons, fountains, and thousands of annoyingly perky squirrels give it an almost park-like appeal, nowhere approaching the bleakness of, say, St. Louis No. 1. Still, it's easy to get disconcerted—even spooked, if you will—at Metairie, mainly because of its sheer size. Get turned around once or twice and you'll begin to feel you're trapped in an endless maze of tombs. In some areas of the cemetery, the tombs reach so high that it's impossible to see around them. You're surrounded; better pray it's not getting dark. . . .

The cemetery site was first laid out in 1838 as the Metairie Race Course. The Civil War reined in racing activities, and in 1872, the land was acquired by Metairie Cemetery Association. Architect Benjamin F. Harrod took advantage of the mile-plus track, mapping it out as the main avenue of the cemetery. Dr. James Ritchie was the first person buried there, in 1873.

Legend has it that Charles Howard, one of the founders of the cemetery, used it to exact an ironic revenge on the Metairie Jockey Club, which owned the racetrack. Howard, who made his millions in the Louisiana State Lottery Co. and was not considered genteel enough for high society, was refused membership in the Jockey Club. The story goes that he swore then to "make a cemetery of the racetrack." He died in 1855 and now rests eternally on the grounds of the club that refused to admit him. The marble figure of an old man with a finger to his lips, perhaps signifying secrets we'll never know, sits inside the Howard mausoleum.

The most visually prominent monument in Metairie Cemetery was designed by Irish businessman Daniel Moriarty to honor his wife. The eighty-five-foot monument, quite possibly the tallest privately owned monument in the United States, also represents a snub at the local blue bloods, who had in life rebuffed the Moriartys (despite their great wealth) as too recently immigrated to be included in New Orleans society. The Moriarty monument literally looks down its nose at the dozens of high-society tombs surrounding it, effectively dwarfed by its magnificence. It cost the then-enormous sum of $185,000 to build.

Moriarty wanted four sculptures at the base of the monument to represent the "four Graces." He was undaunted when told there were only *three* Graces—Aglaia, Euphrosyne, and Thalia, inaccurately translated as "Faith," "Hope," and "Charity" in the monument's inscriptions. The fourth statue represents Memory, but locals will laughingly tell you it's really a statuesque stand-in for the monument's mistress, Mrs. Mary Moriarty. Daniel Moriarty died thirty-six years after his wife, finally joining her in eternal sleep beneath the monument.

Also buried at Metairie is Josie Arlington, who ran one of the most infamous and successful Storyville "halls of pleasure." In 1911, Josie commissioned the construction of a polished red-granite tomb. When she died in 1914, the cemetery wasn't completely built up, and a red light from the toll barrier on New Basin Shell Road supposedly cast a rosy glow on her tomb—Josie's own little red-light district, even in death. Cemetery officials, anxious to disperse any unseemly rumors (even ghosts, it appears, must behave with *some* decorum), blocked the light with shrubbery and trees.

However, the earthly explanation for Josie's red-light tomb could not account for the other, oft-repeated tales of haunting at her burial site. For instance, many cemetery visitors reported seeing the tomb burst into flames, and the robe-draped, bronze maiden outside Josie's tomb has been the subject of considerable spectral speculation. Numerous accounts, including the terrified recounting of at least two cemetery sextons, describe the statue leaving her post and wandering among the adjacent tombs.

Author Victor C. Klein, while researching his book *New Orleans Ghosts*, saw the several-hundred-pound, supposedly secure statue fall in his direction on one visit to Metairie Cemetery, and on another trip, he was startled by a flashing red light near the grave. On both trips, Klein was accompanied by a friend; for the second visit they crept in after hours to see what happened after midnight during a full moon (on a Friday the thirteenth, yet). Although this sort of behavior is stringently discouraged by cemetery officials, as a fellow author I must admire someone willing to go so far for accurate research! In a fitting tribute to his experiences, a photo of the bronze statue at Josie's tomb graces the cover of Mr. Klein's book.

Josie's relatives, apparently unamused by the tales surrounding their ancestor, eventually removed her remains to a more ordinary vault, and the original red-light tomb was sold to another family.

One can visually explore the world's architectural styles via a two- or three-hour visit to Metairie, and cameras are an essential accessory. (I found one woman perched precariously on top of her minivan, aiming her Nikon at one of the hundreds of statues of angels.) Mausoleums can be found in the form of exquisitely replicated Greek or Roman temples, Egyptian sarcophagi and pyramids, Gothic and Moresque temples. The statuary are particularly striking, often hauntingly emotional. A mounted horseman, representing Confederate general Albert Sidney Johnston, trots eternally atop the tomb of the Benevolent Association of the Army of Tennessee, Louisiana Division. Inside the Chapman Hyams tomb, lit by diffused sunlight through a blue stained-glass window, an angel lies weeping in abject misery, one slender arm flung out in a universal gesture of despair. Two bronze children, the boy holding the little girl's hand, both faces devastatingly somber, sit outside the Vonderbank tomb. Small lambs and cherubs gaze protectively down at the many tombs of children.

The Army of Northern Virginia tomb at Metairie served as a transitory resting place for Jefferson Davis, president of the Confederate States of America. (Davis probably would have found this especially appropriate, since at the onset of the Civil War, the Metairie Race Course was briefly used as a staging area for the state's Confederate troops.) Davis died in New Orleans on December 6, 1889, in the home of a friend at First and Camp streets (the same block of First as Anne Rice's Garden District home). Davis had become ill aboard a steamship traveling upriver on the Mississippi and was brought to New Orleans because he was too sick to be taken home to Beauvoir on the Gulf Coast.

After Davis's death, a cacophony of well-bred disagreement ensued as to the proper resting place for the much-revered daddy of the Confederacy. Southern governors competed for the honor of burying him in their states. Joseph Shakspeare, mayor of New Orleans, wrote Mrs. Davis a note requesting that he be buried in the city: "While the entire South claims him as her own, New Orleans asks that Jefferson Davis be laid to rest within the city where he fell asleep." Mrs. Davis consented, and the city went into a delirium of despair.

Streets were draped in black, and hotel rooms quickly filled with out-of-town mourners. As many as 150,000 people were reported to have paid tribute at City Hall (now Gallier Hall), where Davis's body lay in state. The funeral procession included Confederate generals and soldiers, elderly veterans of the Mexican War, and even fifteen Union soldiers. One observer remarked that the day of the funeral, December 11, 1889, was the day they finally "buried the Confederacy." After the four-hour funeral and procession, Davis was laid to rest at Metairie Cemetery. Four years later, however, Mrs. Davis succumbed to pressure to move the body to Richmond, Virginia, capital of the Confederacy, where Jefferson Davis was reburied in Hollywood Cemetery. The vault in Metairie where his body lay has been permanently sealed.

Many other famous Louisiana figures found their final rest at Metairie—reading the names inscribed on the elaborate tombs is akin to scanning an historical social register. Buried here are nine Louisiana governors, seven New Orleans mayors, three Confederate justices, and four chief justices of the Louisiana Supreme Court. Dozens of members of Carnival "royalty"—the kings and queens who reign at Mardi Gras—also arrived at Metairie after tossing their final beads and trinkets into the throngs.

Odd Fellows Rest

A secret benevolent society, the Independent Order of Odd Fellows, founded this triangular-shaped Canal Street cemetery in 1847. The land, at Canal Street and Metairie Road (now City Park Boulevard) was relatively high, and the Odd Fellows site has remained dry through some of New Orleans's worst flooding, including the 1849 deluge caused by a Mississippi River crevasse.

Later in 1849, when the cemetery was dedicated, a hearse pulled by six horses transported the remains of sixteen deceased Odd Fellows (previously buried elsewhere) to the new cemetery; they became its first permanent residents. The "funeral car" bearing the remains was preceded by two circus (yes, circus) bandwagons, drawn by a total of twenty magnificent steeds. The ceremonial procession to the cemetery—including hearse, circus wagons, carriages, and thirty-five chartered omnibuses packed with Odd Fellow brethren—began at Jackson Square and wound through the main streets of the city before proceeding up Canal to its final destination. The Odd Fellows may be secret, but it seems they are certainly not boring (or shy).

By 1852, 200 vaults had been built in Odd Fellows Rest, along with wall vaults on two sides of the cemetery, and by the 1930s, it was nearly full. In the late twentieth century, vandals and neglect have tormented the cemetery, and pedestrians waiting for buses often squat atop the boundary walls. Huge chunks are missing from the lovely cast-iron gates, which feature intricate renderings of I.O.O.F. symbols such as a widow and her children, a beehive, and a Bible.

Many of the I.O.O.F. tombs have become dingy and strangled with weeds, but somehow manage to retain their inherent dignity. The Howard Association tomb features a sculptured bas-relief of John Howard, the eighteenth-century English social reformer for whom the society was named. The Howard Association, however, died out after its mission—giving emergency care to yellow fever victims—became obsolete in the early twentieth century, and no one is left to take care of the tomb. Today, the somber sculpted face of John Howard barely peeps above the weeds and shrubbery tangled around the tomb. Another spectacular tomb is that of the Southwestern Lodge No. 40, which probably originally was the tomb of the I.O.O.F. Teutonia Lodge No. 10. The center panel's carving reads, in German, "*Freundschaft Liebe und Warheit.*" Friendship, love and truth.

St. John Cemetery

St. John Cemetery, in the 4800 block of Canal Street, was the second Protestant cemetery established in New Orleans. Christ Church (Episcopal) founded the first Protestant burial site, Girod Street Cemetery, which opened in Faubourg St. Mary in 1822 and was deconsecrated and abandoned in 1957. St. John, originally called the First German Evangelical Lutheran St. John Cemetery, was founded in 1867 by the St. John Evangelical Lutheran congregation. It originally had space for about 750 six-by-nine-foot lots, as well as vaults along the perimeter walls.

In the 1920s, the cemetery was sold to the Huber family, who renamed it simply St. John Cemetery and made it nonsectarian. Inspired by community mausoleums he had seen on a visit to the West Coast, family patriarch Victor Huber decided to build something similar at St. John. Construction on Hope Mausoleum, which now occupies more than half the land in present-day St. John Cemetery, was started in 1931. The first crematorium in Louisiana was built here, and the mausoleum now contains several thousand crypts. When Girod Street Cemetery was closed in the late 1950s, many of the remains were reinterred in Hope Mausoleum.

St. Louis No. 2

St. Louis No. 2, the second-oldest surviving cemetery, is bounded by North Claiborne Avenue and South Robertson, Iberville, and St. Louis streets, just off of Interstate 10. Founded in 1823, it bears much in common with No. 1 and was opened at the behest of the City Council in response to citizens' fear of spreading disease. New Orleanians were clueless as to what caused the diseases—cholera and yellow fever primarily—that regularly ravaged the city. One suggestion was that the epidemics might be spread by fumes emanating from the burial crypts. A new cemetery located farther outside the city, officials reasoned, might halt or at least delay further outbreaks. Originally, St. Louis No. 2 ran all the way from present-day Canal Street to St. Louis Street. The cemetery's present tri-squared shape came into being when Iberville, Bienville, and Conti were cut through. The area between Iberville and

Canal was used only for a few scattered burials and is not part of the present-day cemetery.

The layout of St. Louis No. 2 resembles the haphazard arrangement of No. 1—possibly from the hasty burials accompanying the many epidemics. Some summers saw hundreds of people dying each day; the last thing on anyone's mind was the convenience of twentieth-century tourists who would prefer more orderly pathways. A straight center aisle and parallel side aisles help visitors maneuver through the cemetery, but placement of the tombs still seems random. Architecture, too, is similar to St. Louis No. 1, with dozens of simple stepped-top tombs constructed of slave-made bricks, marble, or granite. Wall vaults surround all three squares, with the exception of the Robertson Street side of Square 2.

St. Louis No. 2 is the final resting place of such luminaries as three mayors, James Pitot, Nicholas Girod, and Charles Genois; and Oscar Dunn, a black lieutenant governor of the Reconstruction period. Also buried here, in a small, simple tomb, is Dominique You, a pirate captain, smuggler, and artillerist who commanded a battery during the Battle of New Orleans. You was a close affiliate (some say brother) of the notorious pirate Jean Lafitte, whose band of seagoing scoundrels helped Andrew Jackson trounce the British in early 1815's dramatic epilogue to the War of 1812. After the Battle of New Orleans, the city gratefully pardoned the pirates for all crimes, real or imagined. Dominique You died in 1830, receiving full military honors and numerous public tributes. Banks and businesses closed, and flags flew at half-mast on harbored ships and at half-staff on public buildings. More than a century later, in 1938, Dominique was immortalized in that quintessentially twentieth-century way: Cecil B. De Mille made a movie, *The Buccaneer*, about the pirate's adventures.

Other prominent New Orleanians whose remains rest in St. Louis No. 2 include John Davis (1773–1839), owner of the Theatre d'Orleans; architect James Freret (1838–97); and Claude Tremé, owner of the tract where the cemetery was located and developer of Faubourg Tremé.

In 1832, just nine years after St. Louis No. 2 opened, a horrific epidemic swept the city, followed by an even worse plague in 1833. The cemetery, overwhelmed by an influx of hundreds of bodies each month, quickly filled. A city ordinance in 1835 required that anyone dying in New Orleans or the vicinity be buried in a new cemetery on land purchased from Evariste Blanc near Bayou St. John. This presented a transportation problem, since the Blanc land was considerably removed from New Orleans proper. A pragmatic entrepreneur named John Arrowsmith supplied the ghastly answer: a corpse-carrying railroad running from St. Claude Street, out Orleans Street, to the cemetery at the bayou. Although the City Council authorized the railroad in March 1835 (carefully specifying that the corpses of whites, free colored people, and slaves would be segregated on even their final ride), no record of either the "railway of the dead" or the bayou cemetery exists today.

St. Louis No. 3

Still more epidemics, particularly those during the deadly decades of the mid-nineteenth century, created the need for St. Louis No. 3, on Esplanade Avenue near Bayou St. John. The cemetery was consecrated in 1854, following the cataclysmic yellow fever outbreak of 1853. Before St. Louis No. 3 opened, an area along Orleans Avenue from Broad Avenue to Bayou St. John served as a temporary burial ground.

St. Louis No. 3 appears more orderly than the other two St. Louis cemeteries, with wide, straight aisles that traverse several city blocks. Planners showed much the same diligence as Pauger had demonstrated in originally laying out the Vieux Carré. The cemetery "streets," or main aisles, were named for Saints Louis, Peter, and Paul. The smaller parallel aisles honored Saints Mary, Joseph, Magdalene, and Philomene. Cross aisles were named for bishops and archbishops of the New Orleans diocese.

Tombs found in St. Louis No. 3 include those of sugarcane king Valcour Aime (1798–67) and Father François Isidore Turgis (1805–68), a Confederate chaplain who following the Civil War was pastor of St. Anthony's Church (the old Mortuary Chapel). The remains of Colonel D. Dreux, the first Confederate officer from New Orleans to die in the Civil War (on July 5, 1861), originally were interred at St. Louis No. 3, but were moved on July 4, 1896, to the Army of Tennessee tomb at Metairie Cemetery.

Architect James Gallier Jr. erected a monument at St. Louis No. 3, dedicated to the memory of his father, renowned architect James Gallier Sr., and stepmother, who were lost at sea. The inscription reads: "This monument is erected to the memory of James Gallier, architect of New Orleans, born at Ravensdale, Ireland, July 24, 1795, by his son as a tribute to his genius, integrity and virtue, and of Catherine Maria Robinson, born at Barre, Massachusetts, wife of James Gallier. They were lost in the steamer *Evening Star* which foundered on the voyage from New York to New Orleans October 3, 1866."

St. Patrick Nos. 1, 2, and 3

St. Patrick Cemeteries Nos. 1, 2, and 3 (actually one cemetery with three numbered sections), also at the junction of Canal Street and City Park Avenue, accommodated many of the Irish immigrants who settled in the American sector of Faubourg St. Marie in the 1830s. The Catholic Celts soon founded their own church, St. Patrick's on Camp Street, and bought the land for their own cemetery from a free man of color named Gabriel Jason. The three sections sprang from the site's division by Canal Street and City Park Avenue (which was then Metairie Road).

After only a dozen years in service, the St. Patrick Cemeteries did overtime duty during the horrific yellow fever epidemic of 1853, many of whose victims were the recently immigrated Irish. In August 1853 alone, more than 1,000 people were buried in the St. Patrick Cemeteries. The enormous toll on the cemetery keepers during this time most likely accounts for the haphazard layout of St. Patrick No. 1, where most of the yellow fever dead were buried. St. Patrick No. 2 has more conformity of plan and more above-ground tombs (St. Patrick No. 1 features almost exclusively below-ground burial, which worked fairly well in this part of town, one of the few areas of "high ground").

Among those buried in the St. Patrick Cemeteries are Emile "Stalebread" Lacoume, a pioneer jazz musician of the early twentieth century; and William Blair Lancaster (1826–96), a Florida native who converted to Catholicism and helped found the first New Orleans branch of the Society of St. Vincent de Paul, a men's benevolent organization.

Sculpted stations of the cross adorn the entrances to the St. Patrick Cemeteries. In 1966, care for the St. Patrick Cemeteries was taken over by the Archdiocese of New Orleans, and No. 3 was reserved primarily for burial of members of religious orders. At this time, the archdiocese also assumed responsibility for St. Louis Cemeteries Nos. 1, 2, and 3, the St. Roch Cemeteries, St. Joseph Cemeteries, and St. Vincent So-niat Street Cemetery.

St. Roch Nos. 1 and 2

St. Roch Cemetery, on St. Roch Avenue near North Robertson (north-west of the French Quarter), was started in 1874 by Father Peter Leonard Thevis, pastor of Holy Trinity Catholic Church in lower New Orleans. During a devastating yellow fever epidemic, Father Thevis and his congregation prayed to St. Roch, one of the Catholic Church's "Fourteen Holy Helpers," to protect them from the plague. The priest swore that if his parishioners were spared, he would build a shrine and cemetery dedicated to the saint. Legend claims that none of Father Thevis's flock died, and he made good on his word with the opening of St. Roch Cemetery, which was modeled after the famed Campo Santo dei Tedeschi near St. Peter's Cathedral in Rome.

St. Roch's Chapel, resembling a miniature Gothic chancel, rises in a blaze of white behind the front gates of the cemetery. A statue of St. Roch and his faithful dog adorn the altar, and Father Thevis was buried under the altar. In 1895, the equally stunning St. Michael's chapel-tomb was built in the new section of the cemetery (St. Roch No. 2). The sense of peace and comforting sanctity at St. Roch's Chapel have made it a popular shrine for the faithful throughout its 120-year history.

St. Vincent de Paul Nos. 1, 2, and 3

These cemeteries, in lower New Orleans (northeast of the French Quar-ter, near the river), probably opened in the 1840s and may have been founded by a priest. In 1857, the St. Vincent cemeteries were acquired by Señor José Llula (called Pepe Lula), a famous Spanish duelist of the era. The cemeteries, apparently, were simply one of Pepe's many business endeavors. Hundreds of relatively simple tombs line the rows of the St. Vincent de Paul cemeteries, which are enclosed by brick walls. A few large family tombs stand out, many with distinctly German names such as Zaeheringer, Frantz, and Schoen. Also buried here are the remains of Mother Catherine Seals, a black spiritual leader of the early twentieth century. Marie, queen of the Tinka-Gypsies, was entombed at St. Vincent de Paul in 1916.

The similarly named St. Vincent Cemetery, in the 1900 block of Soniat Street (Uptown), is operated by the Archdiocese of New Orleans.

5

Altar Images: The Churches

The soaring spires and architectural majesty of New Orleans's churches confirm its identity as one of America's most Catholic cities. The Crescent City's religious identity, indelibly forged by those first eighteenth-century French and Spanish settlers, remained stubbornly Catholic despite the wave of Protestant immigration following the Louisiana Purchase. Thousands of Irish, German, and Italian settlers also came to New Orleans in the nineteenth century, strengthening the Catholic foundation of the religious community and raising glorious new churches despite enormous economic and cultural hardships. In fact, the first organized Protestant service did not take place until two years after the Louisiana Purchase, in 1805.

Of the dozens of glorious New Orleans churches worth exploring, three in particular will beckon fans of Anne Rice's *The Vampire Chronicles* and *Mayfair Witches* series—St. Louis Cathedral in the French Quarter, and St. Mary's Assumption and St. Alphonsus in the Irish Channel.

The triple-spired **St. Louis Cathedral**, officially a minor basilica since 1964, is actually the third St. Louis Church to hover serenely at the edge of Jackson Square, gracefully dominating the Vieux Carré sky-line and serving as the true soul of the old city. The church site, facing the river with the Place d'Armes as its "front yard," was first designated for a church in 1721 by Adrien de Pauger, the French engineer whose meticulous grid pattern of streets still survives in the Quarter.

The Church of St. Louis is mentioned many times in the *Vampire Chronicles* series, notably as the site where Louis slays a priest, with the vampire taking his blood nourishment at the communion altar in a gory parody of the Christian mass.

Like all old buildings, particularly in New Orleans, St. Louis Cathedral has its share of rumored ghosts, most of whom seem to pre-fer the outdoors near the church to the cathedral itself. Many a startled onlooker has described seeing a monklike gentleman strolling along the misty Père Antoine Alley—claimed by some to be the beloved Ca-puchin priest himself.

On rainy nights, another Capuchin, Père Dagobert, who arrived in New Orleans in 1745, is said to wander the streets between St. Louis Cathedral and St. Louis Cemetery No. 1 singing the *Kyrie*. Dagobert was

St. Louis Cathedral glows in the dusk.

The ornate interior of St. Louis Cathedral.

the parish priest when news arrived that the Louisiana colony had been ceded from France to Spain in a secret treaty. A short-lived rebellion was squelched by the arrival of Don Alexander O'Reilly, who mercilessly executed the six rebel leaders and allowed their bodies to decay in the rain and heat of the Place d'Armes. Père Dagobert, unable to withstand such horror in his parish, secretly gathered the bodies and sang the funeral mass for the dead, then walked with the dead men's families through a pounding storm to St. Louis No. 1, where the fallen rebels were buried in consecrated ground.

Construction on the first Church of St. Louis did not start until 1724, six years after the city was founded. An earlier, temporary worship house was destroyed by the hurricane of 1722, which flattened nearly everything in its path. Following the hurricane, a warehouse, tavern, and military barracks took their turns as temporary worship centers.

Pauger's original St. Louis Church, dedicated to the sainted French king Louis IX, was one of the first Vieux Carré buildings constructed in the *briquete-entre-poteaux* ("bricks-between-posts") method. This original church was cruciform in plan, with a nave 112 feet long, 32 feet wide,

Cathedral Garden behind St. Louis Cathedral contains a monument (foreground) honoring a group of French marines, as well as a striking marble statue of the Sacred Heart of Jesus.

and 24 feet high. Two bells perched in a tiny belfry over the entrance. Eighteen pews were assigned to worshipers, based on the highest bid. Democracy in worship, apparently, was deemed unnecessary, or at the very least unprofitable.

Pauger, who planned and oversaw construction of the church, died in 1726, before its completion. His will asked that his remains be interred within the foundation of the building—Pauger, having seen the results of attempted below-ground burials at St. Peter Cemetery, no doubt saw the wisdom of something more permanent. A year and a half after Pauger's death, Father Raphael de Luxembourg dedicated the church just before Christmas 1727.

The brick-and-wood St. Louis Church was used until the mid-1760s, when it was abandoned because of disrepair and neglect. A royal warehouse on Dumaine Street was used for worship while the church was repaired, but the restoration could not save it from the Good Friday fire of 1788, which destroyed most of the Vieux Carré. Ironically, reports indicate that the fire spread so quickly because residents had no warning—church officials were reluctant to ring the church bells on Good Friday, when all bells are silent according to Catholic tradition.

Father Antonio de Sedella (lovingly called Père Antoine by his parishioners) was parish priest when the Good Friday fire engulfed the city. Père Antoine managed to save a few church records by tossing them into the square, then rushed to help the Ursuline nuns save their convent—a feat that allows twentieth-century New Orleans to claim it as the oldest surviving building in the Mississippi River Valley. The church, however, was lost to the flames. Masses took place at governmental buildings, the Ursuline chapel, at Charity Hospital, and in a building where the Cabildo now stands. Construction of a new church finally began in early 1789, but it was five years before New Orleanians had a dedicated place of worship again.

Père Antoine, by the way, served the church from 1785 to 1790, and again from 1795 until his death in 1829. Following an enormous funeral, held in a black-draped St. Louis Cathedral echoing with the sobbing of Antoine's devoted parishioners, Père Antoine was interred beneath the church he loved and served for more than forty years.

The second Church of St. Louis was built through the benevolence of Don Andrés Almonester y Roxas (father of Micaela de Pontalba). Almonester was one of New Orleans's wealthiest citizens, due to canny investments in real estate and the beneficence of powerful friends. Almonester undoubtedly had philanthropic urges—he already had built a chapel for the Ursuline Convent and a retreat for lepers on the edge of town (on his own land) and had rebuilt Charity Hospital after a hurricane damaged it. But his charitable inclinations went only so far—when it came time to build a new church, Almonester requested "a title of Castile" from the king of Spain. If Almonester decided the king and his officers weren't taking the request seriously, his money dried up and work shut down on the church, only to be revived when word arrived that Spanish officials were "discussing" it again.

The new church was finally completed in autumn 1794. It was considerably different from the first church—much larger, with a flat roof and twin hexagonal bell towers on its front corners, but no central spire. The bell towers were empty until July 1804, when the bells (christened St. Joseph and St. Anthony) finally arrived to summon worshipers to mass. The church was built of bricks, some of which were "recycled" from the walls of St. Peter Cemetery, which had by then been abandoned. The interior was distinguished by a marble floor and exquisite altar paintings and sculptures, with the church's total cost weighing in at about $100,000, a tremendous amount at the time.

The second Church of St. Louis, not yet even dedicated, escaped the December 1794 fire, which seized an adjacent guardhouse but miraculously left the new church unscathed. On Christmas Eve 1794, the new church was dedicated as a cathedral. Louisiana and the Floridas had been made a diocese in 1793, and New Orleans was the headquarters city for Bishop Luis Peñalver y Cárdenas. Almonester, the church's on-again, off-again benefactor, received a special "seat of honor" in the new cathedral and also finally received his long-desired title from Spain. He died in April 1798, and his remains were interred in a crypt beneath the church's floor.

The new Cathedral of St. Louis quickly took its rightful place as centerpiece of community activities and celebrations. On January 23, 1815, a spectacular victory festival on the square outside the church greeted General Andrew Jackson, hero of the Battle of New Orleans. Historian Charles Gayarré described the happy tumult: "The balconies and windows of the city hall, the parsonage house, and all the adjacent buildings, were filled with spectators. The whole square, and the streets leading to it, were thronged with people." Jackson acknowledged the adoring crowds, then proceeded into the cathedral for a special ceremony honoring his defeat of the British at Chalmette.

A central tower, complete with clock and bell, was added in the early 1820s. The tower was one of the last projects of Benjamin Latrobe, architect of the U.S. Capitol and the Cathedral of Baltimore. Latrobe died in New Orleans, of the pervasive yellow fever, in September 1820, before his cathedral tower was completed. The church bell, the same one which today rings on the hour, lauds the victorious Battle of New Orleans, with both French and English inscriptions. In French, "*Braves Louisianais, cette cloche dont le nom est Victoire a été fondue en mémoire de la glorieuse journée du 8 Janvier 1815.*" In English, "Brave Louisianans, this bell whose name is Victory was cast in commemoration of the glorious 8th January 1815."

Today, a total of seven bells graces the cathedral steeples. Three, including "Victoire," are attached to the great clock; the remaining four are church bells used on various religious occasions. The Angelus bell strikes the notes of the Angelus at 6 A.M., noon, and 6 P.M. daily. Bells are not rung before services these days except on Easter, Pentecost, and Christmas, when all four ring together. On Good Friday, all the bells are silent. The bells named St. Joseph and St. Anthony, installed in 1804, have disappeared.

In the early to mid 1800s, flamboyant memorial services often took place at the cathedral, minus the deceased "honorees." Those memorialized with services at St. Louis Cathedral included Napoleon Bonaparte and the Marquis de Lafayette. A newspaper of the day described Lafayette's 1834 memorial procession: "Next came the citizens representing the States of the Union, all of them in mourning and bearing escutcheons indicative of the twenty-four members. There came in succession, the Civil and Military authorities, the Citizens, and a trail of Artillery. . . . So extensive was the Procession that when the van reached the Public Square, the rear was still opposite the State House on Canal Street."

The central square's appearance changed dramatically in the mid-1840s, after Micaela de Pontalba returned to her native New Orleans from Paris and oversaw the construction of her magnificent row houses along the sides of the Place d'Armes. Probably to conform to the Pontalba Buildings' original design, mansard roofs and dormer windows were added to both the Cabildo and Presbytère in 1847. While effectively enhancing these buildings, the additions dwarfed the cathedral, which also was suffering from cracked walls and general deterioration.

In 1834, church trustees had opened discussions with renowned architect J. N. B. de Pouilly about upgrading or replacing the St. Louis Cathedral to accommodate the demands of a rapidly growing congregation. Pouilly, whose architectural feats included the St. Louis Hotel, the

Dufilho Pharmacy on Chartres, and many of the elaborate tombs in St. Louis Cemeteries Nos. 1 and 2, first suggested enlarging the existing church by lengthening the nave and adding galleries. Church officials nixed the plan.

Pouilly came up with a much more drastic solution in 1839—one that, if put in place, would have altered completely the look of the French Quarter as we now know it. Pouilly this time suggested demolishing St. Louis Cemetery No. 1 and building a new church and rectory on that land. "Galleries" of vaults would be included in the church plans, so that human remains could be reinterred there and remain in sacred ground. He proposed a church with at least four entrances, built to contend with the hot, humid climate. After this new church would be finished, Pouilly suggested that the old cathedral be demolished and Orleans Street be extended to Jackson Square. Once again, though, church leaders cried, "Non!"

For Pouilly, the third time was indeed the charm, although another decade would pass before his final proposal was accepted and work begun, in early 1849. The new plan called for extensive reconstruction of the existing church, including a longer nave, heightened facade, and open central steeple. The plans were eventually amended to include replacement of all the walls, which were dilapidated and might have weakened the church structure if any were left intact. Foundation trenches for the new side walls were lined with flatboat planks, harvested from flatboats coming down the Mississippi. (Much of the uptown suburb of Lafayette, which saw its heyday a decade earlier, also was constructed of the sturdy flatboat remnants.)

While the new cathedral was being built, the remains of the illustrious citizens interred in the church—Père Antoine, Don Almonester and one of his daughters (a sister of Micaela), and others—were temporarily moved to St. Louis Cemetery No. 1; they were reinterred in the new cathedral in November 1852.

As building progressed at a snail's pace, the *Daily Picayune* commented on the efforts: "Even in its present rough and incomplete state, the loftiness and lightness of the main portion of the interior edifice are very striking to the eye of the beholder. . . . A view of the front of the cathedral is not altogether destitute of a pleasing effect; but that of the rear suggests other ideas," the paper noted in November 1850. It would be more than another year, in December 1851, when the diocese's arch-bishop finally blessed the reconstructed church. The elaborate baroque altars, however, were not part of the celebration—they didn't arrive from Ghent, Belgium, until mid-1852.

Not everyone was charmed by the new building. Historian Charles Gayarré, for instance, in his *History of Louisiana* (1854), remarked: "The monumental and venerable relic of the past was pulled down in 1850 in the mere wantonness of vandalism to make room for the upstart pro-duction of bad taste."

Modifications of St. Louis Cathedral have continued through the years. The open central spire, constructed of wood and wrought iron, was enclosed in slate in 1859 to protect it from the weather. The slates on the smaller side steeples were modified to include double-barred archiepiscopal crosses, indicating the church's status as a metropolitan cathedral, seat of an archbishop.

In the late 1800s and throughout the twentieth century, efforts have continued to preserve the rich history evident in the walls, ceil-ings, and spires of St. Louis Cathedral. To the unparalled delight of wor-shipers, air-conditioning was added in 1956, and the entire exterior was restored and weatherproofed that same year.

The historic murals can be enjoyed more fully since the mid-1970s, when a major restoration included installing chandeliers at evenly spaced intervals above the main aisle. The mural above the great altar shows St. Louis, king of France, announcing the Seventh Crusade. The Latin lettering on the cornice can be translated to "My Blood Is Drink Indeed; I Am the Way, the Truth and the Life" and "My Flesh Is Food Indeed." The original 1852 baroque altar centerpiece, which had been moved to the priests' sacristy, has been put back in place. A freestand-ing sacrifical altar in front of the centerpiece was added following the Second Vatican Council.

Dignitaries who have visited St. Louis Cathedral in modern times include French president Charles de Gaulle in 1960, French president and Madame Valery Giscard d'Estaing in 1976, and Pope John Paul II in September 1987. St. Louis Cathedral was the only Catholic church in New Orleans until 1833, when St. Patrick's Catholic Church was built on Camp Street for English-speaking Catholics in the new Amer-ican sector.

The two Irish Channel churches, **St. Mary's Assumption** and **St. Alphonsus**, are especially significant to Anne Rice's *Mayfair Witches* series and played a large role in her own religious upbringing.

Both built in the 1850s, St. Mary's and St. Alphonsus originally comprised two-thirds of a unique three-church parish that was split along national, rather than religious, lines—St. Mary's for the Germans, St. Alphonsus for the Irish, and Notre Dame de Bon Secours for the French. Notre Dame, on Jackson Avenue, was demolished in the 1920s.

St. Mary's Assumption Church in the Irish Channel boasts exquisite baroque styling and brickwork.

The first chapel of the St. Mary's Assumption German Catholic congregation was built in 1844. The small frame building, which seated eighty, was moved in the mid-1860s, after the new St. Mary's church opened. The original chapel still exists; it was moved uptown to a permanent resting place at St. Joseph No. 1 cemetery on Washington Avenue (the same cemetery, incidentally, where Anne Rice's mother is buried).

Both St. Mary's and St. Alphonsus benefited from the influx of skilled brick masons into the city from the 1850s to the 1870s. Both churches are recognized as outstanding examples of brick architecture, with bricks used as both decorative and structural elements. Advanced technology in brick making, with kilns producing brick strong enough to withstand the elements, allowed for exposed surfaces rather than the traditional plaster covering.

Steadfast in their refusal to worship with their German-speaking neighbors, the Irish immigrant population started construction on St. Alphonsus in 1855, finishing in 1857. The cornerstone for St. Mary's was laid in April 1858, and the church was finished in 1860. Both churches were built by the Redemptorist Fathers as part of a large religious complex—dubbed Ecclesiastical Square—that at one time included boys' and girls' schools, St. Katharine's College, the Convent of Mercy, and a rectory.

Both Anne Rice and her protagonist Michael Curry of the *Mayfair Witches* series attended Redemptorist School, and services at both churches were part of their religious instruction. Unfortunately, in the late twentieth century, most of the surrounding buildings have been turned into public housing, and the area is not considered particularly safe. St. Mary's still has a small congregation; St. Alphonsus is struggling for survival in the face of possible demolition.

St. Mary's Assumption Roman Catholic Church, on the downtown riverside corner of Josephine and Constance, is considered the city's most impressive example of German Baroque brick construction. Sadly, the name of the designer of this magnificent red brick structure has been lost to time. The St. Mary's facade teems with interesting niches and molding in brick—crosses, arches, and other details create a visually intriguing veneer. Although primarily baroque in style, it also incorporates many Italianate features.

Buried beneath the St. Mary's altar lies one of the city's most beloved priests, Father Francis Xavier Seelos, who valiantly ministered to the yellow fever victims during the vicious 1867 epidemic before succumbing to the disease himself.

The stunning St. Mary's tower, visible from every corner of the Irish Channel, rises 142 feet skyward at the rear. Inside, plaster ornamentation, gleaming carved wooden pews, and dozens of life-size statues of the saints create a breathtakingly gorgeous tableau. This is a place where one's voice automatically drops to a reverent whisper.

St. Mary's is mentioned in the *Mayfair Witches* series, although the Mayfairs express a distinct preference for St. Alphonsus and, later, Our Mother of Perpetual Help Chapel in the Garden District. When Rowan Mayfair comes to New Orleans, she witnesses the funeral of her mother, Deirdre, at St. Mary's. "Footfalls echoed softly and loudly under the graceful Gothic arches, light striking brilliantly the magnificent stained-glass windows and the exquisitely painted statues of the saints," Rice writes in *Witching*. Later, Rowan and Michael Curry are married here, because St. Alphonsus is closed for repairs when their wedding takes place.

The church was condemned following Hurricane Betsy in 1965, but has since been gloriously restored and reopened. The ornate altar from Notre Dame de Bon Secours now resides in the St. Mary's sanctuary. Most masses, however, take place in the small chapel behind the main sanctuary. The sanctuary glows with a rainbow of colors—peach, blue, green, and lilac robes adorn the saint statues, along with the more typical white and gold.

Visitors can view the interior of St. Mary's by visiting about fifteen minutes before scheduled masses; call the church office at (504) 522-6748 for a schedule. Congregation members are wonderfully friendly, and understandably pleased to show visitors their beautiful church. The church is protected from future development in the area, earning National Historic Landmark status in 1974.

St. Alphonsus Roman Catholic Church, on the lakeside of Constance between Josephine and St. Andrew, was built in predominantly Italianate style between 1855 and 1857, under the direction of Baltimore architect Louis L. Long. Twin towers crown the roof; baroque

The gloriously restored interior of St. Mary's Assumption Church.

spires originally were planned for the church but never were completed. The church was named for St. Alphonsus Liguori, founder of the Redemptorist Order. St. Alphonsus remains with "his" church; a statue depicting the Italian priest was installed in an outdoor niche over the front doors in 1871.

St. Alphonsus is somewhat simpler in design than St. Mary's, both interior and exterior, and has not been as sumptuously restored. Still, its beauty is undeniable, and it retains a hushed, almost haunted air of solemnity and dignified grandeur. Stained glass, frescoes, and ornate wood carvings peek from every corner, patiently awating rediscovery. Wandering through its echoing, dust-filled nooks and crannies, one becomes very grateful for the laughter and squeals of children in the yard at St. Alphonsus School next door.

Many of the church's religious and decorative artifacts were auctioned at a Redemptorist Parish fund-raiser in 1990, but some of those items have been retrieved or donated back to the church. One remaining artifact is the gilded Victorian baptismal font, which was recently

St. Alphonsus Church was built for the Irish immigrant population, right across the street from St. Mary's, where the Germans worshiped.

restored. The font is enclosed by its own little wrought iron fence. Gorgeous stained-glass windows depict the life of Christ and life of Mary on opposite sides of the church.

Katherine and Howard O'Brien, Anne Rice's parents, were married at St. Alphonsus, and this is one of the churches that Anne attended as a child. Many of the fictional Mayfair family were married here, including flamboyant Mary Beth. Those baptized under its arched ceilings include the "legacy witches" Stella, Antha, Deirdre, and Rowan, presumably in that same Victorian font. As a child, Michael Curry serves as an altar boy here, and has a creepy Christmastime encounter with

Lasher inside St. Alphonsus. In one of the century-old wooden confessionals at St. Alphonsus, Deirdre murmurs her fears of Lasher to a priest, who pays little attention to what he considers a child's fabrication.

Even on a sunny twentieth-century afternoon, it's not difficult to imagine Lasher lurking around any of St. Alphonsus's shadowy corners. While researching this book, I was left alone in St. Alphonsus for a few moments, and although I tried to retain some sense of dignity, getting spooked was almost inevitable. I was inexpressibly glad when my tour guide returned.

A nonprofit organization, Friends of St. Alphonsus, has been formed to renovate and restore this landmark church to its former glory as the St. Alphonsus Art and Cultural Center. Although restoration is still in progress, the church has been used for several cultural events such as concerts, Irish genealogy seminars, antique auctions, and social events. Recently, the group applied for National Historic Landmark status for the church, which would ensure its protection in future years.

The interior of St. Alphonsus is being restored for use as a cultural/arts center. In *Witching*, St. Alphonsus is where Michael Curry, as a child, sees Lasher.

A decaying but still lovely angel adorns the main altar of St. Alphonsus.

As of this writing, Friends of St. Alphonsus had announced plans to keep the building open two days a week to share their treasure with the public. For information about open days, or to arrange a tour, call (504) 456-5315. If you request a tour, remember that your tour guide is a volunteer with Friends of St. Alphonsus, and although they're far too polite to ask, a small donation for the continuation of the society's work is always appropriate.

Ironically, the parish is still officially called St. Alphonsus Parish, although services take place only at St. Mary's Assumption

The ornate Victorian baptismal font at St. Alphonsus. Many of Rice's Mayfair characters are baptized in this church.

Church and Our Mother of Perpetual Help Chapel in the Garden District.

New Orleans can claim dozens of other historically significant houses of worship in an amazing array of styles. Any of the following are worth a visit if time permits.

Christ Church Cathedral, 2919 St. Charles Avenue. The Christ Church congregation was the first officially organized Protestant group in New Orleans. The congregation held its first service November 17, 1805, in the Cabildo. The present Christ Church, the fourth worship house for this congregation, was built in 1886. The building received landmark designation in 1972.

A wooden confessional at St. Alphonsus, perhaps the very one where Deirdre Mayfair confessed her fears of Lasher to a sympathetic but disbelieving priest.

Church of the Immaculate Conception, 140 Baronne Street, built in 1929–30 by architects Victor Wogan and Joseph Bernard. The design closely followed that of another church, built between 1851 and 1857, that originally graced this site. Cast-iron columns and pews from the original church were reused in the new building. In 1977, it was designated a New Orleans Historic District Landmark.

Coliseum Place Baptist Church, 1376 Camp Street, built in 1854 in Gothic Revival style. The tower steeple was destroyed by Hurricane Betsy in 1965 and never replaced. It was designated a landmark in 1976.

Felicity United Methodist Church, 1226 Felicity Street, built in 1888 in Gothic Revival style after a fire destroyed its predecessor. The present building's double towers originally had steeples, which were destroyed by a hurricane in 1915. Felicity Methodist was given landmark status in 1976.

Holy Redeemer Church, 2122 Royal Street, built in 1858–59 as the Third Presbyterian Church, now Catholic.

Holy Trinity Catholic Church, 721 St. Ferdinand Street, built 1853.

Our Lady of Guadalupe, 411 N. Rampart, built from 1826 to 1827 as a mortuary chapel for yellow fever victims—fearing spread of the disease, city leaders passed an ordinance banning funerals from taking place in St. Louis Cathedral, where the living worshiped. This church, erected in 1826 near St. Louis No. 1 Cemetery, is the oldest surviving New Orleans house of worship. Père Antoine himself laid the cornerstone on October 10, 1826. In 1875, the old Mortuary Chapel became a church for Italians. It was renamed Our Lady of Guadalupe in 1918 and became the official chapel of the New Orleans police and fire departments in 1931.

Rayne Memorial Methodist Church, 3900 St. Charles Avenue, built in 1875 for the St. Charles Avenue Methodist Episcopal Church South by architect Charles Hillger. The church is named in memory of William Rayne, a Confederate soldier who died on a Civil War battlefield. William's father, Robert, was a major benefactor of the church. In the evenings, Rayne Memorial's lighted steeple glows through the enormous oak trees lining St. Charles Avenue.

St. Augustine's Catholic Church, St. Claude Avenue at Gov. Nicholls Street, built 1841–42. This church, rectory, and school were built on land purchased by the Ursuline nuns, who then donated it to the diocese for a church. J. N. B. de Pouilly designed St. Augustine's, which was built next door to Claude Tremé's plantation home, which stood through the 1930s. The church was designated an historic landmark in 1977.

St. John the Baptist Catholic Church, 1101 Dryades Street, built 1869–72. St. John's is distinguished by its guilded, onion-shaped baroque tower. The impressive brickwork is similar to that of St. Mary's Assumption, and St. John architect Albert Diettel is often mentioned as the possible designer of St. Mary's (although this cannot be confirmed). In 1977, St. John the Baptist was designated a New Orleans Historic District Landmark.

St. Joseph's Roman Catholic Church, 1802 Tulane Avenue, built 1869–92. Original plans for this church, the largest in New Orleans, are

Our Lady of Guadalupe Church on Rampart Street. The oldest surviving church in New Orleans, it was built as a mortuary chapel for yellow-fever victims.

credited to Viennese architect Carl Kaiser and builder Thomas O'Neil. After the walls were erected in the 1870s, building ceased until the 1880s, when a new architect and builder were hired. Services began in 1893 in the still-unfinished church, and the towers never were built. The Romanesque-style building seats 1,600 to 1,800 worshipers and was designated a New Orleans Landmark in 1977.

    St. Patrick's Catholic Church, 724 Camp Street, built in 1838–39 as the first uptown church for the Irish immigrant population. For many years, this landmark was the tallest building in New Orleans. The original architects were Charles and James Dakin, but James Gallier Sr. took over in 1839 after a dispute with the contractors. In 1974, St. Patrick's was designated a National Historic Landmark.

Sts. Peter and Paul Catholic Church, 2317 Burgundy Street, built 1848–60.

St. Roch's Catholic Chapel, St. Roch Avenue between Derbigny and Roman streets, built 1875.

St. Stephen's Roman Catholic Church, 1025 Napoleon Avenue at Camp Street, built 1871–88. This is one of the churches mentioned in the "Nine Churches" ceremony described in *Lasher*. This Catholic Lenten-season tradition requires participants to walk to nine designated churches and perform a prescribed ritual at each one. St. Stephen's boasts the tallest spire of any New Orleans church, constructed in 1905–8. St. Stephen's received landmark status in 1979.

St. Theresa's Roman Catholic Church, Camp Street at Erato, built 1848–49 on part of the old Saulet plantation. This Gothic Revival landmark is another of Rice's "Nine Churches."

St. Vincent de Paul Roman Catholic Church, 3053 Dauphine Street, built 1866. Like the Irish Channel churches of St. Alphonsus and St. Mary's Assumption, St. Vincent's boasts ornate German Baroque brickwork, here designed by architect Lewis Reynolds. The St. Vincent congregation dates to 1838.

Trinity Church (Episcopal), 1329 Jackson at Coliseum, built 1852–54. The soaring entrance tower was added in 1873. Trinity Church received landmark status in 1986.

6
Swamps and Plantations: The Outskirts

In Louisiana, the phrase "a walk on the wild side" can conjure a variety of diverse meanings, each alluring in its own way—from a midnight dinner at a Bourbon Street restaurant, to an afternoon among the chimps at Audubon Zoo, to an evening of delirious twirling to the infectious rhythm of Cajun swing. But New Orleans offers more than urban adventures; truly intrepid souls can venture just a few miles outside the city for a glimpse at *genuine* bayou wildlife—the alligators, wild boars, snakes, and nutria roaming unfettered through the Louisiana swampland. As far as they're concerned the prehistoric era never died—they live almost exactly as they did thousands of years ago.

Visitors willing to go beyond the bounds of New Orleans proper also can get a remarkably detailed, precise glance at antebellum plantation life by way of more than three dozen restored estates along the historic River Road, which hugs the banks of both sides of the Mississippi upriver from the city. Several of these plantation homes, many of which are now open to the public, served as Anne Rice's inspiration for her richly envisioned, fictional plantations at Riverbend, Pointe du Lac, and Oak Haven.

This chapter explores the swamps, where Claudia and Louis dumped the body of a supposedly destroyed Lestat, as well as many of

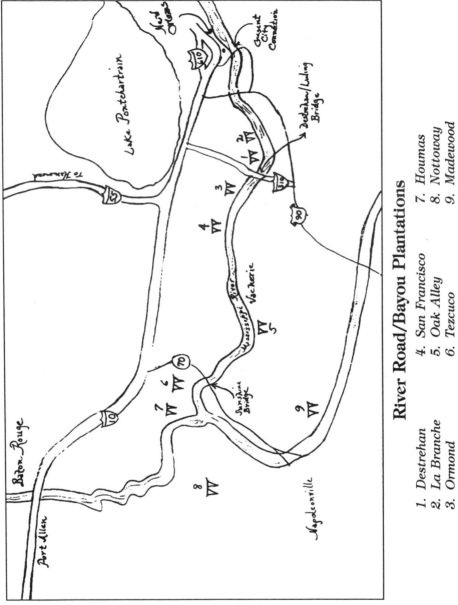

River Road/Bayou Plantations

1. Destrehan
2. La Branche
3. Ormond

4. San Francisco
5. Oak Alley
6. Tezcuco

7. Houmas
8. Nottoway
9. Madewood

those sumptuously restored mansions along the River Road. It also includes sites closer to the center of New Orleans, such as Pitot House on Bayou St. John and Chalmette Battlefield, which are nevertheless outside the "main drag" frequented by tourists and require a little extra effort (but well worth it) to visit.

Secrets of the Swamp

The abundant, primitive swampland just north of New Orleans is kept at bay only by the most sophisticated engineering and modern design. If all the humans suddenly left New Orleans, it probably wouldn't be ten years before the modern city reverted to the oozy sludge encountered by Bienville and his crew in 1718.

Driving along Interstate 10 on the way out of New Orleans, one is struck by two vivid reminders of nature's dominance. First, bright blue signs posted every few miles identify I-10 as the "Hurricane Evacuation Route" out of the city. Second, and even more unsettling, whole sections of the highway itself are built on concrete pilings sunk deep into the mucky wetlands. You can drive here, but you couldn't walk two feet off the highway without being at least waist deep in water, duckweed, and water hyacinth, with who knows what swimming or creeping past your unseen knees.

Those flying for the first time into New Orleans International Airport, perched on the edge of the swampland, often glance down just prior to landing and wonder aloud exactly where the plane will find a dry place to land.

Just outside New Orleans looms the second-largest swamp in Louisiana, the 400-square-mile **Honey Island Swamp**, named for its large population of honeybees. Only the Atchafalaya Swamp, near Lafayette, is larger than Honey Island. Some 35,000 acres of the Honey Island Swamp are owned by the State of Louisiana, which has turned it into a thriving wildlife-management area. Because Honey Island is a "river overflow" swamp, flowing out of the Pearl River, the water remains in a healthy, constantly moving state. Still, it's disturbingly easy to imagine a wounded Lestat flailing beneath the gently rippling waters; an undercurrent of menace pervades the wetlands, perhaps because we humans feel so out of place. In addition to serving as Lestat's temporary

Ancient moss-draped cypress trees create a ghostly cathedral in Honey Island Swamp.

grave, the swamps north of New Orleans also were the site of a bloody duel in *Interview*.

A wide variety of swamp tours are available, from one-hour jaunts to in-depth afternoon-long journeys. Some operators provide custom tours for bird-watchers or those brave enough to travel through the swamps after dark. Some tours also go into marshlands, which are another type of wetlands environment, the primary difference being that swamps have trees, and marshes do not. Marshlands actually are future swampland; the base land of a marsh is still too soft to support trees, but will inevitably firm up as the centuries glide by. The marshes provide a rich habitat for thousands of migratory birds; Louisiana attracts some 5 million ducks and geese every winter, more migratory game birds than any other state.

I took two mesmerizing tours with Honey Island Swamp Tours Inc., which was founded by environmental expert Dr. Paul Wagner. The shallow, gas-powered boats put guests "up close and personal" with the wildlife, including an unforgettable visit with "El Whoppo," also known as "Handsome," a fifteen-foot alligator who'll dart out of the water with frightening speed when the tour guide throws a whole, skinned chicken onto a bank. The chicken disappears in one fast gulp, no chewing necessary. We had several other gator sightings on our tours, including two smaller reptiles who circled the boat in not-so-friendly competition for the marshmallows our guide tossed into the water. Alligators, it seems, have lousy eyesight but an extraordinary sense of smell. It's not that they have an inherited sweet tooth; it's merely that the large white marshmallows are easy to spot on the murky green-gray water, and they float. Guides use them to lure shy alligators out of their hiding places into clear view. Because gators are extremely territorial, guides have a good idea of where to spot them.

The swamps, eerily quiet at times, quiver with unseen life and a peculiar beauty all their own. No matter how perfect the silence, there is always the feeling that you're never quite alone. At intervals, the tranquility is broken by the strident screeching song of millions of cicadas, Southern insects similar to locusts (just as

A Honey Island Swamp Tours boat cruises alarmingly close to the alligator-infested waters.

destructive, and twice as noisy!). Blue and white egrets, barred owls, and dozens of other birds glide overhead. If you're lucky, you might even catch a quick view of the bald eagles that have tended a nest in the area for decades.

Plant life also thrives in the unspoiled swamp. Flourishing cypress, red maple, water elm, and tupelo gum trees poke through the water like frozen water ballerinas, twisting and stretching in a macabre, dazzling imitation of dance. Cypress "knees," offshoots of the profuse bald cypress trees, surround their "parents," nudging through the hazy water like tiny, misshapen sentinels. Millions of tiny duckweed plants combine to make a bright green blanket over sections of water, parting delicately to allow passing boats, then closing up seamlessly as if completely unperturbed.

Clumps of lacy, pearl-gray Spanish moss shroud the ancient trees, creating a cool green cave of leaves and gnarled branches. Spanish moss, by the way, is neither indigenous to Spain nor moss. The moss actually is a bromeliad, an airborne plant that uses the trees for support only and gets all its nourishment from the air. Although Spanish moss is not a parasite, it eventually will kill some trees by "accident," completely covering the leaves, thus depriving them of needed oxygen. Spanish moss was once a million-dollar business in Louisiana, used for upholstery stuffing in train and car seats, in mattresses and cloth dolls, and as filler in floral arrangements (where it is still frequently found). Legend insists that unless stuffed with Spanish moss, voodoo dolls lose their potency and become powerless to harm the intended victim.

Honey Island guides also take passengers past many of the fishing camps along the Pearl River, which feeds the swamp. These camps, accessible only by water, appear rundown and crude, but have served their purpose for decades. Deserted camps quickly fall victim to the elements; one shack sports a tree sticking through its roof.

Of course, the swamps hide many secrets, including the source of a reported "swamp monster" along the lines of Bigfoot. A fisherman told Dr. Wagner (of Honey Island Tours) that he's seen the beast, and that it was about seven feet fall, weighed 300 to 350 pounds, and had orange-brown fur and big eyes. Dr. Wagner has nicknamed the questionable creature Wookie, after the lovable *Star Wars* mascot.

Information on swamp trips available from New Orleans (many operators pick up customers at local hotels) is included in chapter 7.

Not Quite Gone With the Wind

The gracious antebellum lifestyle along the River Road virtually disappeared after the Civil War. Hundreds of prosperous indigo, cotton, and sugarcane plantations once lined the Mississippi River upriver from New Orleans. The plantation parcels were long and narrow, with each landowner claiming a slender slice at riverside; trade routes along the Mississippi made access to the waterway absolutely essential to maintain a profitable plantation. The family residences were usually built near the levee and docks, with slave quarters and acres of fields beyond the homes and farther away from the river. This land arrangement makes it understandable how plantation homes might be quite close to one another, even though the holdings of each landowner could climb into thousands of acres.

Although many of the splendid plantation residences were desecrated by Union troops during the Civil War, others were spared by chance or, in at least one case, through intervention by a Yankee officer who had once been a guest on the plantation and didn't want to see it destroyed. The war was devastating to the local economy, and most of the plantation homes left standing fell into disrepair during Reconstruction and after, victims of vandals, vagrants, and sheer neglect.

During the late 1800s and on into the twentieth century, families again occupied many of the stately mansions, once more filling the galleries and oak-draped lawns with children's laughter and elegant social events. But the plantation way of life was forever gone, and today most of the homes are vacant. In *Lestat*, our vampire hero keeps his band "holed up in a lovely old plantation house north of New Orleans," perhaps referring to one of the many vacant dwellings—or maybe band members were bed-and-breakfast guests at Madewood or Oak Alley, two of several restored plantations that offer sleeping quarters. Fortunately for history lovers, numerous mansions all along the River Road, from just outside New Orleans clear to Baton Rouge, have been maintained by nonprofit foundations and are open to the public. Addresses and phone numbers for plantations are listed in chapter 7. A directional note: Strictly speaking, the Mississippi River actually runs from west to east for a good deal of its course from New Orleans to Baton Rouge, so plantations are situated either north or south of the river. However, residents of the area stick to the traditional designations of east bank and west bank, based on the river's more familiar north-to-south route farther upriver. (This also explains why the "west bank" of New Orleans, where the city of Algiers lies directly across the river from the French Quarter, is in reality almost due south.)

Of the dozens of River Road plantations, **Ormond, Oak Alley**, and **Madewood** are specifically mentioned in *The Vampire Companion* and *The Witching Companion* as having influenced Anne Rice in her depiction of the darker side of plantation life. In addition, Pointe du Lac

The eighteenth-century Destrehan Plantation, near New Orleans on the east bank of the River Road, was used for several scenes in the film version of *Interview With the Vampire*.

(which translates to "Point of the Lake"), Louis's indigo plantation in *Interview*, was partially based on **Pitot House**, which still stands on the Bayou St. John near City Park in New Orleans, and Madame John's Legacy in the French Quarter (discussed in chapter 2). Bayou St. John is often referred to in Rice's works by its old French translation, Bayou St. Jean. **Destrehan Plantation Home**, although not specifically mentioned by Rice, is the oldest documented plantation home still standing in the Lower Mississippi Valley, and was used in the filming of *Interview With the Vampire* in 1993.

So we begin with **Destrehan**, which is one of the most easily accessible plantation homes from New Orleans. It's about a ten-minute drive past New Orleans International Airport, or thirty minutes from the French Quarter. To reach Destrehan, take I-10 west to 310, turning south toward the river. Take the last exit before the Destrehan/Luling Bridge, and turn left (east). Destrehan is at 9999 River Road (State Highway 48), on the east bank of the River Road.

Destrehan, built in 1787–90 in the French Colonial style, is fascinating for both its grand historic legacy and the rumors that it may well be the most haunted house along the Mississippi River. The house was built for Robert Antoine Robin de Logny by a master builder known only as "Charles." One book about Destrehan, *Past Masters*, speculates that this may have been Charles Paquet, a free black who lived in the area and employed runaway slaves to cut cypress posts for him, indicating that Paquet may have been a builder. Another clue: Destrehan featured hand-carved cypress posts along its upstairs gallery.

Typical of West Indies plantation dwellings, Destrehan's original design had two stories of six rooms each, with no central hall or interior stairs, surrounded by 12-foot wide galleries. Most of the living quarters were on the second floor, except for the formal dining room downstairs. After Logny's death, just two years after the house's completion in 1790, his son-in-law, Jean Noel Destrehan, purchased the indigo plantation. Destrehan was a New Orleans native of noble Creole ancestry, and his older sister, Jeanne Marguerite, was married to Étienne de Boré, New Orleans' first mayor. Boré's experimentations in crystallization of sugarcane helped that crop become dominant over "King Cotton" and indigo, a dye-producing plant that was so toxic it eventually killed those who worked with it over long periods of time.

Destrehan, a highly influential statesman as well as successful planter, helped draft Louisiana's first state constitution. He later became the state's first elected U.S. senator, but did not accept the job. He remained in Louisiana and served as a state senator from 1812 to 1817. Destrehan and his wife, Marie Celeste de Logny, had fourteen children, most likely prompting the expansion of the family home to include *garçonnières* on either side of the main building. *Garçonnières*, from the French word *garçon* for "boy," were essentially bachelor's apartments for the young gentlemen of the family. They could basically do as they pleased in these attached apartments, while the young ladies were kept safely ensconced within sight of Mama and Papa.

In January 1811, the largest slave uprising in U.S. history began about thirty miles upriver from New Orleans. Slaves at Manuel André's plantation revolted, wounding André and his son. The rebellious band then began marching toward the city via what is now the River Road. Eventually other runaway slaves joined the group, which numbered between 150 and 200. Two days later, the Louisiana militia put a quick end to the incident, killing dozens of the runaways and taking the twenty-one leaders for trial at nearby Destrehan. They all were found guilty and taken back to their own plantations for speedy, if not exactly painless, execution. Following the bloody tradition of the French Revolution, their heads were stuck on poles along the River Road as an example to others who might consider rebellion, which included two slaves from Destrehan who took part in the insurrection, and whose sentence was carried out at the plantation.

Jean Noel Destrehan died at his plantation home on October 4, 1823 (coincidentally the same month and day as Anne Rice's birth date). His descendants continued to live at Destrehan until 1910. Those who made their home there included Nicolas Noel Destrehan, a son of Jean Noel and Marie Celeste. Nicolas Noel, who was strikingly handsome and often wore a black cape, has been identified by many as one of the ghosts of Destrehan. He certainly had a life haunted by catastrophe—his fifteen-year-old bride, Justine Fortier, died soon after their marriage, leaving Noel alone and childless. A few years after that, Nicolas's right arm was cut off when his cape got snagged in some plantation machinery. Nicolas eventually married again and moved to a plantation across the Mississippi from New Orleans, where the city of Harvey is now. His second wife also died young, of yellow fever in 1836.

Nicolas Noel never actually owned Destrehan; after Jean Noel and Marie Celeste's death, the plantation passed to their daughter Elinore Zelia Destrehan and her husband, Scots merchant Stephen Henderson. Indeed, the marriage between the beautiful, Catholic Zelia Destrehan and the suspiciously unattractive, Protestant Henderson may have been arranged in a deal to keep the plantation in family hands. Destrehan was advertised for sale in 1815; by 1816, Zelia had married the wealthy Henderson and the For Sale notices mysteriously disappeared.

The Destrehan tragedies continued when, in 1830 at a relatively young thirty, Zelia Destrehan died of unknown causes while on an extended visit to New York City—a visit that did not include her husband, who was, nevertheless, named as her sole heir. Six years later, Zelia's brother René Noel, twenty-eight, also died at a New York City hotel. In both cases, the cause of death was omitted from the death certificate. Henderson died in 1838, stipulating in his will that he be buried with Zelia and that the slaves of Destrehan were to be freed. He wanted each slave given one hundred dollars and free passage, if desired, back to Africa. This being a few decades prior to the Emancipation Proclamation, however, the New Orleans courts quickly overturned the provisions regarding the slaves.

In 1839, Henderson's heirs sold the plantation to Judge Pierre Adolph Rost, husband of Zelia's younger sister Louise Odile, thus keeping it in the Destrehan family. The Rosts undertook an extensive remodeling of Destrehan in 1840, converting it to the more popular Greek Revival style. Doric columns were built around the cypress colonettes, and interior ceilings were plastered over. Doors and windows were replaced with taller models, surrounding the popular keyhole-style moldings.

In addition, the rear gallery was enclosed, and two winding staircases were constructed on either side of the newly created foyer. The family became connected by marriage to neighboring Ormond Plantation when Nicolas Noel's daughter, Adele (Louise Odile's niece), married Samuel McCutchon of Ormond. When the Civil War started, Rost was appointed minister to France by Confederate president Jefferson Davis. The entire Rost clan left for France in 1861, leaving Destrehan to be snatched by the Federal government. For four years, Union soldiers lived in the house, which was then made into a Freedman's Bureau. The family returned in 1866 and eventually regained their holdings, including Destrehan. Their youngest son, Emile Rost, was the last Destrehan descendant to live in the house. In 1910, he sold the plantation and house to a sugar corporation, and 123 years of Destrehan history ended.

Destrehan's colorful, often tragic past may account for its reputation as being tormented by otherworldly spirits. Madeline Mansure Levatino and Phyllis Barraco, both of whom have worked at Destrehan, wrote *Past Masters: The History & Hauntings of Destrehan Plantation* to document some of these ghostly tales. Levatino recounts her own encounter, manifested in the form of an unnatural cold on the downriver foyer staircase, which followed her through a twilight preclosing check of the upstairs rooms.

Most of the sightings have been reported in the back hall and upriver side of the house, although inexplicable incidents have taken place in almost every section of the house. Barraco, the gift shop manager at Destrehan for more than a decade, tells in the book of a tourist who met a tall, French-accented man on her way downstairs from a guided tour. When Barraco showed the woman a picture of Jean Noel Destrehan, the tourist claimed he was the man she had just spoken with. The staircase ends just outside the gift shop, which occupies the section of the house in which Jean Noel reportedly died. Many tourists have reported similar encounters with a courtly gentleman who strongly resembles Jean Noel. Others have seen a staring specter identified as probably Nicolas, as one woman said the man had no right hand (Nicolas's right arm, remember, was severed in an accident). Two ghostly little girls also have been spied playing at Destrehan.

Several of the upper-level rooms at Destrehan were transformed into eighteenth-century ballrooms for the film adaptation of *Interview*. The white walls were painted a deep burgundy, then restored to their original colors.

Just a short distance west on the River Road, on the other side of the Destrehan-Luling Bridge that transverses 310, lies **Ormond**, which also was built in the late 1780s or early 1790s. The positions of Ormond and Destrehan as neighboring plantations recalls Rice's placement of

Pointe du Lac and its neighbor, the Freniere Plantation. Like the fictional Freniere house in relation to Pointe du Lac, Ormond is a short ways upriver of its similarly constructed neighbor, Destrehan. Because the exact date of Ormond's construction is unknown, neighboring Destrehan can claim "oldest plantation" honors. Ormond was built by Pierre d'Trepagnier, who had been granted the land by Spanish governor Don Berndardo de Galvez to reward Trepagnier's service in the American Revolution. Trepagnier planted indigo and then sugarcane. Ormond physically resembles Destrehan, built in the same Louisiana Colonial style that mimicked West Indies architecture.

Ormond also had its share of tragedy and mystery, beginning with the into-thin-air disappearance of the master in 1798. While enjoying a meal with his family, Pierre d'Trepagnier was called away to meet a caller, supposedly a man dressed like a Spanish official. Trepagnier left with the man and never returned, and no trace of Ormond's master was ever found.

Ormond, near Destrehan on the River Road, is another late-eighteenth-century plantation that recently has been opened to the public.

In 1805, Colonel Richard Butler bought the land from the (supposedly) widowed Mrs. Trepagnier. Although "Ormond" has a French sound, Butler actually named his new home after Ormonde Castle in Ireland, the Butlers' ancestral home. Butler eventually sold Ormond to his business partner, Samuel McCutchon, whose oldest son (also named Samuel) married Adele Destrehan. Ormond's adjoining *garçonnières*, like those at Destrehan, were added sometime early in the nineteenth century, either by Butler or McCutchon.

The home suffered during the War Between the States and was sold at public auction in 1874 and 1875. In 1898, it was purchased by state senator Basile La Place Jr., son of the landowner for whom La Place, Louisiana, is named. La Place Jr., who supposedly had made enemies with the local Ku Klux Klan, was murdered October 11, 1899, by unknown assassins. Ormond's owner was shot, then hanged from an oak tree fronting River Road. The tree still stands.

The plantation eventually passed to the Schexnaydres, whose large extended family lived there from 1900 to 1926. During the Roaring Twenties and Depression, Ormond was abused or neglected by a series of tenants, including hobos who camped out in the once elegant rooms.

Ormond was saved from further humiliation by Mr. and Mrs. Alfred Brown, who restored and made major improvements to the plantation beginning in 1943. The Browns enclosed the carriageways on either side of the house, converting the *garçonnières* to the equivalent of wings instead of separate buildings. The Browns also added modern amenities such as indoor plumbing, gas, and electricity. After the Browns died, Ormond was sold to a developer and then to Betty R. LeBlanc, who was then executive vice president of Barq's Beverages in New Orleans. Mrs. LeBlanc died of cancer in 1986, before she could complete her plans for restoring the house. At this writing, LeBlanc's son, Ken Elliott, is renewing his mother's renovation efforts and has opened Ormond to the public for the first time in its two-century existence.

The Witches' Companion speculates that La Victoire at Riverbend, the Mayfair family plantation just north of New Orleans, may have resembled Ormond in its West Indies style of construction.

About sixty miles upriver from New Orleans, on the west bank of the Mississippi just outside Vacherie, is one of the prettiest views in the United States. **Oak Alley**, probably the most photographed and well-known of all the River Road plantations, owes its fame more to its landscaping than to the plantation house itself. The house is visually dwarfed by the twenty-eight live oak trees that extend for one-quarter mile to the river levee. The trees, planted by an unknown Frenchman at least one hundred years before the house was built, are evenly spaced at eighty feet apart, with a one-hundred-foot-wide leaf-draped avenue between the two rows.

Oak Alley was used for several scenes in the movie of *Interview*, including the first "flashback scene" of Louis at Pointe du Lac, which in the book is indeed described as featuring an "avenue of oaks before the plantation house." In the film, actor Brad Pitt, as Louis, is shown on horseback, trotting through a man-high crop of sugarcane. He rides up over the river levee, then dramatically gallops down the alley of oaks, which are dripping with ringlets of atmospheric, creepy Spanish moss. Visitors to Oak Alley may be surprised at the real-life view—the sugarcane was planted especially for the movie, and the levee offers an unobstructed view of both the house and the Mississippi River. Also, that's faux Spanish moss; Josephine Stewart, the last resident owner of Oak Alley, didn't like the moss because she said it made her home look spooky (what's not to like?). The trees were chemically treated to remove the moss, and once gone, it doesn't grow back. For *Interview*, movie crew members perched in cherry pickers to drape fake moss on the ancient limbs (probably the first time those trees felt dressed in several years).

According to *The Witches' Companion*, Oak Alley also was the model for Oak Haven, the Talamasca retreat house where Aaron Lightner takes Michael Curry to read the file on the Mayfair Witches. Michael instantly adores the house, "lavishly dreamlike in its southern Gothic perfection, the gargantuan black-barked trees extending their gnarled and heavy limbs to form an unbroken ceiling of crude and broken arches." Rice's description of the house and its environs is so accurate that her fans probably would recognize it as Oak Haven's real-life counterpart even without being told.

Centuries-old oak trees dwarf Oak Alley Plantation near Vacherie. Oak Alley was a filming site for *Interview*, and served as Anne Rice's inspiration for "Oak Haven" in the *Witches* series.

The Oak Alley mansion was built by Jacques Telesphore Roman and his wife, Celina. The architect may have been Celina's father, Gilbert Joseph Pilie; master builder George Swainy oversaw construction. The house was built in the classical style, with twenty-eight eight-foot-round columns surrounding it. The columns were built with brick made on the plantation, baked in pie-shaped molds to conform to the circular structure of the columns. Oak Alley is a model of form adapting to climate—its galleries extend more than a dozen feet beyond the outer walls, keeping the interior in shade nearly all day. Tall windows and doors are placed to allow cross-ventilation, and the ceilings are fifteen feet high. Sixteen-inch walls throughout the house helped Oak Alley residents stay cool in summer and warm in winter.

Celina Roman called her beautiful new home Bon Sejour, which means "pleasant sojourn," but the admiring travelers viewing the house from Mississippi riverboats dubbed it Oak Alley, and the name has endured ever since. The family remained at Oak Alley throughout the

Antique dolls and mosquito netting create an eerie atmosphere in a bedroom at Oak Alley.

Civil War, but soon after succumbed to a downward spiral that had begun years before, when Jacques died in 1848. Oldest son Henri took over the plantation business, but was unable to curb his mother's lavish spending. The economic turmoil caused by the war eventually caught up with the Romans, and Henri sold everything at auction in 1866 for a scant $32,800.

The plantation then changed hands several times, and Antonio Sobral (later called Antoine) purchased it in 1881. The Sobrals lived at Oak Alley for twenty-four years, restoring it to a flourishing plantation. The large family apparently lived with uncommon zest and enjoyment of everyday life; one account tells of the Sobral boys racing, horseback, through Oak Alley's paved center hallway. One of the girls' many suitors scratched the family name in a windowpane, presumably with a diamond ring.

Josie Sobral, Antoine's daughter, especially adored Oak Alley and often assisted her father with plantation business. In fact, Josie, an apparent forerunner to today's "workaholics," irritated her fiancé, Sidonius

Goette, with her frequent wedding postponements until she finally gave in to his "now or never" ultimatum. Their wedding was attended by the governor of Louisiana, and the newlyweds went on an extended honeymoon to St. Louis. While they were away, Josie's father decided to sell her beloved Oak Alley, and the Goettes' telegram offering to buy it themselves arrived too late. Josie's cherished childhood home passed out of Sobral hands in 1905.

The next family to occupy Oak Alley for an extended period were the Hardins. Patriarch Jefferson Davis Hardin Jr. worked diligently from 1917 to 1924 to save the plantation and was especially concerned for the trees, battling the Corps of Army Engineers twice. The engineers wanted to move the levee inland, which would have meant uprooting several oaks on either side of the alley. In the end, Hardin won the dispute and saved the centuries-old live oaks. Hardin also had the mansion's deteriorating roof replaced, which necessitated eviction of a huge bat population. Although Rice's immortals refrain from the indignity of turning themselves into bats, it still seems ironic that this "batty" mansion would one day host a movie crew devoted to celluloid vampires.

During Hardin's restoration of Oak Alley, the family lived in what once had been the old plantation jail. This building is now the Oak Alley Foundation office. Although Hardin hoped to transform the plantation into a working twentieth-century farm, a series of misfortunes prevented him from fulfilling that ambition. In 1925, Andrew and Josephine Stewart bought Oak Alley and transformed the former sugar plantation into a cattle ranch, bringing a herd of Santa Gertrudis from Josephine's family ranch in Texas. Pictures of Oak Alley taken in the late twenties and thirties show a herd of contented cows grazing beneath the famous oaks. Mrs. Stewart, called Tita, cultivated a magnificent 500-bush rose garden and revived the old custom of using the plantation bell to summon family members. Tita and Andrew labored hard to renovate Oak Alley to its former glory and made it the first modern example of antebellum restoration.

Tita outlived her husband by twenty-six years. Before she died in October 1972, she founded the Oak Alley Foundation to ensure that her sumptuous home could be shared and enjoyed by future generations of history buffs. Plantation tradition dictated that clocks should be stopped at the time when the owner died and remain there until a new owner took over. Hence, time stands still at Oak Alley, with all time-pieces frozen at 7:30, the time Josephine Stewart died. Her sister, Julia Kaufmann, served on the Oak Alley Foundation board until 1986, then was a member emeritus until her death in December 1992.

In addition to *Interview*, Oak Alley has provided a graceful setting for many television shows and movies over the years, including the NBC soap opera *Days of Our Lives*; the 1983 CBS film *Dixie: Changing Habits*, starring Suzanne Pleshette and Cloris Leachman; and the NBC remake of *The Long Hot Summer*, starring Don Johnson, Judith Ivey, and Cybill Shepherd. The earlier version, a theatrical movie starring Paul Newman and Joanne Woodward, is based on three short stories by Southern writer William Faulkner.

Like virtually every surviving plantation along the River Road, Oak Alley has its share of ghost stories, including that of a young woman in an old-fashioned dress who showed up in a tourist's photograph. When the photo was taken, the blonde was nowhere in sight. With luck,

Twenty-eight gigantic oaks line the path from Oak Alley to the Mississippi River levee.

several more generations will have the chance to gaze at that extraordinary, unique alley of oaks and listen for the whispers of generations past among their tangled branches. The trees are approximately 300 years old, and barring disease or the ravages of mankind, should have a life span of about 600 years.

Some seventy-five miles from New Orleans, on Bayou Lafourche south of the Mississippi, is exquisite **Madewood Plantation**, said to be one of Rice's prototypes for Fontrevault, the plantation owned by generations of "country" Mayfairs. The fictitious Fontrevault has been ruined by water and time, swallowed up by the surrounding swampland. It's where Mary Jane Mayfair takes her cousin Mona to give birth to her Taltos offspring, Morrigan. Rice describes Fontrevault as being up the River Road and over the Sunshine Bridge, near Napoleonville, an exact description of Madewood's geographic location.

Madewood, however, is far from descent into ruins. It's one of the most lovingly restored of the New Orleans–area plantations, and several of its antique-furnished rooms provide overnight accommodations to bed-

Madewood Plantation, near Napoleonville, was one of Rice's models for Fontrevault, the ruined bayou home of a branch of the Mayfair family.

and-breakfast guests—a rare chance to experience a touch of plantation life firsthand. Most of the other plantation guest quarters are in cottages or former slave quarters, rarely in the main house as at Madewood.

The sugar-white, Greek Revival house features wide front galleries supported by six unbroken Ionic columns. The home was built in 1846, and was designed by New Orleans architect Henry Howard, the man responsible for many of the Garden District's antebellum masterpieces. Colonel Thomas Pugh, who commissioned the building of Madewood, died before it could be completed, and completion was overseen by his widow, Eliza Foley Pugh.

Moss-covered oaks guard the antebellum-era cemetery on the grounds at Madewood.

An English walnut staircase curves upward at the end of the wide first-floor central hallway, with a Baccarat crystal chandelier dangling from the twenty-five-foot ceiling. Two Corinthian columns also grace the breathtakingly lovely entry hall. The home's designation as "Madewood" probably stems from the fact that it was built entirely from locally harvested cypress wood. The bricks were hand-made by plantation slaves and fired in on-site kilns. In 1964, Madewood was bought by the Harold K. Marshall family, who were generous and meticulous in its restoration.

Guests at Madewood can pay tribute to many past residents by visiting the plantation cemetery, which rests peacefully under ancient oak trees at the rear of the house. Madewood served as the setting for the acclaimed Cicely Tyson film *A Woman Called Moses*.

For Rice fans whose appetite for plantation history and culture has been whetted by visits to Destrehan, Ormond, Oak Alley, or Madewood, dozens of other River Road and bayou homes deserve a visit or drive-by, even though they are not explicitly related to Rice's works.

Listed below (in alphabetical order) are several to consider if time and energy allow. All of these homes offer public tours (tour details described in chapter 7).

Houmas House Plantation, on the River Road's east bank near Darrow, about sixty miles from New Orleans. Houmas House, a magnificent one-and-a-half-story Greek Revival mansion, was built in 1840. It was completely restored in 1940 and is furnished with period antiques. Houmas, named for the Houmas Indians who originally owned the land on which it sits, was built by Colonel John Smith Preston of South Carolina. Irishman John Burnside bought Houmas House Plantation in 1857 and turned it into a leading sugarcane producer. Burnside saved Houmas from Civil War devastation by claiming immunity as a British citizen.

After Burnside died, the home changed hands and eventually fell into disrepair. In 1940, it was bought by Dr. George B. Crozat of New Orleans, who returned it to splendor befitting its century-old heritage. Doric columns surround the house on three sides, supporting wide galleries and a hipped roof. A glass-enclosed belvedere towers above arched dormer windows. Houmas House served as the setting for 1964's lurid

Gothic thriller *Hush, Hush Sweet Charlotte,* starring Bette Davis and Olivia de Havilland.

La Branche Plantation Dependency House, about twenty miles from New Orleans in St. Rose, near Destrehan and Ormond on the east bank, east of 310. La Branche, built in 1792, is listed on the National Register of Historic Places. Tours include the interesting slave quarters and gazebo. For hungry River Road travelers, La Branche has an on-site restaurant.

Nottoway Plantation, about seventy miles from New Orleans in White Castle, south of the Mississippi and west of Bayou Lafourche. Nottoway, finished in 1859, was commissioned by John Hampden Randolph. The architect was Henry Howard, who also designed Madewood. Randolph christened the Greek Revival–Italianate Nottoway in honor of his original home in Nottoway County, Virginia. The home is surrounded by twenty-two unbroken columns, with ornate "iron lace" adorning the galleries. During the War Between the States, Nottoway was spared burning or destruction by a Union gunboat officer who remembered once having stayed there as a guest. Nottoway's 53,000 square feet and sixty-four rooms have earned it recognition as the "largest plantation home in the South." One of Nottoway's most impressive rooms is its captivating White Ballroom.

San Francisco Plantation, in Reserve, about forty-five miles from New Orleans, is on the River Road's east bank. San Francisco, built between 1853 and 1856, is a remarkable example of "steamboat architecture," constructed with the idea of eliciting sighs of admiration from passing riverboat passengers. It undoubtedly succeeded. The owner's dedication to finery nearly exhausted his resources, leading to the house's original name of "Sans Frusquin," which translated into the French slang of the day meant "one's all," or "without a penny in my pocket." Today, San Francisco sits in the unsettling shadow of an oil refinery, whose owners admittedly restored the house, now operated by the San Francisco Plantation Foundation. Of particular interest are its five handpainted ceiling frescoes. Frances Parkinson Keyes made San Francisco the setting for her novel *Steamboat Gothic.*

Tezcuco Plantation, in Burnside on the Mississippi's east bank, fairly close to Houmas House, about sixty miles from New Orleans.

Tezcuco Plantation House was started in 1855 and finished in 1860 by Benjamin F. Tureaud and his wife, Aglae Bringier. It was owned by their descendants until the mid-1940s, when it was bought by the Rouchon family. The raised-cottage, Greek Revival home was built of cypress and plantation-made brick. Sixteen-foot ceilings and extravagant interior architectural touches, such as ceiling cornices and rosettes, give Tezcuco its unique charm. The name stems from an Aztec word meaning "place of quiet rest."

Although those listed above are probably the most easily accessible (on tours) and most often visited of the River Road's plantation homes, dozens of others (some private, some open to the public) line the route from New Orleans to Baton Rouge and are worth a glance or a short stop. So, for the "can't get enough" plantation groupie:

Ashland–Belle Helene, in Darrow on the east bank of the River Road, was completed in 1841 as a gift from Duncan Kenner to his wife, Anne Bringier. The plantation, an austere Greek Revival showplace, originally was named after Henry Clay's Kentucky home, Ashland. Kenner was one of Louisiana's most prominent sugar growers and, in 1865, was recruited by Confederate president Jefferson Davis to help win support from France and England for the South's fight (clearly, Kenner was either unsuccessful or too late). In 1889, Ashland was bought by John Reuss, who renamed it in honor of his granddaughter, Helene Reuss Hayward.

The imposing home is surrounded by double galleries, twelve feet wide, supported by twenty-eight three-foot-square, thirty-foot high brick columns covered in stucco. In the 1940s, the house was unoccupied and suffered major deterioration from neglect. The Haywards began restoration in 1946. Ashland–Belle Helene was abused again in 1959, this time at the hands of vandals who destroyed all eight Italian marble fireplaces.

The stately home has survived adversity, however, and was entered on the National Register of Historic Places in 1979. An old slave cabin still stands just behind the house. Visitors will also be impressed by the spiral staircase at the rear of the central hall, said to be one of the finest in the state. The Ashland–Belle Helene grounds include cypress swamps, and the plantation has been used for filming several movies.

Bagatelle sits on the east bank, curled up in a sharp curve of the river near Sunshine, below Baton Rouge. The planation home was originally located near the Sunshine Bridge (close to Darrow, downriver), but was transported by barge in the late 1970s to its current site.

Belle Alliance, near Donaldsonville on the east bank of Bayou Lafourche, was built in 1846 for Belgian aristocrat Charles Kock. The Kock family lived there until 1915, building a sugarcane plantation that at one time spread over 7,000 acres. The thirty-three-room Greek Revival mansion features double galleries all around, with an unusual stairway on the front facade that allows access to the upstairs gallery. Decorative ironwork is featured on the gallery balustrades and stairway.

Bocage, near Darrow on the Mississippi's east bank, was built in 1801 by Marius Pons Bringier as a wedding gift for his daughter, Françoise, and her fiancé, Christoph Columb of Carbeille, France. Columb was said to be a relative of Christopher Columbus. Bringier was either unusually generous to his children or exceedingly glad they were getting married—he also built the nearby L'Hermitage as a wedding gift for his son.

An 1837 fire spurred extensive remodeling, under the direction of architect James Dakin, who also designed many New Orleans homes and the Old State Capitol in Baton Rouge. The two-story home features eight square, plastered-brick columns across the front facade, with the two innermost pillars considerably smaller than the other six. The plantation's name, Bocage, translates to "shady retreat" in French.

The Cottage, on the east bank a few miles downriver from Baton Rouge, was a magnificent twenty-two-room mansion constructed in 1823. The house had two-story Doric columns and two-foot-thick brick walls on the ground floor. Like so many of its River Road neighbors, The Cottage was built as a wedding gift, for Frances and Frederick Conrad. But after a happy beginning, years filled with parties and entertaining, The Cottage entered a period of great sadness.

During the Civil War, Federal soldiers arrested and imprisoned Frederick Conrad and occupied the great mansion, at one time using it as a hospital for wounded troops. Henry Holt, Conrad's personal secretary, also was arrested and tossed into a Federal prison. Mr. Conrad died in prison, and after the war, Henry Holt returned to live at the empty Cottage, where he died in 1880.

In the twentieth century, The Cottage was restored and used as the site for several movies, including *Band of Angels*, starring Clark Gable. The Cottage burned in 1960, but its columns and brick walls still stand as testament to the great house that once graced the spot. Some say the columns aren't all that stayed—neighbors and visitors have reported seeing the ghost of Henry Holt prowling the grounds, and hearing the unearthly strains of invisible musicians, with unseen guests twirling in a flurry of prewar bliss.

Evergreen, near Edgard on the west bank of the Mississippi, is considered one of the finest remaining plantation compounds in the state. The architect and exact date of completion are unknown, but "best guess" estimates date it about 1830, when Michel Pierre Becnel married Desirée Brou. The couple's descendants held on to the land for some six decades, building an expansive, prosperous sugar plantation.

The Evergreen grounds include the Greek Revival mansion, guest houses lining a double garden, and a double row of slave cabins. Eight unbroken Doric columns extend from ground to roof on the main house, and a graceful double-curved staircase extends from the upper gallery to the ground on the front facade. The house is topped by a delicate belvedere, flanked by twin chimneys. In 1946, following years of deterioration, Evergreen was purchased by Matilda Geddings Gray, who began the meticulous restoration. Mrs. Gray's descendants continue to maintain the home in pre–Civil War elegance and style.

Felicity Plantation Home, near Vacherie (close to Oak Alley) on the west bank of the river, was built by Valcour Aime as a wedding gift (another proud papa!) to his daughter, Felicité Emma, and her spouse, Septime Fortier. The Greek Revival mansion, built of native cypress, features six wooden columns supporting a gabled, slanting roof adorned with dormer windows.

Felicity changed owners several times from 1873 to the 1890s, when it became the property of Saturnine Waguespack. Felicity and the next-door St. Joseph Plantation were combined in 1901 to form the St. Joseph Plantation and Manufacturing Co. Waguespack family descendants still live at Felicity.

Forest Home, near Plaquemine and the west bank of the Mississippi, was built about 1830. The quaint two-story home, fabricated of native cypress wood, is elevated about three feet from ground level by a foundation of handmade bricks and features a steeply pitched roof. Virginian John Randolph grew cotton at Forest Home until his fortunes allowed the family to move in 1859 to a new, considerably grander home, Nottoway, several miles downriver.

Federal troops "visited" Forest Home during the Civil War, encountering only Mrs. Randolph and her daughters—Mr. Randolph had taken the best furniture, silver, and slaves to Texas for safety until the war was over (one has to wonder if he considered the well-being of his silver paramount to his wife and children). The Yankees took food and cattle from Forest Home, but did no damage to the home or its occupants.

Glendale, in Lucy on the River Road's east bank, was built in 1805–7 by David Pain and his wife, Françoise Bossier. It changed hands many times in the 1800s, and was purchased by the Lanaux family in 1922. The Lanauxs, who also owed an Esplanade Avenue mansion in New Orleans, furnished Glendale with antiques and restored it to its original beauty.

The French Colonial house, similar in style to Destrehan and Ormond, is two rooms deep, with front and back galleries and a window between each front and back room. This clever detail allows refreshing cross-ventilation even if the doors are closed. Glendale, still a productive sugarcane plantation, remains in the Lanaux family.

L'Hermitage, near Darrow on the east bank, was constructed in 1812–14 on land owned by Marius Pons Bringier, who gave the property to his son and daughter-in-law, Michel Doradou Bringier and Louise Elizabeth DuBourg, as a nuptial gift. Michel's place in history was secured in January 1815, when he fought under General Andrew Jackson at the Battle of New Orleans. Following the war, Jackson visited the Bringiers at their riverside home, inspiring Michel to name his plantation after Jackson's Nashville home.

L'Hermitage and its owner survived the War of 1812 unscathed, but the next war brought devastation. The plantation was confiscated and damaged by the Union army in 1863 during the Civil War, but the Bringiers returned and rebuilt during Reconstruction. The building reflects the Greek Revival style that became popular during the early 1800s, with massive Doric columns and a steep roof with dormer windows. Another restoration took place in the early 1960s, and L'Hermitage is now listed on the National Register of Historic Places.

Homeplace-Keller House, near Hahnville on the west bank of the river, was built by the Fortier family around 1801. The French Colonial raised cottage, now unoccupied, boasts sixteen-foot-wide galleries on all sides, with round-brick columns on the ground floor and thin wooden colonettes above. The austerity of the sharply slanting roof is offset by simple, pretty dormer windows. Exterior scenes for the film *Interview With the Vampire*, depicting a rowdy riverside tavern, were shot at Homeplace in the fall of 1993.

Indian Camp, near Carville on the east bank of the river, was built in the late 1850s. In 1894, Dr. Isadore Dyer of Tulane University Medical School leased the plantation home to open a treatment center for Hansen's disease (leprosy). In November 1894, Dr. Dyer and his patients made the eighty-five-mile trip up the river from New Orleans on a coal barge. The manor house was in a state of decay, so the patients initially lived in slave quarters.

Indian Camp was purchased by the State of Louisiana in 1896 for the Louisiana State Leprosarium. In 1921, the U.S. government purchased the center, and it now houses the National Center for the Treatment of Hansen's Disease.

Longwood, built in 1803, is on the east bank near Baton Rouge. The house may have been named to honor Napoleon Bonaparte; Longwood also was the name of the house to which the French leader was sent in exile. The rear section of the house was added in 1835.

Magnolia Lane, near Westwego on the west riverbank (two miles downriver from the 310 bridge), was built about 1784 for Edward Fortier and originally was called Fortier Plantation. It faces the Mississippi River's Nine Mile Point, so dubbed for its distance by water from Canal Street in New Orleans. Magnolia Lane was bought in 1867 by the Naberschnig family, who renamed it for the exquisite trees growing on the property.

The French Colonial–West Indies style dwelling is constructed of brick and cypress, with a double-pitched roof dotted with dormer windows. The Magnolia Lane house still contains more than 800 panes of original glass in the windows and doors. Magnolia Lane, used in the twentieth century as a nursery, was the first plantation in Louisiana to grow orange trees and strawberries.

Magnolia Mound, at 2161 Nicholson Drive in Baton Rouge, is tucked between the Louisiana State University campus and the downtown business area. The circa-1791 raised cottage, one of the oldest wooden buildings in Louisiana, was built on the cotton and indigo plantation of John Joyce. After his death, his widow remarried and she and her new husband, Armand Allard Duplantier, extensively remodeled and restored the home during the early 1800s.

Magnolia Mound nestles comfortably atop a natural ridge, safely above the Mississippi River floodplain. Its walls were constructed of *bousillage* (a nasty-looking mixture of mud and Spanish moss between cypress studs). Its side-by-side rooms, lacking hallways, are typical of the period. The house was saved from demolition in the late 1960s and is now listed on the National Register of Historic Places.

Mount Hope, at 8151 Highland Road in Baton Rouge, was built on a 400-acre parcel of land granted by the Spanish government to Joseph Sharp. The German-born Sharp, who acquired his land in 1786, built Mount Hope in 1817 in what became known as the Dutch Highlands area of the state. As in many parts of the United States, Germans in Louisiana often were called Dutch because of confusion with the word *Deutsche*, for "German."

Mount Hope was painstakingly restored in the 1970s and furnished with mid-1800s antiques. The raised-cottage farmhouse features a hipped roof and recessed galleries on the front and sides. "Nineteenth-Century Christmas" tours are offered each December by the current owners.

Mulberry Grove, near Donaldsonville on the west bank, is easy to miss, nearly obscured from view by oak trees and foliage. It was built in 1836 as the manor house for a 700-acre plantation tract. Mulberry Grove was one of several plantation properties bought by John B. Reuss later in the 1800s, which were operated together as the Germania Plantation.

The Mulberry Grove part of the land was inherited by one of Reuss's daughters, who sold it in the 1950s to Mrs. C. C. Clifton. The lovely plantation home was being used for hay storage when Mrs. Clifton began a yearlong restoration. The three-story house sports a steeply pitched roof and wide galleries on both floors at front and back.

Palo Alto, near Donaldsonville on the west bank of Bayou Lafourche, was constructed about 1850 and bought in 1852 by Pierre

Oscar Ayraud and his wife, Rosalie Rodriguez. Palo Alto, which in Spanish means "high tree," and the adjacent St. Emma Plantation were the site of several Civil War battles, in which Confederate forces beat the Yankees to the tune of some 465 casualties on the Union side.

The one-and-a-half-story house is lifted about four feet above the ground by brick piers. A twelve-foot-wide gallery sits beneath the gabled roof and dormer windows. Palo Alto, set on lavishly landscaped grounds, remained a productive sugarcane plantation well into the late twentieth century.

Judge Poché Plantation House, in Convent on the Mississippi's east bank, was built for Judge Felix Pierre Poché in about 1870. Seven years later, Poché gained national recognition as a founder of the American Bar Association. The judge moved to New Orleans in 1880, but the plantation remained his summer home until 1892, when it was sold.

Poché did a tremendous service to future historians through his Civil War diary, copies of which can be purchased at the house. The dwelling, in a distinct departure from the West Indies and Greek Revival dominance of remaining plantation homes, reflects the Victorian Renaissance Revival style popular in the late 1800s. The house sports nine-foot galleries on three sides, a kitchen wing, and an upper half-story set under a gabled roof. A brick-and-wood cistern sits at the rear of the home. The interior is light and airy, featuring fourteen-foot ceilings and the original *faux-bois*, or painted false wood grain, in the dining room.

St. Emma, on the west bank of Bayou Lafourche, was built circa 1854 by Charles A. Kock, a sugar grower who owned several area plantations. In 1862 and 1863, St. Emma and neighboring Palo Alto were the site of several Civil War conflicts, and Confederate troops were quartered in the sugar houses of both plantations. The raised cottage features wide central hallways on both floors, with main living quarters upstairs.

St. Joseph Plantation House (also called Josephine House), near Vacherie on the Mississippi's west bank (between Felicity and Oak Alley), was built circa 1820 by Cazamie Bernard Mericq, a native Frenchman. Double outdoor stairways grace the lower rear gallery, typical of West Indies architecture. The open ground floor was enclosed in the late 1850s or 1860s by Alexis Ferry, who had purchased the home from Mericq's widow. Joseph Waguespack bought the plantation following the Civil War.

St. Louis Plantation, near Plaquemine on the west bank of the Mississippi, was built in 1858 by Edward James Gay, who had come to Louisiana from St. Louis. Gay, who was the first president of the Louisiana Sugar Exchange of New Orleans, escaped fighting in the Civil War due to bad health. His son, however, served in the Confederate army.

The unusually lovely exterior of St. Louis sports six Ionic columns on the first floor gallery and six fluted Corinthian columns on the upper gallery. The balustrades on both galleries are of lacy cast-iron filigree. Unlike the "musical owners" game seen by many plantation homes, St. Louis has remained in the Gay family since its construction.

Tally-Ho, near Plaquemine on the west bank, was built in the early 1800s in typical colonial style—brick construction for the lower floor, cypress for the upper levels. Five simple brick columns support the galleries. The plantation received its smile-evoking name from the Murrells of Lynchburg, Virginia, who bought the plantation in 1848 and whose descendants have remained ever since.

A couple of wonderfully unique restaurants lie along the River Road. On the east bank, **The Cabin**, near Burnside, was constructed from slave cabins off of three local plantations. The restaurant specializes in seafood, steak, and Cajun cuisine.

Lafitte's Landing Restaurant lurks just off the River Road at the Sunshine Bridge near Donaldsonville. The building originally was the manor house of Viala Plantation. It was moved from its River Road site more than thirty years ago and converted to the restaurant, which tempts hungry visitors with Creole and Cajun specialties. Jean Pierre Lafitte, who some claim was the son of pirate Jean Lafitte, married Marie Emma Viala in this building when it was the Viala manor house.

(More restaurant information is included in the Plantation Homes section of chapter 7.)

For those attracted by the possibility of ghostly inhabitants, one other plantation home bears mentioning although it's a good ways from New Orleans and not on the River Road. **The Myrtles**, on Highway 61 near St. Francisville (north of Baton Rouge), has earned a reputation as "America's most haunted house." It even has a sign outside its gates proudly proclaiming that distinction.

St. Francisville sits in the midst of "English Louisiana," the area settled by English colonists who arrived when this was still Spanish territory. The Myrtles was built in the late 1790s for General David Bradford, who was one of George Washington's officers in the American Revolution.

The house may have been built over a sacred Indian burial site, which, as anyone who has seen *Poltergeist* knows, doomed it as cursed for anyone daring to build there. When Bradford died in 1818, he left the plantation (apparently unhaunted to that point) to his daughter, Sarah Mathilde, and son-in-law, Judge Clarke Woodruffe.

A nasty story of punishment and revenge ensued. Judge Woodruffe disciplined an eavesdropping slave, Chloe, by cutting off one of her ears; she exacted revenge by poisoning a birthday cake with oleander juice. The judge's wife, Sarah, and two of their daughters died from the deadly confection. The plantation's other slaves, horrified by what Chloe had done, hanged her from a tree and tossed her body in the river.

Chloe's ghost has been frequently spotted; you can tell it's her by the scarf she wears to hide the scar of her missing ear. Two spectral girls, presumably the doomed Woodruffe's daughters, also have been seen. Other ghosts (as many as ten have been identified) may include Union soldiers, a murdered attorney, and a couple of stabbing victims. Ghostly piano playing and crying babies also have been reported.

For the truly intrepid, The Myrtles offers year-round bed-and-breakfast accommodations, mystery weekends (reenactments of the murders that have occurred on the premises), and ghost tours.

Bayou St. John and Downriver

Anne Rice imitated the simple, West Indies style of **Pitot House**, at 1440 Moss Street on Bayou St. John in New Orleans, in creating her fictional Pointe du Lac, the plantation home of Louis and Lestat before they flee to the French Quarter. The house earned another notch as an

The West Indies–style Pitot House, constructed in the late 1700s, was one of Rice's models for Pointe du Lac, the indigo plantation in *Interview*. Several interior scenes for the movie version of *Interview* were filmed here.

Anne Rice sight when it was used for filming several interior scenes in the *Interview* movie. The bayou itself also is mentioned in the *Vampire Chronicles*, usually by its French name of Bayou St. Jean.

Pitot House is about a 10-minute northwesterly jaunt from the French Quarter, near City Park. This two-century-old house, although virtually surrounded by residential development, still retains an expansive, country feeling—standing on the upper gallery, gazing out over the azure waters of the bayou and relishing the fresh breeze that floats off the water, it's disarmingly easy to slip into an eighteenth-century frame of mind. Bring on those mint juleps!

This area along Bayou St. John was settled at least a decade before Bienville founded La Nouvelle Orleans on the Mississippi River. French settlers from Mobile, Alabama, received land grants along Bayou

St. John as early as 1708, although most of them left within a few years, defeated by the unfamiliar and somewhat hostile climate.

A few sturdy individuals stuck it out, though, and a small plantation community flourished along the bayou. In 1799, Santiago Bautista Lorreins sold a bayou-edge parcel of his planation to Don Bartholemé Bosque, a New Orleans merchant and ship owner. Bosque already owned a New Orleans townhouse, at 619 Chartres Street, on the same site where the disastrous fire of 1788 began.

Bosque's country home along Bayou St. John was designed in typical colonial style of the time—mimicking the West Indies houses that had proven appropriate to the humid, tropical environment. The house had three rooms across the front, all opening onto the wide gallery. Two smaller rooms, called *cabinets* (pronounced "cabee-nays"), were built at either end at the back, with a smaller, recessed gallery between them. Ground-floor walls were plastered brick, as were the columns. Upper floor walls are bricks-between-posts. The overall style is a mixture of French Colonial and West Indies, with the French contributing the large downstairs columns and smaller colonettes upstairs, and the West Indies influence seen in the high ceilings and spacious, ventilating galleries.

Typical of the era, the family's main living quarters were upstairs, reached by way of an outdoor stairway in the back gallery. The center room on the ground floor was used as a dining room; others served as offices, pantry, and storage area. For safety reasons, the kitchen was in a separate outbuilding away from the main house. Upstairs, the central room served as the parlor, and other rooms were family bedrooms.

Myrna Bergeron, director of Pitot House for the Louisiana Landmarks Society, seemed amused by some of the changes made to the home's interior during the filming of *Interview*. "Here we have this very simple, West Indies house, and they're bringing in all this ornate Louis XVI furniture," she said with a laugh. The lovely nineteenth-century piano in the upstairs parlor was replaced by yet another nineteenth-century piano, apparently deemed more appropriate by the moviemakers for Claudia's music lessons. Bergeron said the *Interview* company was "wonderful to work with," but she did get a bit nervous about all those candles burning in a house constructed largely of wood.

The possibly haunted master bedroom at Pitot House. One of the house's mistresses died after giving birth to twins, probably in this bedroom. An unidentifiable, sweet scent sometimes drifts through the air here.

Bergeron gives a lively, engrossing tour of the house, tossing in fascinating tidbits from her years working there. She has displayed her own historic items at the house, including several intriguing morsels from her collection of mourning memorabilia. If gently pressed, Bergeron also will confide a few tales sure to entertain and captivate Anne Rice fans—Pitot House, it seems, may have retained some . . . er, essence . . . of its

The ground-floor dining room at Pitot House. The *punkah* fan above the table was pulled by a servant child with an attached rope, shooing flies away during family meals.

former occupants. While on a private tour researching this book, with only me and Bergeron in the house, we had passed through the office and dining room and were standing in the pantry. We both distinctly heard a door open, as though someone had come into the office. Bergeron left me for a moment to check; no one was there.

She said a feminine, floral scent is frequently noticed in the dining room and master bedroom. "We have ladies' teas sometimes in the dining room, and someone will often ask me what kind of potpourri we use, because the scent is so nice," Bergeron said. "But we don't have any

The upstairs parlor at Pitot House, where several scenes from *Interview* were filmed.

potpourri. And other people won't smell it at all." A psychic once visited the house, and became visibly disturbed in the master bedroom—probably the same room in which Mrs. James Pitot died after giving birth to twin daughters, both of whom also died soon after.

The name of Pitot House's builder has been lost to time, but speculation points to Hilaire Boutté, a well-known New Orleans builder of the period. Boutté's work included a building that is now part of Le Petit Théâtre du Vieux Carré in the French Quarter. Whether or not he actually built Pitot House, he is recorded as having done remodeling work on the home for a subsequent owner.

Pitot House's first master did not linger long on the bayou—Bosque sold the plantation in less than a year to Joseph Reynes, one of his Chartres Street neighbors, for the relatively small sum of $1,525. Bosque's daughter Susanne, who spent her toddler years at Pitot House, became the third wife of William C. C. Claiborne, Louisiana's first American governor. Bosque didn't live to see this wedding, however; Susanne married in 1812, two years after her father had died.

Joseph Reynes expanded his plantation holdings by purchasing land behind Pitot House. In 1805, Reynes sold the land and home to Marie Rillieux, wealthy widow of Vincent Rillieux, who owned a good deal of prime French Quarter real estate. Marie's granddaughter, Marie Celestine de Gas, was the mother of French Impressionist Edgar Degas. Madame Rillieux substantially remodeled and added to Pitot House, probably including the construction of the south gallery. When she sold the house in April 1810, it looked much as it does today.

Pitot House's next owner was its present-day namesake, James Pitot, a native Frenchman who had prospered in the sugar industry in Saint-Domingue until the slave uprisings of 1792. After a brief return to France, he immigrated to the United States and became an American citizen. Perhaps in deference to his adopted country, Pitot changed the pronunciation of his name from the French "pea-toe" to the more American-sounding "pea-tot." After a short while in Philadelphia, Pitot and his family arrived in New Orleans in August 1796, via Bayou St. John, where they would one day make their home.

Pitot eventually became president of Orleans Navigation Co. and was elected to the Spanish Cabildo as ward commissioner. The goal of the Orleans Navigation Co. was to create a complete Mississippi River–to–Lake Pontchartrain waterway, from the lake to Bayou St. John, which connected to Carondelet Canal and then on to the river via Canal Street. That ambitious aim never materialized, however, and the most water Canal Street ever saw was after a hard rain. (Too bad one of Rice's Mayfair Witches couldn't have died nearby; perhaps the resultant storm would have created the longed-for canal.)

In 1804, following the Louisiana Purchase, Pitot became a member of the New Orleans Municipal Council and the city's first elected mayor. Pitot and his family lived at 630 Royal Street near St. Peter, in a house that no longer stands. He and his partner, Jean Lanthois, also owned lots at the corner of Burgundy and Toulouse (part of the old St. Peter Cemetery), where they built warehouses.

As mayor, Pitot instigated vast improvements in his newly American city, establishing a mounted patrol for the town's unruly sectors and ferry services on the Mississippi, as well as improving hospital service and building city schools. He also started pavers to work on New Orleans' treacherously muddy streets and ordered an 1805 census that showed a total population of 8,475. Despite his accomplishments, however, Pitot resigned after less than two years in office to turn his attentions back to his own business.

Pitot bought the house on Bayou St. John, along with thirty acres of land, from Madame Rillieux in 1810, and apparently he and his family enjoyed the country life more than they expected, for they soon moved into it full-time and leased, then sold, the Royal Street residence. In 1813, he sold the bayou house to two investors, who subsequently sold it to the Bank of Louisiana. The Pitot family, however, remained as occupants of the house until 1819.

Pitot and his first wife, Marie Jeanne Marty, had four children, all New Orleans natives, before moving out to Bayou St. John. Five years after moving to Pitot House, in November 1815, Marie Jeanne gave birth to twin girls. She died in the process, probably in the master bedroom with the unidentifiable feminine scent. Marie's babies fared little better than their mother—one little girl died in December; her sister followed in January. In July of that year, James Pitot married Geneviève-Sophie Nicolas, and the couple had two more children. Both Sophie-Gabrielle-Marie, born in 1817, and Henri-François, born in 1819, probably came into the world at Pitot House. In June 1819, just three days before the birth of Henri-François, the house was sold by the Bank of Louisiana. The Pitots then moved back to the French Quarter, purchasing a home at Bourbon and Hospital (Gov. Nicholls) streets. Pitot died there in 1831.

Other nineteenth-century owners of Pitot House included Albin Michel, whose family lived there from 1819 to 1848. Felix Ducayet purchased the house in 1848, becoming a successful hog and poultry breeder. In 1854, he placed a six-page ad in *Cohen's New Orleans Directory*. "Choice pigs only are sold, and are carefully cooped before shipment, if desired," the ad expounded. Purchasers could also put their pig on a leash, one presumes. Ducayet was the industrious sort; at the same time he was thriving in the pig-and-poultry trade, he also worked as a deputy storekeeper in the new Canal Street customhouse, which was built in 1849.

Despite being the nineteenth-century version of a workaholic, Ducayet fell on hard times in the mid-1850s, and the Bayou St. John property was seized and sold in 1857. It was bought by Paul Joseph

Gleises, whose wife was Marie Ducayet, either a daughter or sister of Felix, and Felix continued to live there. The home's roof was substantially altered, probably during the Ducayet years. Among other modifications, three dormer windows were added, two in front and one in the rear.

In 1858, the home was bought by Jean Louis Tissot, whose son Aristée Louis served the Confederate army in the Civil War and fought at Vicksburg. After the war, the younger Tissot and his new bride bought a house adjacent to his parents' Bayou St. John home. This other dwelling had been built about 1800, in a similar style to Pitot House.

The younger Tissot's house and land were sold to Columbia Brewing Co. in 1903, which may have planned to establish a brewery on the site. Instead, the property was sold again in 1905, this time to Mother Frances Xavier Cabrini. In 1904, Mother Cabrini had purchased Pitot House and its accompanying land from Joseph Steckler, a nursery–poultry farm operator.

Mother Cabrini had founded the Missionary Sisters of the Sacred Heart in 1891 and had established schools and an orphanage in the Vieux Carré. A new orphanage at 3400 Esplanade Avenue opened in 1906, and in 1959, that building was converted to Cabrini High School, established by the Missionary Sisters of the Sacred Heart. In the 1930s, Pitot House and the adjacent Tissot House on Moss Street were connected by a covered walkway and served as a convent for the nuns of the order. Mother Cabrini, who died in 1917, was canonized in 1946, the first American citizen declared a saint by the Roman Catholic Church.

Interestingly, Pitot House has a twentieth-century twin, a nearly identical structure at the corner of Moss and St. Ann streets. Before using the Pitot House as part of its convent, the religious order had briefly rented out the house. The last tenants were the Pollatsex-Reynolds family, including a blind family member who had become quite accustomed to maneuvering around the house. When the family moved out to accommodate the nuns, they built an exact replica of Pitot House so that their blind relative would still feel at home. The elegant mantel in the upstairs parlor of Pitot House was removed at this time and given by the sisters to the Pollatsexes as a token of the original house.

In 1963, the Sisters of the Sacred Heart made plans for a new high school building on the Pitot-Tissot site, which would require that both historic houses be demolished. The Louisiana Landmarks Society stepped in, trying to preserve the two historically significant buildings. The nuns offered to donate both buildings to either the city or the Landmarks Society, with the stipulation that the buildings must be removed from the property.

The Society, with no alternative, did what they could afford— saved Pitot House—but Tissot House was doomed. Pitot House was painstakingly taken apart, moved a few hundred feet down Bayou St. John, then put back together like a giant jigsaw puzzle by loving, careful hands. The first-floor brick masonry walls could not be moved and were replaced at the new site with brick and concrete blocks. Restoration of Pitot House included installation of a duplicate of the mantle which had been taken to Pollatsex House. The roof also was restored in its original style, without the dormer windows. Hurricane Betsy, ripping through the city in September 1965, blew away the old slates that were to be used on the roof, making it necessary to use asphalt shingles instead. The work of the Louisiana Landmarks Society was rewarded in 1971, when Pitot House was placed on the National Register of Historic Places.

Several other historically significant homes have survived in the Bayou St. John area. **The Sanctuary**, at 924 Moss Street, was built sometime between 1816 and 1822. The land was acquired by Louis Antoine Blanc in the 1790s, then sold to his son, Evariste Blanc, who is the first documented resident of the house. The younger Blanc built another house along the bayou, selling The Sanctuary to the city in 1834. The Sanctuary was used as an orphanage and school until the 1970s. The building was named a New Orleans Historic District Landmark in 1984.

The **Old Spanish Custom House**, at 1300 Moss, originally was part of the land granted to Antoine Rivard de la Vigne and other settlers in 1708. The French Colonial–style house probably was built or remodeled sometime after 1807. Robert Alexander, who had built the first U.S. Custom House in 1807–9 on Canal Street (same site as the current Custom House), also built the Bayou St. John bridge about this time. Alexander had demolished the old Spanish customhouse (behind the Canal Street site), and speculation is that he may have designed the house at 1300 Moss, using materials left over from the old customhouse (hence the Moss Street house's nickname). The house was named a New Orleans Historic District Landmark in 1984.

The **Evariste Blanc House**, at 1342 Moss Street, was built about 1834 for Evariste Blanc (who had previously lived at The Sanctuary farther up the bayou). This house retains some West Indies influence, but also reflects the classic revival elements that were becoming so popular throughout New Orleans at this time. The home remained in the Blanc family until 1905, then was donated to the Roman Catholic Church. The church has used it as a rectory for the Our Lady of the Most Holy Rosary Roman Catholic Church, which is adjacent on Esplanade Avenue.

The **Christoval Morel House**, at 1347 Moss Street, is a one-and-a-half-story Greek Revival house built in the 1840s. It was named a New Orleans Historic District Landmark in 1978.

Another historically intriguing site near New Orleans, and easily accessible by riverboat, is **Chalmette Battlefield**, where General Andrew Jackson staged his explosive finale to the War of 1812. A Battle of New Orleans Festival takes place annually at Chalmette, on the weekend closest to January 8, the date in 1815 when the American forces beat the British to a bloody pulp in the last battle of the last war ever fought between the two countries. British casualties exceeded 2,000, including Major General Sir Edward Pakenham, commander of the British forces. The Americans reported fewer than twenty dead.

Chalmette, now a unit of Jean Lafitte National Historical Park, is six miles downriver from New Orleans. Many of the passenger boats leaving from docks near the French Quarter stop at Chalmette (see the list in chapter 7). The battlefield also is accessible by car—take St. Bernard Highway (State Highway 46) east to Chalmette; the highway passes directly in front of the park. A campground is available nearby, and a small picnic area is provided in the park.

At Chalmette, visitors will see the Chalmette Monument, the cornerstone for which was laid in January 1840, twenty-five years after the battle. Construction of the monument didn't begin until 1855, however, and wasn't completed until 1908. The Greek Revival home on the grounds, called Beauregard House, was built eighteen years after the Battle of New Orleans and is named for its last owner, Judge René Beauregard. Interestingly, this house was never part of a plantation; instead, it served as a country home for several prominent nineteenth-century families.

Chalmette National Cemetery, established in 1864, serves as the final resting place for Union soldiers who died in Louisiana in the Civil War, as well as veterans of the Spanish-American War, World Wars I and II, and Vietnam. Four soldiers who fought in the War of 1812 lie here, but only one participated in the Battle of New Orleans.

National park rangers conduct excellent tours of Chalmette Battlefield, bringing the clash of 180 years ago to such vivid life that you can almost see the smoke and smell the blood. If ghosts wander anywhere in Louisiana, visitors are almost certain to encounter one or two here. And they're probably British, so try to rein in any hint of a Southern drawl.

If you travel by riverboat to Chalmette, pay particular attention to the New Orleans side (east bank) of the river as you head downstream. Just below New Orleans, you can catch a quick glimpse of two unusual, identical houses that perch at the river end of Egania Street. The **Steamboat Houses**, distinguished by strands of wooden "pearls" draping the upper galleries and fanciful octagonal belvederes, were built by the Doullut family.

The first Steamboat House was built in 1875 by Milton P. Doullut, a riverboat pilot who had immigrated to New Orleans from France. Doullut wanted his home to look like the whimsically adorned steamboats that cruised the Mississippi River. Practical concerns were addressed by the spacious, airy interior of four rooms on each floor, dissected by a wide central hallway. Galleries and floor-length windows provide excellent ventilation. In 1912, Doullut's only child, Paul, paid tribute to his father's idea and built an identical house a block away.

Just a few miles farther downriver, you'll see a cluster of buildings on your left that look like red-brick houses fronted by plain white columns. This is **Jackson Barracks**, at 6400 St. Claude Avenue, a nineteenth-century military base that is still used. Many of the exterior scenes for *Interview* were filmed here, including the spectacular "French

Jackson Barracks viewed from the Mississippi River. The spectacular "French Quarter" fire in the film of *Interview* was shot here.

Quarter" fire that precedes Louis and Claudia's escape to Paris. Most riverboat narrators will point out Jackson Barracks on tours; if they don't, just ask.

Two other noteworthy plantation homes lie south of New Orleans on the River Road downriver of Chalmette Battlefield.

Kenilworth, in St. Bernard east of the Mississippi, may predate Destrehan Plantation, but its exact date of construction cannot be verified. Some sources date it as early as 1759. The charming house sits on equally fetching grounds, planted with lush oak, magnolia, and pecan trees. The land around Kenilworth was acquired through French and Spanish grants by Pierre Antoine Bienvenu, whose family lived there for decades. Legend has it that Kenilworth once served as a temporary capital for the French colony of Louisiana and that it was also the home of a Spanish governor at one time.

The house, constructed of native brick and cypress, is surrounded by twenty-four cement-covered brick columns, which taper inward toward the top of the ground floor. The second-floor gallery features much thinner, wooden colonettes. As with any self-respecting plantation home, Kenilworth has had its share of ghost stories. In one, a white-clad figure has been spotted hovering near the jasmine bushes during the full moon.

Mary, built toward the end of the eighteenth century, perches on the east bank River Road near Dalcour. Some sources date the construction of Mary, which is surrounded by especially lush grounds, as early as 1773. The West Indies–style home is surrounded by twenty-four Doric columns on the ground floor and tapered wooden colonettes above. The central chimney connects to all four fireplaces inside. The lower floor is constructed of plantation-made brick, and the upper portion is built of native cypress.

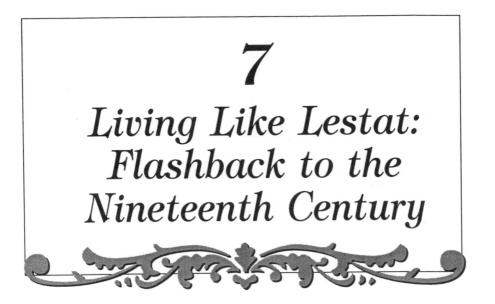

7

Living Like Lestat: Flashback to the Nineteenth Century

Opportunities abound in New Orleans to physically and emotionally lose oneself to the gentler rhythm of the eighteenth and nineteenth centuries or to mix a penchant for the past with a love of modern amenities. This chapter lists accommodations, restaurants, tours, and shopping venues. Historic sites are favored, although more modern choices also are included, for those whose love of nostalgia doesn't extend to sleeping arrangements. Prices are deliberately *not* listed, as they are subject to great fluctuation depending on season and specials. In general, New Orleans accommodations will generally run slightly less than comparable rooms in other large American cities; the hotel industry went crazy building for the 1984 World's Fair and was left with a glut of rooms.

General Information

Climate: The most comfortable times to visit New Orleans are spring and autumn, when the rain lessens a bit and the humidity isn't quite so stifling. Average temperatures from October to December are in the high fifties to low seventies; from March to May temps run from the low sixties to high seventies. Summer highs can soar into the mid and high nineties in July, August, and September—the same months that generally get five to six inches of rain. If you like your saunas al fresco, this is the time to visit. Whenever you visit, it's wise to carry an umbrella or light wrap with a hood; you'll almost certainly get rained on at least once.

Driving: Most major car rental companies have bureaus at New Orleans International Airport, but driving is not one of the city's charms. When it rains, the streets flood, and *quickly*. Left turns are forbidden at most major intersections, making New Orleans the land of the U-turn. If you absolutely must drive, be extremely careful about where you park; if you have the slightest indication or even intuition that you shouldn't park in a particular spot, *don't*. Police and meter readers are especially diligent in ticket writing and towing here. If you think your car has been towed, call (504) 565-7450 for information on how to retrieve it (and pray you have a trust fund handy). Large public parking lots for the French Quarter are located on Decatur Street near Jackson Brewery. In the Garden District and Uptown, on-street parking is generally available.

Public Transportation: The Regional Transit Authority (RTA) runs four tourism-related routes—the Riverfront Streetcar, St. Charles Streetcar, and shuttles in the Vieux Carré and along Magazine Street. Visi-Tour passes are available for unlimited one- or three-day use on all RTA routes. For fares, routes, and schedule information, call the RTA Ride Line at (504) 569-2700, twenty-four hours a day.

Taxicabs: At this writing, the standard fare from New Orleans International Airport to the downtown–French Quarter area is $21 for up to two people; $8 per person for three or more people. Meter fares within the city start at $1.70, plus 20 cents every one-fifth of a mile or forty seconds; 50 cents extra for each additional passenger. For taxi information, call the New Orleans Taxi Cab Bureau at (504) 586-4621.

Tourist Information: Greater New Orleans Tourist and Convention Commission, 1520 Sugar Bowl Drive, New Orleans, LA 70112; (504) 566-5011 or 566-5031. Publishes an excellent brochure with self-guided walking and driving tours.

Louisiana Department of Tourism, 1051 N. Third Street, Room 337, Baton Rouge, LA 70804; (800) 33-GUMBO.

Louisiana Office of Tourism Visitor Center, 529 St. Ann Street on Jackson Square; (504) 566-5031.

Accommodations

Bed-and-breakfast information: Bed and Breakfast Inc., 1021 Moss Street, Box 52257, New Orleans, LA 70152-2257; (504) 488-4640, (800) 749-4640.

New Orleans Accommodations and Bed and Breakfast Reservation Service, 671 Rosa Avenue, Suite 201, Metairie, LA 70005; (504) 838-0071 or 838-0072.

Southern Comfort Bed and Breakfast Reservation Service, 8300 Sycamore Place, New Orleans, LA 70118; (504) 861-0082, (800) 749-1928.

Central Business District

CLARION HOTEL NEW ORLEANS, 1500 Canal Street; (504) 522-4500, (800) 824-3359. Eighteen-story historic landmark hotel with 759 rooms. Free French Quarter shuttle, rooftop pool and hot tub, exercise room.

FAIRMONT HOTEL, University Place, 123 Baronne Street; (504) 529-7111, (800) 527-4727. Twelve-story, historic hotel one block from the French Quarter. Built in 1893, pool, rooftop tennis courts, three lounges and two restaurants. 660 rooms, 72 suites.

HOLIDAY INN CROWNE PLAZA, 333 Poydras Street; (504) 525-9444, (800) 522-6963. Near Riverwalk, Convention Center, and Superdome. Lounge, two restaurants, outdoor pool, exercise facilities. 439 rooms.

HOTEL INTER-CONTINENTAL NEW ORLEANS, 444 St. Charles Avenue; (504) 525-5566, (800) 332-4246. In the heart of the financial district, three blocks from the French Quarter. Twenty-four-hour room service, 480 rooms, 32 suites. Cast and crew of *Interview* bunked at this luxurious CBD hotel during filming in autumn of 1993.

HYATT REGENCY NEW ORLEANS, 500 Poydras Plaza; (504) 561-1234, (800) 233-1234. Five restaurants and lounges, including Top of the

Dome revolving rooftop restaurant and Hyttops Sports Bar. Outdoor pool, fitness center. Free shuttle to the French Quarter, Aquarium of the Americas, and riverfront. More than 1,000 rooms, 100 suites.

ITT SHERATON NEW ORLEANS HOTEL, 500 Canal Street; (504) 525-2500. Near the French Quarter and CBD. Fitness center, pool, three restaurants, and two lounges. More than 1,000 rooms, 53 suites.

LAFAYETTE HOTEL, 600 St. Charles Avenue; (504) 524-4441, (800) 733-4754. Small hotel with 44 rooms, including 20 suites. Five blocks from the French Quarter, on St. Charles Avenue streetcar line.

LA SALLE HOTEL, 1113 Canal Street; (504) 523-5831, (800) 521-9450. Small, 60-room hotel near the French Quarter and CBD.

LE MERIDIEN NEW ORLEANS, 614 Canal Street; (504) 525-6500, (800) 543-4300. Luxury, European-style hotel with health club, business center, pool, and jazz club. La Gauloise Restaurant, twenty-four-hour room service. Nearly 500 rooms, 7 suites.

LE PAVILLON HOTEL, 833 Poydras Street; (504) 581-3111, (800) 535-9095. Elegant, historic hotel near Superdome, St. Charles Avenue streetcar, riverfront attractions. Restaurant and lobby lounge, rooftop pool, and patio. 220 rooms and 7 suites.

NEW ORLEANS HILTON RIVERSIDE, Poydras at the Mississippi River; (504) 584-3848, (800) HILTONS. Adjacent to Hilton's Queen of New Orleans Riverboat Casino and Festival Marketplace. On the Riverfront streetcar line. Restaurants include Kabby's on the River, Kabby's Sports Edition bar, Pete Fountain's, and Horizons on the 29th floor. Two outdoor pools.

NEW ORLEANS MARRIOTT, 555 Canal Street; (504) 581-1000, (800) 228-9290. On the edge of the French Quarter, across the street from St. Charles Avenue streetcar line. 1,200 rooms, 54 suites.

THE PELHAM HOTEL, 440 Common Street; (504) 522-4444, (800) 659-5621. Small luxury hotel in heart of CBD. 60 rooms, all have marble baths.

RADISSON SUITE HOTEL NEW ORLEANS, 315 Julia Street; (504) 525-1993, (800) 333-3333. In warehouse/arts district. Near Convention

Center, Riverwalk, Aquarium of the Americas, and French Quarter. Restaurant, lounge, pool. 226 suites.

WESTIN CANAL PLACE, 100 Iberville Street; (504) 566-7006, (800) 228-3000. Deluxe hotel above Canal Place Shopping Center, on the upriver edge of the French Quarter. All rooms have marble baths, private bars, European appointments. 397 rooms, 41 suites.

WINDSOR COURT HOTEL, 300 Gravier Street; (504) 523-6000, (800) 262-2662. An AAA Five Diamond hotel (New Orleans's first and only to win this distinction). Five-star restaurant, swimming pool, health club. 58 rooms, 266 suites.

French Quarter/Downtown

THE BIENVILLE HOUSE, 320 Decatur Street; (504) 529-2345, (800) 535-7836. Small, intimate French Quarter hotel near Jackson Square and Café du Monde. Courtyard, pool, Chef Andrea's Anacapri Restaurant. 83 rooms and suites.

BOURBON ORLEANS HOTEL, 717 Orleans Street; (504) 523-2222, (800) 521-5338. Elegant English-European-style hotel on the site of the old Orleans Ballroom, directly behind St. Louis Cathedral and near Royal Street antique stores. Queen Anne furnishings, marble baths. 164 rooms, 47 suites.

BOURGOYNE GUEST HOUSE, 839 Bourbon Street; (504) 524-3621 or 525-3983. Restored 1830s Creole mansion with studio apartments and one- and two-bedroom suites overlooking French Quarter courtyard. All have private baths and kitchen facilities.

CASA DE MARIGNY CREOLE GUEST COTTAGES, 818 Frenchmen Street; (504) 948-3875. Faubourg Marigny near French Quarter. Five 1830–80 cottages surround pool area; all have kitchen facilities.

CHARTRES STREET HOUSE, 2517 Chartres Street; (504) 945-2339. An 1850 private home, located in historic Faubourg Marigny near the French Quarter. Garden and swimming pool, continental breakfast. 2 rooms.

CHATEAU LEMOYNE FRENCH QUARTER (Holiday Inn), 301 Dauphine Street; (504) 581-1303, (800) 522-6963. Pool, restaurant, lounge. 159 rooms, 12 suites.

CORNSTALK HOTEL, 915 Royal Street; (504) 523-1515. Built as a private home in the late 19th century, this Victorian mansion sits behind one of only two cornstalk-pattern iron fences in the city.

A CREOLE HOUSE, 1013 St. Ann Street; (504) 524-8076, (800) 535-7858. Century-old European-style hostelry with 18 rooms. Complimentary continental breakfast.

DAUPHINE ORLEANS HOTEL, 415 Dauphine Street; (504) 586-1800, (800) 521-7111. European-style luxury with accoutrements including courtyards, balconies, hair dryers, robes, safes in all rooms, guest library. Pets welcome. 98 rooms, 11 suites.

DAUZAT HOUSE, 1000 Conti Street; (504) 524-2075, (800) 272-2075. Lakeside edge of French Quarter. Courtyard and pool. All guests receive homemade amaretto in crystal decanters, fresh flowers, and champagne on arrival. Kitchen facilities, fireplaces in some suites. 8 suites.

DUFOUR-BALDWIN HOUSE, 1707 Esplanade Avenue; (504) 945-1503. Antebellum home listed on the National Historic Register. Six blocks from the French Quarter. 4 rooms.

THE FRENCHMEN, 417 Frenchmen Street; (504) 948-2166, (800) 831-1781. Two 1860s Creole townhouses, near the Old U.S. Mint and French Market. Complimentary continental breakfast. Pool, spa, off-street parking. 23 rooms, 2 suites, all have private baths.

FRENCH QUARTER MAISONETTES, 1130 Chartres Street; (504) 524-9918. French Quarter home built in 1820s, at the quiet end of the Quarter. 7 rooms.

GIROD HOUSE, 835 Esplanade Avenue; (504) 522-5214, (800) 544-8808. On the edge of the French Quarter. Built in 1833, Creole architecture, courtyard. 6 antique-furnished suites.

GRENOBLE HOUSE, 323 Dauphine Street; (504) 522-1331. Meticulously restored 19th-century townhouse. 17 suites.

HISTORIC FRENCH MARKET INN—A CLARION CARRIAGE HOUSE, 501 Decatur Street; (504) 561-5621, (800) 548-5148. Historic 18th-century building overlooking the Mississippi River, near French Market complex. Breakfast and cocktails included in rates. 68 rooms, 6 suites.

HOLIDAY INN FRENCH QUARTER, 124 Royal Street; (504) 529-7211, (800) HOLIDAY. Pool, restaurant, lounge. 224 rooms, 28 suites.

HOTEL CHATEAU DUPRE, 131 Decatur Street; (504) 569-0600, (800) 285-0620. Intimate 17-suite hotel three blocks from Bourbon Street. Complimentary continental breakfast and afternoon wine and cheese.

HOTEL DE LA POSTE, 316 Chartres Street; (504) 581-1200, (800) 448-4927. Renovated carriage-house rooms and suites, many with balconies overlooking the French Quarter or courtyard. Pool, Ristorante BACCO and bar, on-site valet parking. 87 rooms, 13 suites.

HOTEL MAISON DE VILLE AND THE AUDUBON COTTAGES, 727 Toulouse Street; (504) 561-5858, (800) 634-1600. Small luxury hotel featuring antique furnishings, continental breakfast. Bistro at Maison de Ville restaurant. 23 rooms, 7 cottages.

HOTEL STE. HELENE, 508 Chartres Street; (504) 522-5014, (800) 348-3888. Complimentary continental breakfast served in courtyard. 15 rooms, 8 suites, decorated in 18th-century style.

HOTEL ST. MARIE, 827 Toulouse Street; (504) 561-8951, (800) 366-2743. One-half block off Bourbon Street. Pool, courtyard, valet parking, valet laundry. Cafe Roux restaurant and bar. 93 rooms with traditional furnishings, most rooms have balconies.

HOTEL ST. PIERRE, 911 Burgundy Street; (504) 524-4401, (800) 225-4040. Eighteenth-century Creole slave quarters converted to guest rooms and suites. Two pools, balconies, complimentary continental breakfast and champagne happy hour.

HOTEL VILLA CONVENTO IN THE FRENCH QUARTER, 616 Ursulines Avenue; (504) 522-1793. European-style pensione, family-owned. Creole townhouse built in 1848; all rooms have private baths, some have balconies. Complimentary continental breakfast. 25 rooms.

THE HOUSE ON BAYOU ROAD, 2275 Bayou Road; (504) 945-0992 or 949-7711. Rural plantation atmosphere 11 blocks from the French Quarter. Just off Esplanade Avenue, this historic plantation house sits on two acres of land. Period antiques, private baths. 4 rooms.

THE INN ON BOURBON (BEST WESTERN), 541 Bourbon Street; (504) 524-7611, (800) 535-7891. Bourbon Street Cafeteria, Ivory's Sing-Along Piano Bar. Among the 184 rooms and 2 suites are 100 balcony rooms overlooking Bourbon and Toulouse.

LAFITTE GUEST HOUSE, 1003 Bourbon Street; (504) 581-2678, (800) 331-7971. Restored French manor house in the heart of the Quarter. Quiet, residential end of Bourbon Street. Complimentary continental breakfast, wine, and hors d'oeuvres. 13 rooms, 1 suite.

LA MOTHE HOUSE HOTEL, 621 Esplanade Avenue; (504) 947-1161, (800) 367-5858. Victorian double townhouse on edge of French Quarter. 11 rooms, 9 suites.

LANDMARK HOTEL FRENCH QUARTER, 920 N. Rampart Street; (504) 524-3333, (800) 535-7862. Traditional courtyard with pool, restaurant, lounge. 98 rooms, 1 suite.

LE RICHELIEU IN THE FRENCH QUARTER, 1234 Chartres Street; (504) 529-2492, (800) 535-9653. Decorated in the European tradition. Room service, concierge, free on-site parking. 69 rooms, 17 suites.

MAISON DUPUY HOTEL, 1001 Toulouse Street; (504) 586-8000, (800) 535-9177. Tropical courtyard, heated pool. Restaurant, lounge, valet parking, health club. 186 rooms, 11 suites.

MAISON ESPLANADE, 1244 Esplanade Avenue; (504) 523-8080, (800) 290-4BED. Restored 1846 home, walking distance to the French Quarter, private baths. 7 rooms, some with balconies.

MARIGNY GUEST HOUSE, 615 Kerlerec Street; (504) 944-9700. In Faubourg Marigny, one block downriver of Esplanade (edge of French Quarter). Circa-1890 house with 5 bedrooms, all with private baths and entrances. Continental breakfast, free parking.

MECHLINGS GUEST HOUSE, 2023 Esplanade Avenue; (504) 943-4131, (800) 725-4131. Historic 1860s mansion near French Quarter. 5 rooms with private baths.

MELROSE MANSION, 937 Esplanade Avenue; (504) 944-2255. Victorian mansion, circa 1884, completely restored with period furnishings. 4 rooms, 4 suites, free parking, heated pool. (Ask about the piano-playing ghost!)

THE MONTELEONE HOTEL, 214 Royal Street; (504) 523-3341, (800) 535-9595. Largest "full-service" hotel in the French Quarter. On-site parking, three restaurants, three lounges, rooftop pool, fitness center. 600 rooms, 35 suites.

NEW ORLEANS GUEST HOUSE, 1118 Ursulines Street; (504) 566-1177, (800) 562-1177. 1848 Creole cottage in the French Quarter, near Old Ursuline Convent. Period furnishings, continental breakfast served on patio daily. 14 rooms.

The Monteleone Hotel in the French Quarter.

Nine-O-Five Royal Hotel, 905 Royal Street; (504) 523-0219. Built in 1890s; courtyard and balconies overlooking Royal Street. Period furnishings. 10 rooms, 3 suites, kitchen facilities in all rooms.

Olivier House Hotel, 828 Toulouse Street; (504) 525-8456. Built as a townhouse in 1836, listed on National Historic Register. Pool, courtyards, high ceilings, antique furnishings. 28 rooms, 12 suites, kitchen facilities in some.

Omni Royal Orleans Hotel, 621 St. Louis Street; (504) 529-5333, (800) 843-6664. Built on the site of the historic St. Louis Hotel. Shares a corner with Brennan's and Antoine's restaurants, one block from Jackson Square and Bourbon Street. Rib Room, Esplanade Piano Bar, and LaRiviera rooftop lounge with a view of the Mississippi River. Fitness center.

P. J. Holbrook's Olde Victorian Inn, 914 N. Rampart Street; (504) 522-2446, (800) 725-2446. Restored 1840s home on lakeside edge of French Quarter, near St. Louis No. 1 Cemetery. 6 rooms with private baths, some have balconies or fireplaces.

Place d'Armes Hotel, 625 St. Ann Street on Jackson Square; (504) 524-4531, (800) 366-2743. Comprises six 18th-century French Quarter buildings surrounding a lush courtyard and pool. Complimentary continental breakfast, valet parking, valet laundry. 74 rooms, 8 suites.

Prince Conti French Quarter Hotel, 830 Conti Street; (504) 529-4172, (800) 366-2743. Historic 50-room European-style hotel, one-half block off Bourbon Street. Off-premise pool, on-site valet parking, valet laundry, and complimentary continental breakfast. Bombay Club restaurant and bar. 48 rooms, 2 suites.

Provincial Hotel, 1024 Chartres Street; (504) 581-4995, (800) 535-7922. Near Old Urusline Convent and Gallier House. Comprises several 19th-century buildings, 97 rooms and 10 suites furnished with period antiques, two swimming pools. Honfleur Bar & Restaurant. On-site parking. (One of the buildings is reputedly *extremely* haunted, with specters that enjoy fiddling with the electricity and plumbing fixtures.)

Quarter Esplanade Guest House, 719 Esplanade Avenue; (504) 948-9328. Greek Revival home within walking distance of the French Quarter. 5 rooms, 1 suite, all with modern kitchens and baths.

RATHBONE INN, 1227 Esplanade Avenue; (504) 947-2100, (800) 947-2101. Three-story restored 1850s mansion. 8 rooms, all with private baths and kitchenettes. Owned by Rue Royal Inn.

ROYAL BARRACKS GUEST HOUSE, 717 Barracks Street; (504) 529-7269. Renovated Victorian house at the quiet end of the Vieux Carré. Complimentary breakfast. 4 rooms, 1 suite.

ROYAL SONESTA HOTEL NEW ORLEANS, 300 Bourbon Street; (504) 586-0300, (800) SONESTA. Iron-laced balconies, courtyard patio, lounge, pool, Desire Oyster Bar. 465 rooms, 35 suites.

RUE ROYAL INN, 1006 Royal Street; (504) 524-3900, (800) 776-3901. 1830s Creole townhouse. All rooms have private bath; most have wet bars. 16 rooms, 1 suite.

ST. ANN MARIE ANTOINETTE HOTEL, 717 Conti Street; (504) 525-2300, (800) 535-9706. Quiet section of the French Quarter, private balconies, courtyard with pool, courtyard restaurant. 65 rooms.

ST. LOUIS HOTEL, 730 Bienville Street; (504) 581-7300, (800) 535-9706. Old-world charm in the heart of the Vieux Carré, rooms furnished with antiques. Louis XVI Restaurant. 71 rooms, 4 suites.

ST. PETER GUEST HOUSE, 1005 St. Peter Street; (504) 524-9232, (800) 535-7815. Early 1800s hotel with 17 rooms, 6 suites, all with private baths. Balconies, courtyard, antique furnishings.

THE SONIAT HOUSE, 1133 Chartres Street; (504) 522-0570, (800) 544-8808. Converted townhouse, built in 1830. Designated a Historic Hotel of America by the National Trust. Wrought-iron balconies, spiral staircases, courtyard, 24-hour concierge. Some suites have jacuzzis. 17 rooms, 7 suites.

SUN OAK INN BED AND BREAKFAST, 2020 Burgundy Street; (504) 945-0322. Faubourg Marigny near the French Quarter. Part of the circa-1836 Nathan-Lewis-Cizek Museum House and Creole Gardens. 2 rooms with private bath, share double parlor, kitchen, and patio.

URSULINE GUEST HOUSE, 708 Ursulines Avenue; (504) 525-8509, (800) 654-2351. 18th-century Creole cottage and slave quarters. Continental breakfast, wine served in courtyard every evening. 13 rooms, 1 suite.

Garden District/Uptown

AVENUE PLAZA HOTEL, 2111 St. Charles Avenue; (504) 566-1212, (800) 535-9575. Rooftop sundeck, courtyard pool, European-style health spa, all rooms have wet bars and refrigerators. 240 suites.

BEAU SÉJOUR, 1930 Napoleon Avenue; (504) 897-3746. Uptown bed-and-breakfast in a renovated turn-of-the-century mansion. Free parking. 4 rooms, 1 suite, private baths.

THE COLUMNS HOTEL, 3811 St. Charles Avenue; (504) 899-9308, (800) 445-9308. Stately turn-of-the-century mansion with 19 guest rooms furnished in period pieces. Some rooms have private baths or fireplaces. Complimentary continental breakfast and paper daily. Victorian Lounge European-style pub, complimentary light buffet served at cocktail hour. Outdoor lounge on downstairs gallery. On St. Charles Avenue streetcar line.

FAIRCHILD HOUSE, 1518 Prytania Street; (504) 524-0154, (800) 256-8096. Circa-1841 Greek Revival home in Lower Garden District. Continental breakfast and tea served daily. Free parking. 7 rooms, private baths.

GARDEN DISTRICT BED AND BREAKFAST, 2418 Magazine Street; (504) 895-4302. Each of the 4 private suites has its own separate entrance. Kitchen and patio.

MCKENDRICK-BREAUX HOUSE, 1474 Magazine Street; (504) 586-1700. Restored 1860s house in Lower Garden District. 2 rooms with private baths and courtyard entrances.

MARQUETTE HOUSE NEW ORLEANS INTERNATIONAL HOSTEL, 2253 Carondelet Street; (504) 523-3014. This 100-year-old home has a community kitchen, dining area, reading rooms, and laundry. One block from St. Charles Avenue streetcar line. 80 beds, both dorm-style and private. 12 suites with private bath and kitchen.

PARK VIEW GUEST HOUSE, 7004 St. Charles Avenue; (504) 861-7564. Built in 1884 as a hotel for the World Cotton Exchange Exposition of 1885. Many rooms overlook Audubon Park. On St. Charles Avenue streetcar line. Continental breakfast served on weekdays. 15 rooms with private baths, 10 with shared baths.

THE PONTCHARTRAIN HOTEL, 2031 St. Charles Avenue; (504) 524-0581, (800) 777-6193. Historic Garden District hostelry on St. Charles Avenue streetcar route. Caribbean Room, Cafe Pontchartrain, Bayou Bar, 24-hour room service and valet parking. Completely restored in 1992. 67 guest rooms and 35 suites.

PRYTANIA INNS, 1415, 2041, and 2127 Prytania Street; (504) 566-1515. Pre–Civil War group of buildings. Nearly 50 rooms total, some in converted slave quarters. One block to streetcar, free parking.

PRYTANIA PARK HOTEL, 1525 Prytania Street; (504) 524-0427, (800) 862-1984. Complimentary continental breakfast, free parking. 13 rooms in restored 1840s Victorian building, 49 in modern building.

ST. CHARLES GUEST HOUSE, 1748 Prytania Street; (504) 523-6556. Cozy European-style pension in Lower Garden District. One block to streetcar, some rooms have kitchenettes. Pool, patio, complimentary bakery breakfast. 23 rooms, 1 suite.

ST. CHARLES INN, 3636 St. Charles Avenue; (504) 899-8888. Complimentary continental breakfast and paper. 40 rooms, on streetcar line.

ST. VINCENT'S GUEST HOUSE, 1415 Prytania Street; (504) 566-1515. Restored orphanage that's been converted to a guest house. Gourmet breakfasts (extra), free parking.

SULLY MANSION, 2631 Prytania Street; (504) 891-0457. Queen Anne Victorian home built in 1890. Antiques mixed with modern furnishings. 5 rooms, 2 suites.

THE TERRELL HOUSE, 1441 Magazine Street; (504) 524-9859, (800) 878-9855. Restored 1858 mansion, furnished with period antiques. Three blocks to St. Charles Avenue streetcar. 6 rooms, 3 suites.

Cemetery Tours

Lakelawn Metairie Cemetery, 5100 Pontchartrain Boulevard; (504) 486-6331. Self-guided cassettes and maps are available for walking tours.

Magic Walking Tours; (504) 593-9693. St. Louis Cemetery No. 1 tours at 10:40 A.M. and 1:40 P.M. daily. Departs from Musée Conti, 917 Conti Street at Dauphine. Garden District Tours at 10:30 A.M. daily, including Lafayette Cemetery and Anne Rice's house (outside only). Reservations not needed.

New Orleans Historic Voodoo Museum, 724 Dumaine Street; (504) 523-7685. Guided, offbeat tours of St. Louis No. 1 Cemetery, with the opportunity to make your own X and wish on the tomb of voodoo queen Marie Laveau. Also offers a five-cemetery van tour every afternoon.

Save Our Cemeteries; (504) 588-9357. Nonprofit organization that has worked to preserve New Orleans's historic burial sites. Offers intriguing, well-researched tours of St. Louis No. 1 near the French Quarter and Lafayette No. 1 in the Garden District.

City Tours

The Friends of the Cabildo; (504) 523-3939. Walking tours of the French Quarter, departing from The Friends of the Cabildo Store at 523 St. Ann Street (Jackson Square).

Gay Nineties Carriages, 1824 N. Rampart Street; (504) 943-8820. Daily tours from 8:30 A.M. to midnight in authentic mule-drawn carriages. Board at Jackson Square or other French Quarter spots; half-hour history-based tours.

Gray Line of New Orleans; (504) 587-0861, (800) 535-7786. Several daily tours of New Orleans and environs, departing from behind Jackson Brewery. Also offers walking tours of the French Quarter and the Garden District, plantation tours, and swamp and bayou tours.

Helicopters Sun West Airways Inc.; (504) 242-4883. Bird's-eye view of the city, departing from the downtown heliport, near the Superdome.

Helicopters Unlimited; (504) 522-6434. Several tours from the downtown heliport—10- to 25-minute aerial explorations over downtown, Chalmette Battlefield, Mississippi River and Lake Pontchartrain, or Louisiana swamps. Nighttime tours give a vampire's-eye view.

Heritage Tours; (504) 949-9805. Walking tours of the French Quarter, focusing on literary personalities who have found inspiration in the city.

Hidden Treasures; (504) 529-4507. Daily tours of the Garden District and Lower Garden District. Motor tours at 10 A.M. with hotel pickup available; walking tours at 1:30 P.M. daily meet at The Rink, Washington at Prytania.

Jean Lafitte National Historic Park and Preserve, French Quarter Unit, 916 N. Peters Street; (504) 589-2636 or 589-3840. Park rangers guide intimate, historically centered walking tours of both the French Quarter and Garden District.

Magic Walking Tours; (504) 593-9693. Entertaining, offbeat tours with extremely well-informed guides. Voodoo Tour; Haunted House, Vampire and Ghost Hunt Tour; Cemetery Tour; Garden District and French Quarter tours. Participants in the evening Vampire and Ghost Hunt Tour receive garlic, stakes, prayer cards, and other "protection."

New Orleans Historic Voodoo Museum, 724 Dumaine Street; (504) 523-7685. French Quarter folklore tours visiting Pharmacy Museum, Congo Square, Marie Laveau's tomb, "Haunted House."

New Orleans Tours Inc., 4220 Howard Avenue; (504) 592-1991, (800) 543-6332. City and plantation tours; Night Life Tour for adults only.

Photo Tours, 724 Dumaine Street; (504) 522-2904. Specially designed for photographers—historic buildings, hidden courtyards, scenic galleries.

Preservation Resource Center, 604 Julia Street (Julia Row); (504) 581-7032. Nonprofit group offering architectural tours of various neighborhoods. Open weekdays only.

Steppin' Out Tours; (504) 488-6400. Three-hour morning city tour covers the Vieux Carré, Garden District, Central Business District. Afternoon tour also includes stop at Longue Vue House and Garden.

Tours by Inez; (504) 486-1123. Fairly intimate New Orleans and French Quarter tours daily. Reservations must be booked in advance.

Tours by Isabelle, PO Box 740972, New Orleans, LA 70174; (504) 391-3544. Personalized guided tours in small groups. City, plantation, and Cajun bayou tours offered.

U.S.A. Travel and Heritage Tours; (504) 523-7818. Well-researched historical tours focusing on black history.

Dining

Note: Dinner reservations are recommended at all but the most casual of New Orleans's eateries. Call ahead to be safe.

Antoine's, 713 St. Louis Street; (504) 581-4422. This is New Orleans's oldest restaurant, a haven of classic Creole cooking that has been setting the local dining tone for more than 150 years. Dessert recommendation: baked Alaska, or the savory bread pudding (a Friday-night-only specialty).

Arnaud's, 813 Bienville Street; (504) 523-5433. A New Orleans tradition since 1918, featuring six public and nine private dining rooms. Also has a fascinating on-site Mardi Gras Museum. "Sunday Brunch and Jazz" in the main dining room.

Bluebird Cafe, 3625 Prytania Street; (504) 895-7166. Casual, inexpensive, and extremely popular. Open for breakfast and lunch only; expect a line on weekend mornings. A terrific starting point for a day spent prowling the Garden District and Uptown. Especially recommended are the "build your own omelet" and butter pecan pancakes.

Brennan's, 417 Royal Street; (504) 525-9711. Spectacular outdoor courtyard as well as 12 elegant indoor dining areas. One of the city's favorite breakfast and brunch spots, with huge servings and attentive (not hovering) service. This is the place that invented Bananas Foster, so save room. Founded in 1946, located in the historic Morphy House.

Broussard's, 819 Conti Street; (504) 581-3866. Founded in 1920, one of New Orleans's perennial favorites. Lovely setting around a traditional Creole courtyard.

Café du Monde, 800 Decatur Street; (504) 525-4544. You won't need reservations, but you'll need a wet napkin to de-fleck yourself of the ubiquitous powdered sugar. Coffee with chicory, fluffy *beignets*, and unlimited atmosphere served 24 hours daily.

Cafe Rue Bourbon, 241 Bourbon Street; (504) 524-0114. Cajun-Continental cuisine in an historic setting; the building was constructed in 1831. Dining balcony overlooking Bourbon; Sunday champagne-jazz brunch.

Cafe Giovanni, 117 Decatur Street; (504) 529-2154. Culinary creativity in a comfy atmosphere.

Caribbean Room at The Pontchartrain, 2031 St. Charles Avenue; (504) 524-0581. Classic and contemporary Creole cuisine at its absolute best. Sunday brunch from 11 A.M. to 2 P.M. weekly. Save room for a slice of yummy Mile-High Ice Cream Pie.

Commander's Palace, 1403 Washington Avenue; (504) 899-8221. Wonderful jazz brunch on Sundays, exquisite Creole cuisine always. One of the Brennan family's group of restaurants.

Copeland's, 4338 St. Charles Avenue; (504) 897-2325. The original Copeland's and still the best. A great spot to try New Orleanians' traditional Monday dinner, red beans and rice, spiced up with andouille sausage. Want inventiveness in your desserts? Try the "sweet potato pecan bread pudding."

The Court of Two Sisters, 613 Royal Street; (504) 522-7261. Elegant Creole dining in a setting rich with romance and intrigue. One of the most beautiful courtyards in New Orleans, best enjoyed by the candles and gaslights that glow after sunset.

Desire Oyster Bar, 300 Bourbon Street; (504) 586-0300. Moderate prices, great atmosphere with streetside tables that look out on lively Bourbon Street. Terrific crawfish étouffée and jambalaya, as well as oysters on the half shell and chilled shrimp.

Galatoire's, 209 Bourbon Street; (504) 525-2021. Especially wonderful seafood in an historic Creole setting.

K-Paul's Louisiana Kitchen, 416 Chartres Street; (504) 524-7394. Still *the* place to go for Cajun, now (thankfully) taking reservations for dinner in the upstairs dining room. Chef Paul Prudhomme changes the menu twice daily to take advantage of the day's catch.

Le Jardin at the Westin Canal Place; (504) 568-0155. Traditional French cuisine with a light touch, with one of the city's most magnificent views from its 11th-floor setting. Specializes in "the flavors of Provence."

Louis XVI at the Saint Louis Hotel, 730 Bienville Street; (504) 581-7000. Wonderful selection of seafood, lamb, chicken, and veal specialties. The "filet de boeuf Wellington Louis XVI" is a scrumptious specialty.

Monroe's, 3218 Magazine Street; (504) 891-1897. Uptown restaurant in an historic building, a good choice for a lunchtime break from antique shopping along Magazine Street.

Mother's, 401 Poydras Street; (504) 523-9656. A local institution for more than half a century, serving up the city's best poor-boys. Great breakfasts as well. Take a hearty appetite—they don't know the meaning of "small portions."

Napoleon House, 500 Chartres Street; (504) 524-9752. Inexpensive, casual atmosphere specializing in great sandwiches. Historic 19th-century building.

Palace Cafe, 605 Canal Street; (504) 523-1661. Casual ambiance, specializing in New Orleans seafood. Special weekly blues brunch. Another Brennan restaurant.

Ristorante BACCO, 310 Chartres Street; (504) 522-2426. Italian and Creole specialties including eggplant ravioli, Creole crawfish pizza. The newest venture from—you guessed it—the Brennans.

Upperline Restaurant, 1413 Upperline Street; (504) 891-9822. This Uptown restaurant (near Magazine Street) features adventurous Creole cuisine in an elegant setting.

Historic Home and Building Tours

Beauregard Keyes House and Garden, 1113 Chartres Street; (504) 523-7257. Open 10 A.M. to 3 P.M., Monday–Saturday (last tour at 3 P.M.). Greek Revival home, listed in National Register of Historic Places. Costumed docent give tours.

Gallier House Museum, 1118–32 Royal Street; (504) 523-6722. Open 10 A.M. to 4:30 P.M., Monday–Saturday (last tour at 3:45 P.M.). Restored 1857 home of architect James Gallier Jr.

Hermann-Grima Historic House, 820 St. Louis Street; (504) 525-5661. Open 10 A.M. to 4 P.M., Monday–Saturday. 1831 French Creole mansion with slave quarters, stable and courtyard. Listed on the National Register of Historic Places. Creole cooking demonstrations on Thursdays, October–May.

Longue Vue House and Gardens, 7 Bamboo Road in Metairie; (504) 488-5488. Historic Greek Revival estate filled with antiques and art, surrounded by eight acres of gorgeously landscaped gardens. Open from 10:30 A.M. to 4:30 P.M. Monday–Saturday, 1 to 5 P.M. Sunday (except national holidays). Longvue, which is listed on the National Register of Historic Places, is included on many of the guided city tours.

Louisiana State Museum properties, all open from 10 A.M. to 5 P.M., Tuesday–Sunday (except state holidays):

1850 House, Pontalba Building, 523 St. Ann Street on Jackson Square

The Cabildo, 701 Chartres Street

Old U.S. Mint, 400 Esplanade Avenue

The Presbytère, 751 Chartres Street

For Louisiana State Museum exhibit schedule, write PO Box 2448, New Orleans, LA 70176-2448, or call (504) 568-6968.

Old Ursuline Convent, 1100 Chartres Street; (504) 529-5040. Tours at 10 and 11 A.M., 1, 2, and 3 P.M., Tuesday–Friday; 11:15 A.M., 1 and 2 P.M., Saturday–Sunday. The oldest building in the Mississippi Valley. Built in 1745, it is a registered Federal Landmark.

Pitot House, 1440 Moss Street; (504) 482-0312. 1799 West Indies plantation house on Bayou St. John, used for scenes in *Interview With the Vampire*. Open 10 A.M. to 3 P.M., Wednesday–Saturday, except major holidays. Admission fee.

Museums

Aquarium of the Americas, Canal Street at the River; (504) 861-2538.

Blaine Kern's Mardi Gras World, 233 Newton Street; (504) 361-7821. Take the free Canal Street Ferry across the river to Old Algiers to see this fascinating exhibit of how Mardi Gras comes to life. Daily tours from 9:30 A.M. to 4:30 P.M.

Confederate Museum, 929 Camp Street; (504) 523-4522. Just off Lee Circle, this is Louisiana's oldest museum.

Historic New Orleans Collection, 533 Royal Street; (504) 523-4662. Complex includes 19th-century Williams Residence and 1792 Merieult House. Tours at 10 and 11 A.M., 2 and 3 P.M., Tuesday–Saturday.

Jackson Barracks, 6400 St. Claude Avenue; (504) 278-6242 or 278-6338. Military museum located in old powder magazine. The French Quarter fire in *Interview* was filmed here.

Louisiana Children's Museum, 428 Julia Street; (504) 523-1357. Strong on interactive exhibits.

Louisiana State Museum, 701 Chartres Street; (504) 568-6968. Historic landmark properties include the Cabildo, Prebytère, Old U.S. Mint, and the 1850 House.

Musée Conti Wax Museum, 917 Conti Street; (504) 525-2605. Excellent wax museum featuring tableaux of Louisiana lore, both real and imagined. Don't miss the dungeon!

The Historic New Orleans Collection includes the eighteenth-century Merieult House (center).

New Orleans Historic Voodoo Museum, 724 Dumaine Street; (504) 523-7685. Includes working voodoo altar, live snakes. Offers walking tours and "voodoo ritual" tours.

New Orleans Museum of Art, City Park; (504) 488-2631. Terrific collections of Fabergé pieces and photography, as well as sculpture, paintings, decorative arts.

New Orleans Pharmacy Museum, 514 Chartres Street; (504) 524-9077. 1823 apothecary shop constructed for Louis Dufilho Jr., the nation's first licensed pharmacist.

Plantation Homes

Plantation Tours

Gray Line Tours; (504) 587-0861. Six-hour guided coach tour of River Road homes.

New Orleans Tours Inc., 4220 Howard Avenue; (504) 592-1991, (800) 543-6332. Wide variety of city and neighborhood tours.

Tours by Isabelle; (504) 367-3963. Seven-hour journey with stops at antebellum mansions and lunch at Nottoway.

Individual Homes

Ashland–Belle Helene, 7497 Ashland Road, Geismar, LA 70734; (504) 473-1328 or 473-1207. Open 9 A.M. to 5 P.M. daily. Admission fee.

Destrehan Plantation; 9999 River Road, Destrehan, LA 70047; (504) 764-9315. 22 miles from New Orleans, 8 miles from New Orleans International Airport. Open daily from 9:30 A.M. to 4 P.M. (final tour at 3:30 P.M.) except for major holidays. Destrehan hosts a fall festival the second weekend of every October. Admission fee.

Houmas House Plantation, 40136 Highway 942, Darrow, LA 70725; (504) 522-2262 in New Orleans, (504) 473-7841 in Darrow. 60 miles from New Orleans. Open from 10 A.M. to 5 P.M. daily, February through October; 10 A.M. to 4 P.M., November through January. Admission fee.

Indian Camp, National Center for the Treatment of Hansen's Disease, Carville, LA; (504) 642-4736, ext. 281. Tours at 10 A.M. and 1 P.M. weekdays; gift shop. Children under 16 not admitted. No admission fee.

Judge Poché Plantation House, PO Box 200, River Road, Convent, LA 70723; (504) 562-3537 or 456-1447. Open 10 A.M. to 4 P.M. Monday–Saturday, 1 to 4 P.M. Sunday. Admission fee.

La Branche Plantation Dependency House, 1168 River Road, St. Rose, LA 70087; (504) 468-8843. 20 miles from New Orleans. Open daily from 10 A.M. to 4 P.M. except major holidays. Restaurant available. Admission fee.

Madewood Plantation, 4250 Highway 308, Napoleonville, LA 70390; (504) 369-7151 in Napoleonville, (800) 375-7151 toll-free. 72 miles from New Orleans. Open from 10 A.M. to 4:30 P.M. daily except Thanksgiving and Christmas. Overnight accommodations in both main house and guest houses; meals optional. Admission fee.

Magnolia Lane, 2141 River Road, Nine Mile Point, LA 70094; (504) 436-4915. Open 9 A.M. to 4 P.M. daily. Admission fee.

Magnolia Mound, 2161 Nicholson Drive, Baton Rouge, LA 70802; (504) 343-4955. Open 10 A.M. to 4 P.M. Tuesday–Saturday, 1 to 4 P.M. Sunday. Closed major holidays. Gift shop; antebellum cooking demos on Tuesdays, Thursdays, and Saturdays, October–May. Admission fee.

Mount Hope, 8151 Highland Road, Baton Rouge, LA 70808; (504) 766-8600. Open 9 A.M. to 4 P.M. daily except Sunday. Bed-and-breakfast lodgings, gift shop, candlelight tours available by appointment. Admission fee.

The Myrtles Plantation, PO Box 1100, Highway 61, St. Francisville, LA 70775; (504) 635-6277. Bed-and-breakfast, ghost tours, mystery weekends.

Nottoway Plantation, Highway 1 at Mississippi River Road, White Castle, LA 70788; (504) 832-2093 in New Orleans, (504) 545-2730 in White Castle. 69 miles from New Orleans. Open from 9 A.M. to 5 P.M. daily except Christmas Day. Restaurant open from 11 A.M. to 3 P.M. and 6 to 9 P.M. daily. Overnight accommodations available. Admission fee.

Oak Alley Plantation, 3645 Highway 18, Vacherie, LA 70090; (504) 523-4351 in New Orleans, (504) 265-2151 in Vacherie. Sixty miles from New Orleans. Open from 9 A.M. to 5:30 P.M. daily March–October, 9 A.M. to 5 P.M. November–February. Overnight accommodations in restored 1880 cabins with air-conditioning. Restaurant open from 11 A.M. to 3 P.M. daily. Admission fee.

Ormond Plantation, 13786 River Road, Destrehan, LA 70047; (504) 764-8544 or 764-0691. 23 miles from New Orleans. Open daily 10 A.M. to 4:30 P.M. daily except major holidays. Overnight accommodations and restaurant available. Admission fee.

San Francisco Plantation, Highway 44, Reserve, LA 70884; (504) 535-2341. 45 miles from New Orleans. Open daily from 10 A.M. to 4 P.M. daily, except major holidays. Admission fee.

Tezcuco Plantation, 3138 Highway 44, Darrow, LA 70725; (504) 562-3929. 60 miles from New Orleans. Open daily from 10 A.M. to 5 P.M., March–October; 10 A.M. to 4 P.M., November–February. Restaurant open from 11:30 A.M. to 2:30 P.M. daily. Closed Thanksgiving, Christmas, and New Year's Day. Overnight stays available in restored, air-conditioned cottages (breakfast optional). Admission fee.

River Road Restaurants

The Cabin, PO Box 85, Burnside, LA 70738; (504) 473-3007. This restaurant, on the east bank near Burnside, is constructed of pieces of slave cabins from several surrounding plantations. Casual Cajun cuisine, seafood, and steaks. Open for lunch and dinner daily; hours vary.

Lafitte's Landing, PO Box 1128, Donaldsonville, LA 70346; (504) 473-1232. Just off the River Road at the Sunshine Bridge near Donaldsonville (west bank), Lafitte's Landing originally was the manor house of Viala Plantation. The house was moved to its present site more than 30 years ago and is now a restaurant specializing in Cajun and Creole cuisine. Open from 11 A.M. to 8 P.M. Sunday, 11 A.M. to 3 P.M. Monday, 11 A.M. to 3 P.M. and 6 to 10 P.M. Tuesday–Saturday.

Riverboat Tours

John James Audubon Riverboat, 1300 World Trade Center (departs from Aquarium of the Americas dock); (504) 586-8777, (800) 233-BOAT.

Daily jaunts between Aquarium of the Americas and Audubon Zoo up-river. Departs Aquarium at 10 A.M., noon, 2 and 4 P.M. Departs zoo at 11 A.M., 1, 3, and 5 P.M.

Cajun Queen Riverboat, Poydras Street Wharf (departs from Aquarium of Americas dock); (504) 529-4567, (800) 445-4109. Replica of a 19th-century steamboat takes three river-plantation-harbor cruises daily, at 11 A.M., 1:15 and 3:30 P.M. Cruises past French Quarter, historic plantations, and Chalmette Battlefield. No stops.

Cotton Blossom Sternwheeler, 1300 World Trade Center (departs from Jax Brewery dock); (504) 586-8777. Three-hour "ecotour" departs at noon daily. Combines historic, cultural narrative with "hands-on" ecological presentation.

Creole Queen Paddlewheeler, Poydras Street Wharf (departs from Canal Street Dock at Riverwalk); (504) 529-4567, (800) 445-4109. Replica of a 19th-century paddlewheeler with departures at 10:30 A.M., and 2 and 8 P.M. Stops at Chalmette Battlefield.

Natchez Steamboat, 1300 World Trade Center (departs from Jax Brewery dock); (504) 586-8777, (800) 233-BOAT. Two-hour cruises aboard New Orleans's only sternwheel steamboat. Cruises at 11:30 A.M., 2:30 P.M. Dinner-and-jazz cruise at 7 P.M. daily. Moonlight dance cruise at 10 P.M. Saturday.

Swamp and Bayou Tours

Bayou Segnette Swamp Tour; (504) 561-8244. Southwest of New Orleans near Bayou Segnette State Park (about 30 minutes from downtown New Orleans). Daily tours at 9:30 A.M. and 1:30 P.M. Transportation available to and from New Orleans hotels.

Cypress Swamp Tours; (504) 581-4501. Southwest of New Orleans at Bayou Segnette. Several tours available, including daylong swampboat and antebellum-home tour, daytime swamp tours, and a sunset swamp tour and Cajun *fais do-do*. Transportation available to and from New Orleans hotels. Call for departure times.

Honey Island Swamp Tours Inc.; (504) 641-1769. 35 miles northeast of New Orleans in Slidell. Daytime tours at 9 A.M. and 2 P.M. daily,

October 1–May 14; 9 A.M. and 4 P.M., May 15–September 30. Evening tours, by reservation, available during summer months only. Transportation available to and from New Orleans hotels. Gift shop and snacks available at tour site. For hotel pickup, call (504) 242-5877 in New Orleans.

Jean Lafitte Swamp Tours; (504) 592-0560 for information, (504) 689-4186 for ticket booth. 20 miles south of New Orleans. Daily tours at 10 A.M. and 2 P.M., seasonal tours at noon. Transportation to and from New Orleans hotels available.

Louisiana Swamp Tours Inc.; (504) 467-8020 for information, (504) 689-3599 for ticket booth. 23 miles south of New Orleans. Daily tours at 9:30 A.M., noon, and 2 P.M. Transportation to and from New Orleans hotels available.

Swamp Monster Tours; (504) 641-5106, (800) 245-1132. Two-hour tours of Honey Island Swamp near Slidell.

Shopping

Antiques

In New Orleans, antiques are the thing, and the two main centers for "flashback furnishings" are Royal and Chartres streets in the Quarter and Magazine Street skirting the Garden District. Merchant associations in these areas provide free brochures listing their members, specialties, etc.

For information, call or write:

The Royal Street Guild, 828 Royal Street, Suite 522, New Orleans, LA 70130; (504) 949-2222.

Magazine Street Merchants Association, Box 15028, New Orleans, LA 70175; (504) 899-4491.

Some personal favorites among the literally dozens of enticing possibilities:

ROYAL AND CHARTRES STREETS

Boyer Antiques & Doll Shop, 241 Chartres Street; (504) 522-4513. Antique dolls, doll restoration, antique jewelry, and bric-a-brac.

Royal Street in the Vieux Carré features dozens of antique stores and the occasional bronze hitching post, left over from days when horses needed tethering.

Owner–doll-maker Karl Boyer made the dolls used in *Interview With the Vampire*, and part of the film was shot in the store.

Dixon & Dixon of Royal, 237 Royal Street; (504) 524-0282; 301 Royal, (504) 529-5660; 321 Chartres, (504) 523-2570; (800) 848-5148. Three elegant stores filled with several lifetimes of English, French, and Dutch antiques from the 17th through 19th centuries, as well as art, Oriental carpets, and estate and antique jewelry. A great place to search out your own "Mayfair Emerald."

French Antique Shop, 225 Royal Street; (504) 524-9851. Cramped, but full of wonderful country French and continental furniture; bronze and crystal chandeliers; mirrors and mantels; porcelains and statuary.

Gerald D. Katz Antiques, 505 Royal Street; (504) 524-5050. Comprehensive collection of antique and estate jewelry.

James H. Cohen and Sons, 437 Royal Street; (504) 522-3305, (800) 535-1853. Rare coins, antique weapons and jewelry. If you need

Boyer Antiques & Dolls, on Chartres Street, was featured in the film version of *Interview*. Proprietor Karl Boyer made the dolls used in the movie.

a rapier, this is the place to look (but remember, dueling is prohibited these days).

Joan Good Antiques, 809 Royal Street; (504) 525-1705. Captivating selection of antique jewelry—sterling silver, gold, marcasite, and semiprecious stones.

Keil's Antiques, 325 Royal Street; (504) 522-4552. Established 1899, specializing in jewelry, chandeliers, silver, furniture, and marble mantels.

Dozens of dolls peer at visitors from the antique cases at Boyer Antiques & Dolls. The tall doll in the center of the case is Claudia's favorite in the film of *Interview*.

Lucullus, 610 Chartres Street; (504) 528-9620. Specializes in 17th–19th-century culinary objects—furniture, cutlery, porcelain servers.

Moss Antiques, 411 Royal Street; (504) 522-3981. 18th- and 19th-century antiques and antique and estate jewelry.

M. S. Rau Antiques, 630 Royal Street; (504) 523-5660, (800) 544-9440. Estate jewelry by Tiffany, Cartier, and others; American and European furniture; Tiffany lamps; walking sticks; sterling flatware and tea sets.

Patout Antiques, 920 Royal Street; (504) 522-0582. Early-19th-century American furniture and decorative arts, emphasizing Louisiana craftsmanship.

Rothschild's Antiques, 241 and 321 Royal Street; (504) 423-5816 or 523-2281. Antique English and French furnishings, chandeliers, mantels; antique, estate, and custom jewelry.

Royal Antiques Ltd., 307–9 Royal Street; (504) 524-7033 or 524-7035. Country French and English 18th- and 19th-century furnishings, chandeliers, brass and copper accessories.

MAGAZINE STREET

Acquisitions Antiques, 2025 Magazine Street; (504) 522-7974. Wonderful gold-leaf frames, furniture, mirrors, pottery.

Antebellum Antiques, 2108 Magazine Street; (504) 558-0208. 19th-century American Victorian furniture and ornamentation.

Antiques-Magazine, 2043 Magazine Street; (504) 522-2043. Specializes in American and Victorian antiques from the 1850s through the 1940s. Marvelous tidbits such as fountain pens, cut glass, and silver.

As You Like It, 3025 Magazine Street; (504) 897-6915, (800) 828-2311. Sterling silver flatware, hollowware, and jewelry.

Bep's Antiques, 2051 Magazine Street; (504) 525-7726. Furniture, china, crockery, pharmacy and medical items.

Bush Antiques, 2109 Magazine Street; (504) 581-3518. French, English, and American furniture and accessories. Auctioned off items used in the film version of *Interview With the Vampire.*

Charbonnet & Charbonnet Inc., 2929 Magazine Street; (504) 891-9948. 8,000 square feet of country antiques and accessories.

Dellwen Antiques, 3954–56 Magazine Street; (504) 891-6603. A delightful hodgepodge, with 10 rooms full of goodies.

Ellan's Antiques, 3858 Magazine Street; (504) 891-6369. 19th- and early-20th-century crystal, glass, porcelain, buttons, bottles; furniture; silver and silver plate.

Jon Antiques, 4605 Magazine Street; (504) 899-4482. Historic home full of 18th- and 19th-century English and French antiques—furniture, mirrors, lamps, porcelains.

Mac Maison, Ltd., 3963 Magazine Street; (504) 891-2863. Specializes in French antiques, lighting, architectural artifacts and ornamentation.

Magazine Arcade Antiques, 3017 Magazine Street; (504) 895-5451. European and Oriental art, furniture, music boxes, Victrolas, and curios.

Magazine Street Antiques, 1829 Magazine Street; (504) 524-2807. Antiques, paintings, and prints. Wonderful selection of glassware and collectible costume jewelry.

Nina Sloss Antiques and Interiors, 6800 Magazine Street; (504) 895-8088 or 895-7668. Specializing in French, Italian, and English 18th- and 19th-century furniture.

Nineteenth Century Antiques, 4838 Magazine Street; (504) 891-4845. Unusual collection of rare clocks; cut glass, china, and bric-a-brac; furniture and antique watches.

Wirthmore, 3900 Magazine Street, (504) 899-3811; 5723 Magazine Street, (504) 897-9727. 18th- and 19th-century French antiques and accessories.

Books

The Antique Book Gallery, 811 Royal Street; (504) 524-6918.

Arcadian Books and Art Prints, 714 Orleans Avenue; (504) 523-4138.

Beaucoup Books, 5414 Magazine Street; (504) 895-2663, (800) 543-4114.

Beckham's Bookshop, 228 Decatur Street and 823 Chartres Street; (504) 522-9875. Decatur location has two floors of vintage and secondhand books and records.

Bookstar, 414 N. Peters Street; (504) 523-6411. Modern, but a great selection of local-interest nonfiction and literature.

Crescent City Books, 204 Chartres Street; (504) 524-4997. Used, out-of-print, and new books.

Dauphine Street Books, 410 Dauphine Street; (504) 529-2333.

De Ville Books and Prints, Riverwalk, (504) 595-8916; 322 Carondelet Street, (504) 525-1846. The CBD location of De Ville Books is mentioned in *Lestat*, as the site where the book's namesake spots a paperback edition of *Interview* and wonders "how many of our kind had 'noticed' the book. Never mind for the moment the mortals who thought it was fiction."

Faulkner House Books, 624 Pirates Alley; (504) 524-2940. Housed in the building where William Faulkner wrote his first novel.

Garden District Book Shop, 2727 Prytania Street; (504) 895-2266. Anne Rice's neighborhood bookstore, in The Rink near Lafayette Cemetery.

George Herget Books, 3109 Magazine Street; (504) 891-5595.

Librairie Book Shop, 823 Chartres Street; (504) 525-4837.

Maple Street Book Shop, 7523 Maple Street; (504) 866-4916.

Taylors, 3119 Magazine Street; (504) 891-6707.

Et Cetera

Some additional shopping venues that might be of special interest to Anne Rice fans:

The Rink shopping center in the Garden District, home of the Garden District Book Shop.

Body Hangings, 835 Decatur Street; (504) 524-9856. Capes and cloaks to do a vampire proud, in an amazing array of styles and patterns. Velvet, silk, even Scottish plaid.

The Centuries, 517 St. Louis Street; (504) 568-9491. Antique prints and maps, going back as far as 1493.

Fleur de Paris, 712 Royal Street; (504) 525-1899. Custom hats, dresses of flowing silk and ribbons, and drawers filled with the most delicate, perfectly feminine lingerie.

Frou Frou, Riverwalk; (504) 586-8215. Light, vintage-looking women's clothing—an abundance of cotton and lace, with everything in cool shades of white, cream, and ecru.

Ginja Jar, 611 Royal Street; (504) 523-7643. Contemporary and vintage dolls, Victorian buggies, doll accessories.

House of Broel's Victorian Mansion and Dollhouse Museum, 1508 St. Charles Avenue; (504) 525-1000 or 522-2220. 1847 mansion, remodeled in the 1890s in the Victorian style. Wonderful collection of miniatures and dollhouses, collectibles.

Maison Blanche, 901 Canal Street; (504) 566-1000. Historic downtown department store, favored by decades of fashion-conscious Mayfair women.

Mardi Gras Center, 831 Chartres Street; (504) 524-4384. Adult and children's masks, makeup, hats, wigs, beads, and magic supplies.

Mignon Faget, Canal Place; (504) 524-2973. This local jewelry artist and designer is renowned for her silver and gold creations steeped in the culture and craftsmanship of old New Orleans.

MGM Costume Rental, 1617 St. Charles Avenue; (504) 581-3999. Nearly 15,000 costumes designed for movies, television, and theater.

Quarter Smith, 535 St. Louis Street; (504) 524-9731. This Vieux Carré silversmith shop made those nifty engraved thumb-pieces (used to conveniently puncture skin without sullying one's fangs) used in the film of *Interview*. Artisan Ken Bowers, owner of the shop, also made antique opera glasses and several crosses for the film.

Rendezvous, Inc., 522 St. Peter Street; (504) 522-0225. Enchanting collection of delicate linens and lace handkerchiefs, doilies, children's clothing.

Street Scene, Jax Brewery, (504) 558-0232; Riverwalk Marketplace, (504) 595-8865, (800) 845-0650. Beautifully detailed, limited-edition wood carvings of New Orleans scenes.

Yvonne La Fleur New Orleans, Riverwalk; (504) 522-8222. Elegant women's clothing, signature fragrance.

The Westgate, 5219 Magazine Street; (504) 899-3077. This gallery specializes in necromantic (death imagery) art and literature, especially the Eros-Thanatos theme. Unusual, to put it mildly.

8
We Can't Wait!
What's Next?

The worst thing about reading Anne Rice's books, of course, is finishing them, knowing that it will be at least another year before a subsequent trip into her eccentric, completely unique universe. Fans conclude a *Vampire Chronicles* or *Mayfair Witches* book with a disconcerting mixture of happiness and distress—a happy sigh merged with a mournful moan.

The success of the 1994 film version of *Interview With the Vampire* virtually assures future movie installments. The movie initially drew Rice's wrath because of director Neil Jordan's casting choice for her vampire-hero, the French, blond, and intriguingly androgynous Lestat. The all-American, dark-haired, and boyishly appealing Tom Cruise wasn't exactly whom Rice had in mind. When the book first came out, in the mid-seventies, she envisioned Rutger Hauer in the part (he later made a particularly memorable villain in *The Hitcher*, disposing of poor Jennifer Jason Leigh in a manner that might have made even Lestat wince). Rice was thrilled with the choice of Jordan as director—the Irish writer-director had attained his own cult status via 1992's smash hit *The Crying Game*, and Rice had even cited an earlier Jordan film, *The Company of Wolves*, as one of Louis's favorites in *Body Thief*. But the "Cruise issue" brought howls of outrage from both Rice and her devoted, very outspoken legion of fans.

Negative publicity and verbal bloodletting followed the film like a demented puppy, eagerly lapping up every bit of controversy. The doom-and-gloom naysayers, who as early as spring of 1994 were predicting a monumental flop, got additional fuel for their flames when River Phoenix, cast as Daniel, the story's interviewer, died of a drug overdose outside a Hollywood nightclub. Christian Slater eventually was cast in the part.

But no one who had followed *Interview's* roller-coaster odyssey from page to screen was prepared for the stunner of September 23, 1994, seven weeks before the film's scheduled release date of November 18. Rice took out a two-page ad in *Daily Variety* (repeated in the October 2 *New York Times*). To everyone's amazement, the author who had so publicly vilified the film now did a complete about-face, praising the director and cast (*especially* Tom Cruise) with glowing, effusive adoration. Cynics cried "insincerity," noting that Rice would receive a substantial percentage of the film's gross. But her fans pooh-poohed that notion, sure that their heroine would never sell out her integrity just for the sake of a profit. After all, if that was her motive, why would she have said anything negative in the first place?

Most fans agreed with Rice that Cruise adroitly captured Lestat's personality, a wickedly appealing blend of charm and menace. Critical reviews were mixed, but most reviewers praised director Jordan, Cruise, Brad Pitt (Louis), and, especially, twelve-year-old Kirsten Dunst, who portrayed Claudia with a creepily adult composure. Many predicted that the prodigiously talented Dunst would be nominated for an Academy Award as Best Supporting Actress. However, the film received just two nominations—for art direction (Dante Ferretti) and original score (Elliot Goldenthal).

Critical success, or lack thereof, notwithstanding, *Interview* sailed through the winter of 1994 to become one of the holiday season's few bona fide smashes. Premiering November 11, 1994 (a week earlier than originally planned, possibly to ride the cape-tails of Rice's compliments), it set several opening-weekend records: best nonsummer opening, best debut of an R-rated film, and the fifth-highest three-day opening weekend in film history. Only *Jurassic Park*, *Batman Returns*, *The Lion King*, and *Batman* opened with bigger numbers.

With a cost of an estimated $60 million, by January 1995 *Interview* had already soared past the industry's "magic number" of $100 million in grosses. *Interview* was tied for the number ten spot as 1994's Top Ten films, in terms of gross profits. In January, the film went over the $100 million mark. And when a film makes that much money, you can count on a sequel, if not two or three.

Interview producer David Geffen owns the rights to both *The Vampire Lestat* and *The Witching Hour* (which may be headed for television-miniseries land). As of late 1994, Geffen had reportedly secured the talents of both director Jordan and star Cruise for another fang-filled romp. Shooting locales almost certainly will include New Orleans once again.

Carolco Pictures owns rights to Rice's 1989 book *The Mummy, or Ramses the Damned* (not related to the *Vampire Chronicles* or *Mayfair Witches* series). According to some reports, Rice already is lobbying for Spanish heartthrob Antonio Banderas (who played a smoldering Armand in *Interview*) to portray her mummified protagonist in that one.

As for the book front, the film of *Interview* propelled a whole new generation of Rice fans into the bookstores. For several weeks in the fall of 1994, *Interview* topped the paperback bestseller lists a remarkable *eighteen years* after its first publication. In a bizarre marketing strategy, Ballantine's movie tie-in version of the novel sported nothing other than an artsy new cover sporting a cross—no fang-modeling Cruise or Pitt on the cover, no center section of stills from the film. Obviously, this edition was planned before Rice's reconsideration of the movie's worthiness. The cross was a particularly odd choice for artwork, however—since the Christian religious symbol holds no power over Rice's vampires.

In November 1994, *Publishers Weekly* reported 6.5 million copies of *Interview* in print, 3.35 million of *The Vampire Lestat*, 3.1 million of *Queen of the Damned*, and 2.25 million of *The Tale of the Body Thief*. By January 1995, all four *Vampire Chronicles* books were staking out spots on the *Publishers Weekly* Top Fifteen list of paperback bestsellers. Fall of

1994 was a bonanza for Rice; the hardcover edition of *Taltos* (released in September) debuted at number one on the bestseller lists, and *Lasher* quickly ascended the trade paperback lists.

In August of 1993, several entertainment publications reported that Rice had signed a $17 million deal with Knopf for three more *Vampire Chronicles* installments. She talked about the fifth in the *Vampire* series, *Memnoch the Devil*, in an October 1994 interview with *TV Guide*, describing it as being "about Lestat's darkest hour . . . *Memnoch* nearly killed me. But you have to fish the deep waters." Portions of the book are set in St. Elizabeth's, the nineteenth-century former orphanage Rice and her husband bought in 1994. (Wonder if they'll let a movie company film there. . . .)

Rice also mentioned another book she is writing, *Servant of the Bones*, a ghost story unrelated to either the vampire or witches series. She also has sometimes discussed wanting to do an update of the Frankenstein story.

If form holds true, fans can expect a new Anne Rice novel every fall for the next few years, usually with a release date of September or October (although *Memnoch* broke the trend with a July release). Whatever the future holds for Rice, half the fun for her fans is anticipating the new twists her fertile, inventive mind will take. And it's almost a sure bet that, through her books, Rice will continue to guide fans, as well as assorted supernatural beings, through the narrow, haunted streets and gardens of her favorite city, New Orleans.

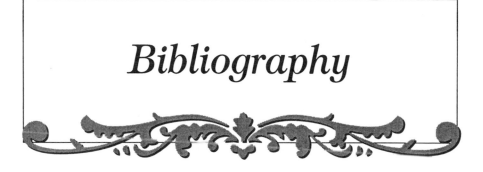

Bibliography

Books

APA Publications. *New Orleans* (Insight City Guides). Singapore: APA Publications (HK) Ltd., 1992.

Arthur, Stanley Clisby. *Old New Orleans*. Gretna, La.: Pelican Publishing Co., 1990.

Birnbaum, Alexandra Mayes, et al., *Birnbaum's New Orleans '94*. New York: HarperCollins, 1993.

Bultman, Bethany Ewald. *New Orleans* (Compass American Guides). Oakland, Calif.: Compass American Guides (Fodor's Travel Publications), 1994.

Cable, George Washington. *Old Creole Days*. New York: Scribner, 1879.

Cable, Mary. *Lost New Orleans*. Boston: Houghton Mifflin, 1980.

Chopin, Kate. *The Awakening*. Chicago, H. G. Stone and Co., 1899.

Cowan, Walter G., et al. *New Orleans Yesterday and Today*. Baton Rouge: Louisiana State University Press, 1988.

Fodor's Travel Publications. *Fodor's New Orleans*. New York: Fodor's Travel Publications, 1991.

Friends of the Cabildo, et al. *New Orleans Architecture. Vol. 1, The Lower Garden District.* Gretna, La.: Pelican Publishing Co., 1979.

————. *New Orleans Architecture. Vol. 2, The American Sector (Faubourg St. Mary).* Gretna, La.: Pelican Publishing Co., 1980.

————. *New Orleans Architecture. Vol. 3, The Cemeteries.* Gretna, La.: Pelican Publishing Co., 1989.

————. *New Orleans Architecture. Vol. 5, The Esplanade Ridge.* Gretna, La.: Pelican Publishing Co., 1977.

————. *New Orleans Architecture. Vol. 7, Jefferson City.* Gretna, La.: Pelican Publishing Co., 1989.

Garvey, Joan B., and Mary Lou Widmer. *Beautiful Crescent: A History of New Orleans.* New Orleans: Garmer Press, 1982 (rev. 1994).

Huber, Leonard V. *Landmarks of New Orleans.* New Orleans: Louisiana Landmark Society, 1984.

————. *New Orleans: A Pictorial History From the Earliest Times to the Present Day.* New York: Crown, 1971.

————, and Samuel Watson Jr. *The Basilica on Jackson Square.* New Orleans: St. Louis Cathedral, 1965.

Jewell, Edwin L., editor. *Jewell's Crescent City Illustrated.* New Orleans: Edwin Jewell, 1873.

Keyes, Francis Parkinson. *Dinner at Antoine's.* New York: Julian Messner, 1948.

Klein, Victor C. *New Orleans Ghosts.* Chapel Hill, N.C.: Professional Press, 1993.

Laughlin, Clarence John. *Ghosts Along the Mississippi.* New York: American Legacy Press, 1987.

Levatino, Madeline. *Past Masters: The History & Hauntings of Destrehan Plantation.* Destrehan, La.: Levatino and Barraco, 1991.

Logan, William Bryant, and Vance Muse. *The Smithsonian Guide to Historic America: The Deep South.* New York: Stewart, Tabori and Chang, 1989.

McAlester, Virginia, and Lee McAlester. *A Field Guide to American Houses.* New York: Knopf, 1984.

Malone, Lee. *The Majesty of the River Road.* Gretna, La.: Pelican Publishing Co., 1991.

Muse, Vance. *Old New Orleans* (Great American Homes). Birmingham, Ala.: Oxmoor House, 1988.

Myers, Arthur. *The Ghostly Register*. New York: Contemporary Books, 1986.

Ramsland, Katherine. *Prism of the Night: A Biography of Anne Rice*. New York: Dutton, 1991.

———. *The Vampire Companion: The Official Guide to Anne Rice's The Vampire Chronicles*. New York: Ballantine, 1993.

———. *The Witches' Companion: The Official Guide to Anne Rice's Lives of the Mayfair Witches*. New York: Ballantine, 1994.

Rice, Anne. *The Feast of All Saints*. New York, Knopf, 1979.

———. *Interview With the Vampire*. New York, Knopf, 1976.

———. *Lasher*. New York: Knopf, 1993.

———. *Queen of the Damned*. New York, Knopf, 1988.

———. *The Tale of the Body Thief*. New York: Knopf, 1992.

———. *Taltos*. New York: Knopf, 1994.

———. *The Vampire Lestat*. New York, Knopf, 1985.

———. *The Witching Hour.*, New York, Knopf, 1990.

Roberts, Bette B. *Anne Rice* (Twayne's American Authors Series). New York: Twayne Publishers (Macmillan), 1994.

Samuel, Martha Ann Brett, and Ray Samuel. *The Great Days of the Garden District and the Old City of Lafayette*. New Orleans: Parents' League of the Louise S. McGehee School, 1961 (rev. 1978).

Sexton, Richard, and Randolph Delahanty. *New Orleans: Elegance and Decadence*. San Francisco: Chronicle, 1993.

Stall, Gaspar J. "Buddy." *Proud, Peculiar New Orleans: The Inside Story*. Baton Rouge: Claitor's Publishing Division, 1984.

Stanforth, Deirdre. *Romantic New Orleans*. New York: Penguin Books, 1979.

Starr, S. Frederick. *Southern Comfort: The Garden District of New Orleans, 1800–1990*. Cambridge, Mass.: MIT Press, 1989.

Twain, Mark. *Life on the Mississippi*. New York: Bantam, 1976.

Viviano, Christy L. *Haunted Louisiana*. Metairie, La.: Tree House Press, 1992.

Wilson, Samuel, Jr. *The Pitot House on Bayou St. John.* New Orleans: Louisiana Landmarks Society, 1992.

Magazines, Newspapers, and Other Sources

Abramowitz, Rachel. "Love Bites." *Premiere* magazine, November 1994.

"Anne Rice." *In Style* magazine, December 1993.

"Anne Rice Buys St. Elizabeth's Compound." *The Times-Picayune*, May 16, 1993.

Atkinson, Mary Lou, et al. "Overview of the Vampire." *The Times-Picayune*, November 10, 1994.

Casey, Constance. "Literary New Orleans." *Publishers Weekly*, May 9, 1986.

Conant, Jennet. "Lestat, C'est Moi." *Esquire.* March 1994.

Conaway, James. "New Orleans Then and Now." *National Geographic Traveler*, September/October 1994.

Dickinson, Joy. "Novelist Anne Rice Recalls Richardson Ties." *Richardson (Texas) News*, November 23, 1990.

Frankel, Martha. "Interview With the Author of 'Interview With the Vampire.'" *Movieline*, January/February 1994.

Friends of St. Alphonsus. *Art Tour of St. Alphonsus.* Undated pamphlet.

Ginsberg, Merle. "Interview With the 'Vampire' Author." *TV Guide*, October 22, 1994.

Gleason, David King. *Plantation Homes Along the River Road.* Map and pamphlet. Baton Rouge: David King Gleason, 1984.

Greater New Orleans Tourist and Convention Commission, Inc. *New Orleans Accommodations.* Booklet, 1994.

———. *New Orleans Visitors Guide.* Booklet, Fall/Winter 1994.

Hobson, Linda Whitney. "A Place to Write: The New Orleans Literary Scene." *New Orleans Magazine*, March 1990.

Interview With the Vampire: The Vampire Chronicles. Film, Geffen Pictures, 1994.

Jensen, Lynne. "Sales From the Crypt." *The Times-Picayune*, December 10, 1993.

———, and Matt Scallan. "Wherefore Art Thou, Lestat?" *The Times-Picayune*, October 20, 1993.

King, Ronette. "Novel End for Landmark." *The Times-Picayune*, May 29, 1993.

McClain, Randy. "At Stake on Screen." *The Times-Picayune*, November 12, 1993.

Mooney, Joshua. "Neil Jordan Bites the Big One." *Movieline*, November 1994.

Nabonne, Rhonda. "They'd Give Their Teeth . . ." *The Times-Picayune*, August 29, 1993.

Oak Alley Plantation. Undated, anonymous pamphlet.

Plume, Janet. "Author Picks Uptown Home." *The Times-Picayune*, March 18, 1989.

Rebello, Stephen. "The Michelangelo of Monsters." *Movieline*, November 1994.

Reed, Julia. "Haunted Houses." *Vogue*, November, 1993.

Ronning, Mary Beth. "The Ghosts of Cemeteries Past." *New Orleans Magazine*, October 1994.

Scott, Liz. "A City of Neighborhoods." *New Orleans Magazine*, June 1992.

Sessums, Kevin. "Cruise Speed." *Vanity Fair*, October 1994.

Virgets, Ronnie. "An Interview With Anne Rice: The New Orleans Experience." *New Orleans Magazine*, June 1991.

———— "Tales From the Tombs." *New Orleans Magazine*, October 1989.

————. "To Look Back Reverentially: Tales From the Crypt—The Sequel." *New Orleans Magazine*, October 1990.

Warner, Coleman. "Rice Plans Museum for Dolls at Home." *The Times-Picayune*, April 26, 1994.